BRIGADISTA

First published in 2006 by
CURRACH PRESS
55A Spruce Avenue, Stillorgan Industrial Park, Blackrock, Co. Dublin

www.currach.ie

1 3 5 4 2

Cover by Sin é Design
Origination by Currach Press
Printed by Betaprint, Bluebell Industrial Estate, Dublin 12
ISBN: 1-85607-937-6

BRIGADISTA

AN IRISHMAN'S FIGHT AGAINST FASCISM

Salud
Bob Doyle

BOB DOYLE

Notes and additional text by Harry Owens

CURRACH
PRESS

CONTENTS

FOREWORD
Paul Preston

Those who volunteered to fight for the Spanish Republic against Spain's reactionary military and their Nazi and Fascist allies made the hazardous journey to that country out of a visionary concern for what defeat would mean for the democracies. The volunteers overcame enormous difficulties to fight for the Republic. Some were out of work, others were intellectuals and there were a few adventurers, but all had come to build barriers against Fascist aggression. For Italian, German and Austrian refugees from Fascism and Nazism, however, the Spanish Civil War was the first real chance to fight back and eventually to go home. For all of them, eventual defeat was a devastating blow but for none quite so bitter as for those who faced Hitler's concentration camps and Mussolini's prisons. Yet, remarkably, those who went on to renege on their anti-Fascist gamble were a tiny minority.

The idea that to have fought in Spain gave meaning to an entire life was captured by the American correspondent Herbert Matthews, a passionate supporter of the Republic both during the war and after. He wrote: 'In those years we lived our best and what has come after and what there is to come can never carry us to those heights again.' Like many correspondents, Matthews never lost his pride in supporting the Republic: 'Those of us who championed the cause of the Republican government against the Franco Nationalists were right. It was, on balance, the cause of justice, morality, decency. All of us who lived the Spanish Civil War felt deeply emotional about it.' That feeling was shared even more intensely by those who fought, and it suffuses Bob Doyle's splendid autobiography.

This is a fascinating memoir, written with honesty and utterly devoid of self-promotion. The Spanish edition was called *Rebel Without a Pause* and that title sums up the endless and heroic struggles of Bob Doyle's life. He was involved in the struggle against Fascism in Dublin, earning vicious beatings from the hands of O'Duffy's Blueshirts. After abortive attempts to find work in Liverpool, he joined the IRA, which gave him a weapons' training that came in useful in Spain. He made Herculean efforts to join the International Brigades in the summer of 1937, stowing away aboard a Greek ship to get to Spain from Marseilles. Unable to make contact with the International Brigades, he was forced to take a job on a ship sailing between Spain and Britain. He learned some Spanish and used his position to liaise with the Spanish Aid Committee in Liverpool, smuggling leaflets and posters in and out of Spain and letters to and from International Brigaders when he called at Republican ports. Finally, at the end of October 1937, he persuaded the recruiting agency at the King Street headquarters of the Communist Party to send him to Spain.

The basic story of his life and of his experiences in Spain is itself astonishing and it is related without pretension and with an acute sense of humour. What is especially remarkable about Bob Doyle's experience is that he is one of the very few brigaders who were imprisoned at Franco's improvised concentration camp in the disused monastery of San Pedro de Cardeña near Burgos. Bob was one of over one hundred British volunteers taken prisoner on 31 March 1938 at Calaceite, between Alcañiz in the province of Teruel and Tortosa on the coast of Tarragona. They were captured by Italians of the Black Arrows Division as the Francoists made their rapid advance through Aragón to the sea. Bob's account of the brutality with which prisoners were treated when they were captured is one of the few by volunteers – that by George Wheeler being another and the one by the American Carl Geiser perhaps the most complete. It was revealing of the Francoist mentality that the officers were convinced that the brigaders were all Jewish.

Prisoners were variously interned in cow sheds, threatened with being burnt alive and suffered horrendous conditions: overcrowding, bitter cold, one thin blanket, little food, thin gruel with bits of stale bread, or a couple of sardines and some beans, daily beatings and tortures for trivial 'offences' like not standing to attention during meals or genuflecting in church. They were subjected to indoctrination and obligatory attendance at Mass. The ferocity of their treatment was seen by Bob as a deliberate strategy to humiliate, dehumanise and demoralise the prisoners. Interestingly, Bob Doyle, like Carl Geiser and others before him, comments on the sinister role of the pro-Francoist correspondent of the *New York Times*, William 'General Bill' Carney, who wrote mendacious accounts representing San Pedro as if it were a relaxing rest home. He reminds us of the Francoist collaboration with the Gestapo agents who came to collect German volunteers and returned them to the Third Reich for execution.

Although Bob himself does not stress the point, these are the memoirs of a man of immense courage and idealism, with great inner reserves of stoicism which enabled him to endure hardship of all kinds. What is especially fascinating is the combination of the deep humanity, warmth and humour familiar to anyone who has ever met Bob Doyle and the utterly serious way he went about his participation in the International Brigades. Evidence from the documents found in the Moscow archives by Irish historian Barry McLoughlin show Bob as a deeply serious Communist, fully aware of, and committed to, the need for discpline within the Brigades.

There have been many profoundly emotional comments made about the Spanish Civil War by those who supported the struggle of the Second Republic against Franco and his Nazi and Fascist allies. Albert Camus came near to accounting for the universal fascination with the Spanish Civil War when he wrote: 'It was in Spain that men learned that one can be right and still be beaten, that force can vanquish spirit, that there are times when courage is not its own reward. It is this, without doubt, which explains why so many men throughout the world regard the Spanish drama as a personal tragedy.' Yet, despite defeat, capture and imprisonment, Bob Doyle emerged from Spain with his faith in humanity undiminished. Relative to what he suffered, the optimism and militancy which pulse through every page of this marvellous book must inspire anyone who did not fight in Spain to know more about the anti-Fascist struggle that unfolded there.

Paul Preston is Professor of International Studies at the London School of Economics. Among his books are Franco a Biography *(1994);* ¡Comrades! Portraits from the Spanish Civil War *(1999);* Doves of War. Four Women of Spain *(2002) and* The Spanish Civil War. Reaction, Revolution and Revenge *(2006) – all HarperCollins.*

PREFACE

This book has been years a-growing. It began when Bob came to Dublin for the 1986 celebration of the Irish who fought for the Spanish Republic. Afterwards a few of us sat down and prompted by our questions Bob told his life story. It filled two ninety-minute cassettes that we gave him saying, 'Right Bob, you do have a story to tell, and it'll fill a book. Here's the start.'

When Bob had finished writing, we did interviews, then research. I noticed that when Bob said he remembered something, however unlikely, it – or something almost the same – had actually happened. Hardly a single fact needed correcting; it was the characters in his colourful life and the background to events that needed explaining for today's readers.

His wife Lola had kept press cutting and some photos, but Bob had nothing left from his time in the war in Spain. Prisoners didn't get to keep souvenirs. With Maria McLaughlin urging us on from London and digging out the journals and biographies from decades past, we ploughed ahead, with the help of Manus O'Riordan and Eugene McCartan; Sinéad McKenna, who took such care in designing the cover; and Jo O'Donoghue, publisher at Currach, among many others. The bibliography at the back is also meant as my sincere acknowledgement to those whose accounts I've used in the notes.

The Doyle family and the many friends I met with Bob are here too, although not all those we really wanted to include. The causes that inspired Bob's struggles in Ireland, in Spain and in Britain, for Nicaragua, for the environment and against exploitation, are growing ever more urgent in today's world of global capitalism. We must never become afraid of idealists or cynical about an earlier generation's sacrifice for the sake of others. Solidarity is within everyone's reach. The International Brigade is not just an association of veterans but one of families, friends and – yes, still – of supporters.

Harry Owens
Dublin
May 2006

A Note on the Text

For the reader for wants to know more, explanatory notes that give information on sources, issues and personalities are available from page 210; the relevant page numbers are noted in the text and an index to all subjects covered by the notes appears on page 236. Notes that are supplied as part of the text, as well as comments by Bob's comrades, are given in brackets.

PART I — BOB'S STORY

AN INHUMAN SOCIETY

OR THE MAKING OF A REVOLUTIONARY

I was born in Dublin on 12 February 1916, one of a family of five, two brothers and two sisters. I was the second youngest to my sister Eileen. It was the time of the 'Troubles'. At that time we were living in the North King Street area in a house like those to be found in Lisburn Street and Linenhall Street today.

Soon after the youngest child, Eileen, was born, my mother, Margaret née Aldridge, whose father was from a mixed marriage, Protestant father and Catholic mother, was found to be incapable of looking after her children and confined as a religious lunatic to Dublin's Grangegorman asylum. My father, Peter Doyle, was a fireman; he shovelled coal into hoppers on ships. While he was away at sea, my eldest sister, Josie, who was about nine, looked after us and tried to run the home when our mother was in Grangegorman. She was the only one who had a bit of sense.

Soon we came under the attention of nuns in nearby Eccles Street, whom I thought to be the Sisters of Charity. My aunt came one day and brought us up to the convent. They took us into their care and that was the last we were to see of any relative for nine years, the nuns having imposed the arrangement of no contact whatsoever. So at the age of five, me and my sister Eileen aged two were placed with the Byrne family of Fern Hill, Sandyford, near Stepaside in County Dublin. My brothers Christie and Peter were sent to some place in Cork. Only Josie stayed at home.

The Byrnes were poor people and had taken us in for the little financial addition to augment the family income of the husband's farm labourer's wage. They had three children of their own, all older than Eileen and myself. We were treated a bit like Cinderellas. Our diet was mainly potatoes and bread. Often allowed to go hungry, the two of us sitting on the doorstep would compete with the hens. I would be sent into the adjoining wood to gather sticks, which was the only fuel for the fire. I would load the sticks on a dried bough and pull them along, often crying in defiance at the strong wind blowing me back.

The mother would go into Bray once a week shopping, leaving the eldest son to look after the cottage. Our greatest treat in her absence was when he raided the cupboard for the sugar and placed little mounds of it on the dirty chairs. We would kneel down to suck it, licking the last grain. This was heaven and we must have looked like we were really enjoying a teddy bear's picnic. But he was a sadist, forcing me to catch the hind legs of the little terrier to swing the poor animal into a heap of briars and watch him struggling to get out. Another kick for him was to make me fetch a bucket of water, which he would throw over the roosting hens in order to watch them scatter.

One day the mother sent me to the fields where her husband worked with his lunch, which consisted of two marmalade sandwiches. I came back later having hidden behind a ditch and eaten the lot, for which I received a beating, but I never forgot the taste or enjoyment of that feast. Eileen and I had not been visited by anyone but after about a year, for some reason or other, we were taken to another family named Fagan in Newtownmountkennedy, in County Wicklow, some twenty miles away. We arrived on a Sunday to the convent and were taken to our new home by Sister Maria Borgia and Sister Mary McCreena. This was another poor family, a farm labourer with six children. Here we were all treated on an equal basis, and it was here that I started my education in the infants' class at the convent.

The door of the cottage opened to a beautiful view of the

Wicklow mountains, Ballinahinch and Ballinasloe. You could not imagine a purer air, yet despite this, I had ringworm, whittles, long tapeworms and boils, which I never mentioned, thinking they were natural. The cure for the latter was generally incision. Our recreation or games would consist of climbing trees, curling yourself in an old motor tyre and racing down a high slope with a ditch and water at the other end, steeplechasing over high fences, ditches and rocks.

We could not afford balls and made them out of old rags. A gun with a bang we made out of an inch-thick elderberry branch with a ramrod of beech; a bow and arrow, we made out of a sally stick and would compete for whose would go higher. We had no toys whatsoever and in retrospect I have no regrets. My greatest delight was to stroll the country lanes and ditches, looking for birds' nests, claiming they were mine, and watching the chicks grow. I would curse the dirty swine that would cut the throats of the young chicks.

During the mushroom season, I would get up at six to beat the other kids and run round the fields for the mushrooms in my bare feet, pissing on my feet to keep them warm in the early morning dew. Recently I revisited my childhood scenes in County Wicklow and went into the same fields. I retraced my steps across the grass to where the mushrooms used to grow when I was seven years old, and there they were, still coming up in the same places many decades later. A local farmer would pay me fourpence a day to frighten the crows off the wheat. With a cocoa tin pierced at the bottom, you'd put a bit of carbide used for bicycle lamps at the time, spit on top of it, and with the lid pressed on, put a lighted match at the bottom and stand clear for the bang. It certainly frightened the crows.

I hated school and would go mitching for the day, poaching the trout hiding under a bridge. Sister Maria Borgia and Sister Mary McCreena were sadistic, never relaxing the use of the stick. Borgia would send me out for a stick to the fields and if I brought a thin one back, I would be the first to be beaten. For the least infringement, like talking, laughing or dropping a note during the singing, she would keep me back after three o clock for a flogging.

Before leaving black and blue welts on my back, she would bow her head in prayer at the table and order me down on my knees with the words, 'Strip off your gansy' and then lay into me with no one present. There was no one to complain to. I was an orphan and nuns were sacred. It was some years later when the parents of some child complained that she was removed to another county.

Schooling consisted of the catechism, ancient Irish folklore, Irish-language and Catholic emancipation and rebel songs like 'The Croppy Boy'. Despite the disadvantages, I have never regretted this part of my formative years. I hated the cruelty and the injustices but these experiences served me well in an urban upbringing and in a better assessment of life in my later years.

It came as no surprise that while I was still attending school and turned ten years of age, the nuns came to the Fagans and said, 'Well, Robbie, you are now a sturdy young lad and fit to go on a farm.' I had noticed some of the older boys go the same way before me. The nuns and the priest used to come round collecting money and read out the names of the contributors at Sunday Mass with heavy emphasis on the biggest contributors. It was highly profitable for the nuns to supply a strong lad to a farmer to replace a farm labourer.

There were tears and protests about my removal from the Fagans and although it was only two miles down the road, it was like being sent to Australia. My life on this farm was lonely and a misery. The farmer had acquired two of us, Martin Grace and myself. Every night before bed we would all kneel on the stone floor to recite the rosary; in the morning, the piss would be collected in which the farmer bathed his feet for some complaint.

There were about one hundred acres and after school I would muck out and prepare the feed for the cattle and pigs and attend to other chores. The farmer would flog us for the least infringement; there was no time for play of any kind. On one occasion coming from 'devotions' in church on a Sunday evening, we stopped and played with the two girls at the nearest cottage. When the farmer heard of it he flogged us both with a strap and made us feel guilty of a crime. We were playing hide and seek, with no intentions of doing whatever was in his evil and hypocritical mind.

Again for some reason, after a year on this farm, I was moved to a farm the other side of Newtownmountkennedy called Hermitage. The name of the owners was Byrne, a middle-aged couple with no children. It was rightly named Hermitage and now I had three miles to walk to school as well as doing the work of a farm labourer. Having to rise at six in the morning, I would go to the fields to count the sheep, remove the snares from their legs and after school assist the farmer with general chores and carry the water from a distant spring.

Sunday I would pass my spare time on a rope swing, which I hung from an oak tree near the house. I was treated as a virtual slave by these two, who would pass me on the way to Mass in the pony and trap. At the end of Mass I would be given twopence as my weekly wages, which bought me a quarter of aniseed balls. We were never served dinner at the same table as the two. One night when I thought they were asleep, I sneaked downstairs and stole some sugar and was caught. I never heard the end of it. Many a time on my way out at six in the morning – I had to be at school at nine – I would take an egg from the barn and boil it in a cocoa tin out of sight of the house. My other enjoyment, apart from the swing, was poaching for trout on the nearby estate, often being chased by the gamekeeper.

I enjoyed going with a load of cabbages to Greystones on a farm dray, while the farmer drove around I would knock at the doors of the houses surrounding the golf course and ask if they wanted cabbage. Other times we went to the Powerscourt estate in Enniskerry for timber. On these occasions I would get twopence for my aniseed balls.

After two years here, I was now over twelve, when out of the blue the Mother Superior told me I was going to Dublin to my parents. My mother was now back home. Her words of advice were, 'Well Robbie, you are now going out into the world, don't forget to make your Easter duty.' This then was the extent of my education: I was now a good Catholic, having been baptised, made my first communion and served as an altar boy. I had been taught the Latin by Father Vaughan, who beat it into us with a cane.

I knew how to read and write, that God made the world, that

Jesus Christ was killed at the desire of the Jews whom I now hated, and I knew what the last word of the catechism was and what it meant, 'Amen – as it is meant to be.' I later became bitter about my education. I knew nothing other than the story of Brian Boru, the King of Munster, and that Daniel O'Connell was the great Catholic liberator. Most of the time we had religion, Irish and Catholic nationalism. The nuns were severe and sadistic.

Sister Maria Borgia, what a name! It was a revelation to me later when I read the history of the Borgia family and the history of the popes and I have often wondered why and how did the nuns adopt such names. In the summer of 2000, a friend, Shay Geraghty, brought me back to my old haunts in County Wicklow and I met a chap called Michael from Newtownmountkennedy when I was going around the grounds of what used to be the old convent.

He said, 'Hello Bob', and told me he'd been in the school under the same nuns for a short time. He swore about the nuns, Sister Maria Borgia and Sister Mary McCreena. He thought they were vicious. I told him how I was beaten and pointed out the room where Sister Maria Borgia kept me in after hours and said her prayers before she laid into me with the stick until my back was black and blue. He told me that upstairs, where my sister was taught, was where he was sent. He was still angry about the convent and those days.

At the age of thirteen I returned home to Dublin. We were in 30 Stafford Street, now Wolfe Tone Street, together with my younger sister who had remained at Fagans for the last couple of years. My parents, brothers and sister were strangers whom I could not recollect ever having seen before. But now my real education began.

I discovered the correct name of the order of nuns only when I was researching this book. Standing in Eccles Street outside the Georgian doorway where my aunt had brought me and my sister, I saw the plaque commemorating St Brigid's Orphanage of the Sisters of The Holy Faith, founded 'for the protection of Catholic orphans and destitute children in danger of loss of Faith'. It was set up under British legislation which allowed guardians to place a child at nurse with foster parents, a system that laster in Ireland from 1862 until the 1950s.

In 1997 I made my way to the current Holy Faith convent in Dublin's Liberties, where Sr Benignus, who was in charge of records, made me welcome. Glad of 'any news of our babies', today's cheerful nuns told me that the Newtownmountkennedy convent had been handed over to lay management. (Renamed Trudder House, it closed after problems emerged in the 1970s and 1980s.) Sr Benignus opened the ledger with its page for each child, My entry read:

> *Report 19 May 1921; Category: Children at Nurse*
> Robert Doyle born 14 [*sic*] February 1916, baptised
> in Marlborough Street (Pro-Cathedral). Both parents
> Catholics, mother in asylum, father lives in Pyles
> buildings, is to pay 18 shillings a week for the support
> of his two children, Mrs Lawlor is the children's aunt.
> Nurse (foster mother) Mrs Byrne, Fern Hill, Sandyford,
> County Dublin. Changed to Newtownmountkennedy,
> confirmed in Kilquade in May 1928. (My date of birth
> is given as 14 February, not 12 February. Dublin's poor
> often had the date of baptism a few days later taken as
> their birth.)

Sr Benignus confirmed that my father had kept up that weekly payment for the nine years, the largest contribution recorded in their ledger, but this was the first time I ever knew that our father had contributed a cent to mine and Eileen's maintenance. When I got up to leave, she carefully tore out my page from the ledger and handed it over as a memento. As a young novice joining in the 1950s, she remembered my two enemies, Maria Borgia and Mary McCreena, recalling one with a tall, stooped figure in old age, the other with a rasping voice and heavily built. That night in the home of the son of my fellow veteran of the International Brigades, Mick O'Riordan, I couldn't stop saying to myself, 'Eighteen shillings!' Since that day my ledger page remains a valued heirloom, and I often show it to visitors.

2

HOME FROM THE ORPHANAGE

After the years of isolation and the constant movement from one household to another, my return to the family was little more than another move. But I felt free at last of the burden of school and the exploitation of the nuns and farmers. Stafford Street then consisted of Victorian tenements, each sheltering four families. All seven of us were now back as a family living in two rooms. The two girls occupied one room and our parents and us three boys the other. Being the smallest I had to sleep with my head between my two brothers' feet. The one water tap and toilet were four flights down in the yard. Fights often broke out between families in the street, sometimes stretching as far as Jervis Street, and police were always present chasing the 'corner boys', the unemployed, stopping them from playing football.

We called the local copper 'Monkey Nuts'. My brother Peter and the crowd in the street would nick his baton and run away, throwing it from one to the other when he tried to stop them playing football in the street. The fights were between the grown-ups of the two streets during the daytime, our street and Jervis Street. There'd be a crowd; we kids wouldn't be in it.

There was a coalman living in our street and since I couldn't get a start in a job I went around a few times with him. He would sometimes stand outside places like the Shelbourne Hotel with a hand on one ear singing for a few pence. I'd stand beside him as 'the child' but he didn't share anything he got with me. I never got inside the doors of the Shelbourne.

Matt Talbot (1856–1925) who was later up for canonising, lived around the corner from us. When he died it was rumoured that he wore chains around his body for penance and that he was spotlessly clean and never had a bath. The Dublin Corporation named a new bridge after him for the city's Millennium Year, 1988. I never knew him to do anything useful to help the deprived of Dublin, but some years later I was to read a pamphlet by Sir Joseph Glynn glorifying the life of the coming saint and holding him out as a shining example to all Irishmen because he refused to take extra payment for overtime while turning round the timber boats of T. and G. Martin to catch the Liffey tide, believing it to be immoral,.

No wonder old McAlpine is reputed to have said on his deathbed, 'Never close the door on Paddy.' The story goes that he never refused an Irish labourer a job. As many Irish were from the rural areas they worked on the 'lump': paid in cash, no tax or welfare deductions and no unions. It became a well-known phrase in England: the folkgroup, the Dubliners, recorded 'McAlpine's Fusiliers', a ballad that satirised this emigrant experience.

My father was now working as a fireman in Lever Brothers soap factory and when I was fourteen he bought me my first pair of long pants, grey flannels, which were the vogue at the time. I now felt grown up and started to look for some kind of job. But nothing was available. I went down to Gardiner Street labour exchange where I used to sign on. There was no dole paid at my age. There was a big queue, right out into Gardiner Street; all ages it seemed to me coming fresh from Wicklow.

To get a job as a messenger boy, which was considered a good job, you would have to get a reference from the parish priest or some other dignitary. Most of our street was unemployed, including my two elder brothers, and many lived by their wits. Even my mother, with the aid of my brother Peter, raided the gas meter. She would enjoy putting the money in the meter to register and then catch it coming out the bottom. There'd be an unholy row when the gasman came and on one occasion my father called the police. From the slums and unemployment many went through the university of reform school, borstal and prison. We were no exception.

My father got me an interview at Lever Brothers and I failed the written examination test. I'd no education practically. The job would have been in the powder section, soapflakes. If I'd got that job I'd have been made – a job for life. My father worked here until he retired; he worked on the boilers stoking, shovelling coal into the hoppers. On Fridays he'd get his money, I'd meet him and we'd walk up from the North Wall, doing all the pubs on the way. I'd wait outside the door. He was known to be a good singer. When we got to our corner, he'd go into the last pub on the corner of Henry Street. My mother got some money but she didn't get enough.

Life was miserable at home for us, the two youngest. My mother would make us go to regular early Mass, which we hated, and while we could only afford condensed milk and meat bits from Moore Street, she would give money to the priests at Dominic Street chapel for masses to be said 'for the repose of the poor souls in purgatory'. At one stage the priest told her that her duty was to her children, and she should keep the money and feed them. Everything pawnable went into Brereton's pawn office in Capel Street on Mondays, even a new pair of sheets. The pawn office is still there in Capel Street but today the pawnshops are full of displays of jewellery, binoculars and cut glass.

My mother would give me a penny to go over to the Whitefriar's Street chapel to light a candle and pray to a certain saint to get me a job. (The Carmelites there have the shrine to the apostle St Jude, popularly known as the 'patron saint of hopeless cases' and opposite in the same side chapel, the shrine with the relics of St Valentine.)

It gradually dawned on me that neither God nor the saints would perform this miracle but I thought perhaps my prayers were answered when I saw the following advert in the Dublin *Evening Mail*: 'Young boy wanted to train as butler.'

The *Evening Mail* was the middleclass unionist paper. In those days unionists weren't just the Ulster loyalists who want to keep their link with Britain, they were the ones here in the South who'd lost the War of Independence only a decade before, who wanted all of

Ireland under the British crown. I replied to the advert and was taken on by a family named Patterson in Sandymount, Dublin.

I went out on the tram to where they lived on the seafront. Here I got a good bed and food for five shillings a week. I found myself being a 'houseboy', doing all the cleaning, polishing the shoes and emptying the chamber pots. On receiving the guests for the weekly bridge party I was instructed when opening the front door to remain unseen by walking behind the door.

Mrs Patterson had a son who was ill. He'd been in the Far East, the colonies, and had caught a disease. He was in bed all the time and I used to bring him up his food. It was 1931–32, the time of the general election when de Valera was making his bid for power under the slogan of 'Get your husbands off to work,' which I took to mean that he would create more jobs. Mrs Patterson hated my support for Fianna Fáil. She thought de Valera was a Communist, the devil in hell. After three months of subservience I had enough. I was a good worker but I was made to feel like a slave.

I told Mrs Patterson I was leaving and asked her for a reference. Furiously she took a piece of paper and wrote 'honest'. I tore it up, slung it on her table and returned to Stafford Street. I knew that her curt reference would be no good to me as proof of experience and character for the next job. In those days you couldn't get a job without a good reference.

(Thom's Directory from 1934-54 shows 'Patterson, ME, 113 Strand Road, Pembroke.' Facing the sea near the Martello tower, number 113 is one half of a late Georgian building, looking out to Howth across Dublin Bay, with two storeys over a basement and granite steps up to the hall door, a side entrance for servants and rear gardens which now have well-built bungalows. The house, now divided into three apartments, is still among the most elegant residences on the Sandymount seafront.)

1932 was also the year of the Eucharistic Congress in Dublin. To ordinary Catholics this was a worldwide Catholic gathering, a bit like the Olympics today. Phoenix Park, Dublin's main open space and the largest park in Europe, was packed. It lasted a full week; there was even a High Mass celebrated on O'Connell Bridge. I didn't go. I preferred to spend my time down at the docks trying to earn a few pence from the huge liners that brought the Catholics from all over the world.

Despite the misery, poverty and religious hysteria, Dublin that summer was great, a unique and beautiful city surrounded by sea and mountains. It was delightful to see the thousands setting out on the weekends towards Blackrock and Dollymount. These were the two huge beaches on either side of Dublin Bay, easily reached by any Dublin family with a pram on a sunny day. We would swim off the Custom House steps, the canal and the rivers. My brother Peter was a strong swimmer; he could swim across the Liffey and back while I could only manage halfway. There were only two public baths in the whole of Dublin so in the winter, when we had four pence, we were off to the one in Tara Street. It was always packed. A bath in the house was a luxury; we didn't have room for a tin one. The claim was that if you built baths for the workers they would only put coal in them.

One day my brother and I decided to nick the B&I mooring boat and row to Liverpool. It was a heavy carvelled rowing boat used by two stevedores to take the lines out for mooring the passenger and freight boats from Liverpool. We nicked it on the early evening tide and set out for where everyone seemed to be emigrating. London was too far away; you never heard anyone saying, 'I'm going to London.'

We rowed down the river; I'd bought some chocolates that were to last us until Liverpool. We got as far as Ringsend at the mouth of Dublin Bay when the tide turned and heavy winds set in. My brother, with more sense than me, decided to abandon ship and pulled in against the seawall, He climbed out while I was calling him a cowardly so-and-so. I too had to abandon ship. We walked back – I doubt if we tied up the boat. I would have to wait for another opportunity to get to Liverpool – the land of hope.

3

STREET POLITICS

By now I had started to take part in the demonstrations by the unemployed for work or full maintenance and to fight against the rising tide of Fascism. By this time Italy had been completely taken over and there were a number of countries that had dictatorships or had gone Fascist, like Portugal, Hungary, Poland and Bulgaria, and from 1933, Germany.

When the Blueshirts, the Irish Fascists, caught me on a demonstration through d'Olier Street I was surrounded by a crowd of them. They got me down a laneway off Dame Street and were hammering me. The police came and they joined in and then arrested me, dragging me up to O'Connell Bridge to an inspector who was sympathetic. When I was alone with the inspector for a moment, he said 'Can you run?' I said 'Yes' and was across the bridge like a hare. Another time we were waiting for a Blueshirt march. We tried to stop them and I got a knuckleduster in the eye and ended up in the Mater hospital.

We had demonstrations in O'Connell Street. It was the time of the 'Boycott Bass' campaign and Bass had offices nearly opposite the present Savoy cinema. They had their head-office in Belfast and one of their directors, a prominent unionist, Colonel Gretton, had made comments attacking Catholics and Republicans, so the IRA began their Boycott Bass campaign. They were following the example of their women's organisation Cumann na mBan who'd begun to boycott British sweets. Both were adopting the tactic first attributed to Jonathan Swift: 'Burn everything English except their coal!'

We'd hurl stones and many a time I was batoned to the ground in the street. The police were really brutal. In the 1932 elections, Sean Lemass said unemployment was the big challenge. Much was made, too, of Fianna Fáil's house building programme. Both had helped to attract Labour votes. The promised jobs never materialised and our attitude to Dev's government continued hostile.

(In 2004, the Taoiseach Bertie Ahern, himself a Bass drinker, contacted the Bass owners to prevent the closure of the 100-year-old plant in Belfast, with the loss of eighty jobs, at the request of Sinn Féin MP Gerry Adams. Opened in 1897 in the west Belfast nationalist heartland of Andersonstown, it is one of the few workplaces to survive the recent Troubles with a cross-community workforce. If closed, Bass ale would be imported from Britain.)

On one occasion we lay down on the tram tracks and then marched to Leinster House. My brother Peter took part in this march. He took a revolver with him and always boasted that he had let off a few shots outside Leinster House.

I had by now acquired a little knowledge of upholstery, working as an apprentice for a little man who was an upholsterer in a basement in a slum in Dominick Street for 2/6 a week and earned a few bob repairing chairs for the rich in Merrion Square. It was 1934 and I had saved enough to make another attempt to get to Liverpool, this time on the B&I cattleboat, which cost about ten shillings at the time. I felt sad as we sailed down the Liffey singing to myself 'Come Back to Erin, Mavourneen'.

In Liverpool I stayed at the Salvation Army in Park Lane at 1/6 a night. I saved the money I could by filling my pockets from the mountains of Brazil nuts on the docks, bound for Libbys, and at night patronising the different Gospel halls which enticed you to come in and pray with tea and sandwiches.

I spent the rest of the days going over and back to Wallasey, Port Sunlight and New Brighton, buying a one-way ticket and staying all day waiting for the Gospel halls to open, enjoying the sight of the big ships entering and leaving the bustling port. I tried for a job on the Mersey Tunnel, which was then being built, but had no luck.

When my money ran out I tried the Sailors Home for a bed and ended up sleeping around the landing stage until I was sent to father Berry's Catholic Home where, after a while, I was given a ticket and sent back home. The whole episode lasted about two or three weeks. I came back again to the North Wall of the Liffey on the cattleboat feeling disappointed. Liverpool was just as hard a place to look for a job as Dublin was, so many there were out of work too.

I didn't last long at home this time. I remember my father chasing me around the two rooms we had. He was wild to get hold of me; I think it was the drink. I managed to escape out the door and got cheap digs around the corner at 112 Capel Street, a two-room flat where I shared a room with Kit Conway. Our landlady was Mrs Sherlock; her daughter worked in the Italian ice-cream place across the street. I got a job as a clothing presser at 25 shillings a week with a little Jewish firm called Berbers in the North Lotts, near the corner with Elvery's. There were about twenty others there and it was a good place to work in.

My roommate, Kit Conway, who was later to die in the Spanish Civil War defending the Republic, was a well-known IRA activist and a legend in his native Tipperary during the fighting against the Black and Tans and the Pro-Treaty crowd. For his troubles he got a bullet through his mouth and ended with a very slight lisp. He was about the same height as me.

By now I too had become a seasoned participant in the political struggle, in all the unemployed demonstrations and in the battles against the Blueshirts, and I looked forward to the meetings in Cathal Brugha Street after Sunday Mass, where famous figures like Maude Gonne, Peadar O'Donnell and other Republicans would attract large crowds. Kit was my inspiration. A military instructor and a strict disciplinarian, he had earlier recruited me into the first Dublin Battalion of the IRA. We used to train in the fields west of Cabra doing barrack-type drilling and extended formations, which was to prove useful later in Spain. On weeknights we practised dry-firing with revolver and rifle in the basement of 41 Parnell Square. I was placed in the Engineers, going out to the Dublin mountains with dynamite and plenty of ammunition for rifle practice. I was surprised we got away with it as we were within hearing distance of Rathfarnham police station and we were supposed to be illegal under de Valera. Perhaps it was our strength in numbers – membership of the IRA was reputed to be 80,000 at that time. There were arms kept in a tent, we dug mines and later when I went to London I brought my notebook with instructions on making explosives. Paxo the breadcrumb mix for fish, was one of the ingredients we used. If I'd been searched and this was found in my pockets I'd have got about ten years.

(A few years later, Brendan Behan was also trained in IRA bomb making. He recalled the procedure: French clocks were preferred because their ticking wasn't loud. They used a cigarette lighter, a bicycle lamp battery and Paxo, a mix of chlorate of potash and paraffin. When the clock struck it connected the current, a low powered wire became red hot which then exploded the Paxo mix.)

At that time there were quite a lot of statues, relics of British Imperialism and the only activity I took part in was blowing up monuments. I was part of the new IRA, the old IRA having been the one that fought between 1916 and 1923. The new IRA was very broadly based but mainly dominated by middleclass officers and those whose concept was solely one of a united Ireland but the left-wing, which included Frank Ryan and Kit Conway, could see that this wouldn't have the appeal to the masses of the Irish people, and it certainly didn't appeal to me. Nationalism always appealed to me, by that I mean the right of Ireland to independence and to conduct its own affairs in the way it wishes. But that alone wouldn't put bread on the table since you would probably have the same shower of capitalists there afterwards. The reason I would later split from the IRA was that I felt the leadership had no social policy. While living in slums I couldn't see what their policy was.

When Kit was drilling us up in the fields in Cabra – there were no houses there at that time – if there was any laughing or talking in the ranks, he'd warn, 'Just because you live with me, don't think you get away with anything.' He used to keep a tommygun under the bed, with a case of ammunition. He'd take it out and clean it. He was an expert – he could take it apart and reassemble it with his eyes closed. He seemed to do a lot of nocturnal work sometimes bringing back a revolver. Being a prominent Republican he was often followed by a Special Branch man. He told me he could sometimes manage to slip around the detective, get him from behind and take his gun off him. He'd come straight back to the flat and pass me the revolver and give me the price of the cinema around the corner in Mary Street, the 'Mare-oh', until the heat died down. On the first occasion as I passed the local cinema I noticed there was a Tom Mix cowboy film on. I went in and sat there watching the film feeling a certain elation with the gun sticking down my trouser belt.

There were two cinemas in the street, the other one was called the Volta. We called it the Louse Bank; it had an old woman who used to play the piano while the silent films were showing. I'd stick the revolver down my trouser belt and forget about it, waiting for the afternoon matinee. Later I'd pass the gun on to Bill Gannon, another senior IRA man, at 41 Parnell Square, and a great friend of Kit's. Paddy Sullivan was there too. Kit remained in his position until the formation of the Communist Party of Ireland and the Irish Republican Congress. He became a founding member of both. He was my hero and I followed every political decision he would take. He was a great friend and a great inspiration. (See note, *Kit Conway*, p. 210.)

4

THE CONNOLLY HOUSE SIEGE

I had attended the evening mission on Monday 27 March 1933 at the Pro-Cathedral, during the period of Lent where the preacher was a Jesuit. The cathedral was full. He was standing in the pulpit talking about the state of the country, I remember him saying – which scared me – 'Here in this holy Catholic city of Dublin, these vile creatures of Communism are within our midst.' Immediately after the sermon everybody then began leaving singing and gathered in a crowd outside, we must have been about a thousand singing 'To Jesus Heart All Burning' and 'Faith of Our fathers, Holy Faith'. We marched down towards Great Strand Street, to the headquarters of the socialist and anti-Fascist groups in Connolly House. I was inspired, if you could use that expression, by the message of the Jesuit. There was no attempt by the police to stop us.

When we got there, the mob attacked and tried to destroy the building. I was pressed up against the wall opposite Connolly House. I couldn't see what was happening at first – we were told that they were spitting on a statue of the Blessed Virgin inside. I remember the fire brigade coming up and stopping in between us, people blocking the brigade, throwing things at them. These were hitting the wall behind me, thrown back from Connolly House. As the injured were taken to the nearby hospital in Jervis Street, I tried to get a good look to see if they had big beards as they were portrayed by the priests. I stayed there watching this for an hour or so and then walked home. I only lived up the road.

I was present only at the first attack. The next morning I was shocked and ashamed to read on the *Irish Press* billboards: 'Hooligans Burn Connolly House.' I was one of the hooligans. I went along to Phoenix Publications to see Seán Murray, a veteran guerrilla fighter in the war against the British and the Civil War, and an outstanding public speaker and socialist. I wanted to find out about his emerging Communist Party of Ireland. I wanted to know if they believed in God? I said to him: 'I have a gun; surely you must need to have people trained in the use of arms in the struggle for socialism and in our defence against the Fascists?' I had been caught by the Blueshirts and beaten up three times.

Seán answered the first question by citing the example of Fr O'Flanagan, the outstanding socialist Republican and anti-Fascist priest, whom I had heard speaking on many occasions and who was suspended by the bishops for his beliefs and yet continued to say Mass. To the second question he pointed out the need to organise, and 'When the time comes to use arms we will have the workers trained.'

Jim Larkin, the trade union leader, had his Workers Union of Ireland office up from the Pro-Cathedral in Marlborough Street. I used to follow him down the street and watch to see did he raise his hat as he passed the church or not; we'd heard so many stories about him being against the church and I still thought this was true. Eugene Downing, who was also to serve in the International Brigade, remembers what it was like inside the besieged Connolly House. This is a translation of his account from his memoir originally published in Irish as *La Niña Bonita agus an Róisín Dubh* (1986):

> For three days in March 1933, Connolly House at 64 Great Strand Street, headquarters of the Revolutionary Workers Groups, was besieged by the city's riff-raff. It would ease off during the day but at night the crowds would gather again, trying to break in and burn the place. In the end the defenders had to yield in the face of these attacks and escape over the rooftops.
>
> On the night of Wednesday 29 March came the

last phase of the attack. That evening Bill McGregor managed to get in with food for the defenders. We had blocks of wood nailed to the floor inside the door for fear the crowd might make a rush and break through, which made the entrance pretty narrow. He was trying to rush in and broke a few eggs, someone made the joke that we'd have scrambled eggs for supper.

Later that night nobody could get in or out because the street was packed. We also had to keep an eye on the back door because there was a way in from the furniture factory on our left; we'd to watch the rear first floor window which overlooked the factory yard. We also had to guard the roof which was accessible from the roofs on either side. Strange to relate, the street entrance was safer than the rest of the building. The police on duty couldn't be distinguished from the onlookers, and were more concerned about the free flow of traffic through Swift's Row and Capel Street than prosecuting the attackers.

During the night many of the mob were injured by the missiles they'd fired through the windows, and which were thrown back at them, and slates taken from the roof. Donal O'Reilly, one of those who'd been sent home during the Easter Rising because he was too young, was in charge. About ten thirty some of the crowd broke the gate into the furniture factory and ran up to the back door of Connolly House. Things got dangerous then. When it seemed we couldn't hold them back any longer Joe Troy fired a shot which wounded one of them in the knee. That stopped them for a while. But then they gathered up things from the factory and piled it up outside the door and set it alight. Burning wood was put through the letterbox at the front door.

The fire brigade arrived on the scene shortly

afterwards, but things were so bad at this stage that it was impossible to defend the building any longer; it was just a matter of time. We had to retreat to the attic and began escaping through the skylights. Brian O'Neill and Christy Clark were already on the roof covering the retreat with revolvers. Charlie Gilmore, a brother of George, was downstairs with a Colt revolver, guarding the rear. As there were at least six armed men amongst us, it shows how disciplined we were, that nobody was killed, despite the mob's fierce attack.

Most of those who got out managed to reach the roof of the St John's Ambulance hall which was conveniently close, and found shelter there. For some reason Tommy Watters and myself with two others continued on across the roofs to Capel Street and eventually we got down into a yard at the rear of shops. There was no exit to the street other than through these shops. We found a back door and knocked. A short fat Italian answered; it was a chipper. Tommy explained that all we wanted was to get out to the street. We were asked to stay there for a while and the door was shut. We weren't sure what would happen but, sure enough, he came back soon after and told us to come into the shop, one at a time, and sit at the table. We did as he told us and we had a nice meal and listened to the racket outside. Then we went out into the storm.

Great Strand Street and the corner of Capel Street were packed with people, screaming and shouting. We walked through them as if it was all nothing to do with us. One of us bumped into someone who knew him slightly and didn't know he'd any connection with the Revolutionary Workers Groups. He began excitedly telling us about the thrashing they were giving the Reds. We listened as although somewhat interested and content with this turn of events, then headed for the quays and home. The same mob marched around the city a few days later, and when passing Unity Hall they threatened to destroy it also. As this held the offices of a trade union, it indicates the anti-democratic spirit which lay behind the violence.

When the storm eased off some of us went back to the wrecked house and Denis Larkin, a brother of young Jim, took photos of the various rooms with everything smashed. I was happy to see the light I'd fixed over the hall door a few weeks before was still intact, I like to think it was due to the quality of my own handiwork. The Blueshirts and the mob were the main elements in that attack. There were some decent people amongst them, swayed by the malicious rumours and extreme language of the clergy.

A few years after the attack on Connolly House, myself and Barney McGinn, on our way to a lecture on the Paris Commune, were in the Pro-Cathedral in Marlborough Street where they were giving a mission. The priest made some reference to the dreadful lecture about to be given in the holy city of Dublin.

'I'm informed,' he said, 'that Brian O'Neill is to give this lecture but I'd be doubtful about that. I'd rather believe his name is really Isaacson or Levinsky or some such.' And then, speaking slowly, energetically and with venom, he said, 'And he should be thrown into the Liffey.' The ordinary people must have been getting a bit more sensible at this stage because the priest's efforts failed to move them to any further violence.

Joe Monks, who later joined the International Brigades as well, was in a house besieged by a similar mob: 'On the night that the immense murmuring mob came to 63 Eccles Street, a collection of old socialists stationed themselves in the hall. The roof party consisted of Bill Tumilson, myself and and three others with handguns, some provided by Lil O'Donnell, to be used if armed Blueshirts attempted to come over the roofs, and buckets of half bricks to be used against the mob. Late in getting up to the roof, we missed an opportunity to frighten off the mobsters. The singers among them had only succeeded in singing half a verse of 'Faith of Our Fathers' then the battering at the hall door began.

The police were conspicuous by their absence although Lil's sister, Nurse Jo O'Donnell who owned a nursing home on the opposite side of the street was all the time telephoning the Castle. She eventually got onto the Government Minister responsible, Patrick Ruttledge.

The veteran suffragette Mrs Despard, aged but unafraid, moved forward to see who it was that was battering at her door. Mary Donnelly followed. The mob, seeing the figures at the window, raised a blood-curdling howl. But Mickey Bleau, a Flanders veteran and, like those outside, one of Dublin's poor, speedily interposed himself between the women and the window. He'd a broom handle which accidentally went through a pane of glass.

A woman mobster mistook his broom handle for the barrel of a gun, and her warning cries mingled with the sounds of the broken pieces of glass clanging down into the area. Panic gripped the foremost mobsters at the door. They hurled themselves down the steps into the bosom of the mob, and we on the roof bombarded the steps with bricks which burst into dust on impact.

Even had the ghost of Lord ffrench, one-time Commander-in-Chief of the British Army in Flanders, and Mrs Despard's brother, come charging at the head of a squadron of cavalry, the area could not have been cleared with such speed. Mob orators rallied the

fugitives outside Molly Bloom's window at no. 7 Eccles
Street but their chances had passed because the 'boys in
blue' like a belated Seventh Cavalry, came on the scene,
they came on motorbikes and sidecars, in Black Marias
and squad cars.

As the journalist Michael McInerney wrote: Paddy
Ruttledge, the Minister of Justice, was one of those
early Fianna Fáil men who had no inhibitions about
'left ideologies' and soon the guards lathered the divil
out of the Animal Gang, and the other hooligans
around the building.

Our activities continued, as did the daily battles with the Blueshirts
and the Animal Gang in O'Connell Street and in the mass
demonstrations for work or full maintenance. The Animal Gang
weren't criminals; they were toughs, and used bicycle chains. We'd
form up at Burton's corner opposite Nelson's Pillar, where the
Kylemore Café is now, they'd form up outside the GPO. They'd
wear British Legion poppies in their lapels and we'd try to snatch
them. We'd be wearing Easter Lilies. They fought for the Blueshirts.
I always thought a priest organised them. They'd a base or office
in Pearse Street and they'd attack anyone of the Left, targeting
meetings, marches and demonstrations etc. There were running
battles between the Fascist movement led by the ex-Chief of Police
in Dublin, General O'Duffy, who formed the Blueshirts with another
one by the name of Cronin. There was no alliance whatsoever with
the IRA.

The Blueshirts mainly comprised the sons of middle-sized and
large farmers; their aims were principally against Communism or
any group of a left-wing direction and against Republicans. Behind
the Animal Gang and Fine Gael's Blueshirts there were some
whose family members served as Irish nationalists in the British
Army during the First World War, and were proud of this. Many
had little confidence in the new Irish Free State that had broken
away from Britain or in Dev who was destroying the remaining

links with the British Empire they'd grown up in. Some supported
Fascism: Professor Hogan said, 'It was the growing menace of the
Communist IRA that had called forth the Blueshirts as inevitably as
the Communist anarchy had called forth the Blackshirts of Italy and
the Brownshirts of Germany.'

Living in the slums as I did, the struggle over the question of
the border became of secondary importance, as it did for the more
socially and politically conscious and progressive elements in the
leadership of the IRA. This difference of priorities caused a build-
up of opposition within the Republican movement which led to the
Athlone Conference in 1934 and the split which followed. A new
organisation, the Republican Congress, was formed and I promptly
joined it. This was more left-wing and not only politically, which
appealed to me. They became more involved in strikes, lock-outs and
defending people being evicted from slum areas for non-payment
of rent. They participated in all kinds of social areas and worked to
prevent black-legging.

This had more appeal for me than the ultra nationalism of certain
factions of the IRA. It was close to the Communist Party, so close
it was denounced by the Church. Though the actual Communist
Party was very much a minority thing, every left-wing movement
was branded as Communist anyway. The congress was a broad-
based organisation embracing the left Republicans, the unemployed,
tenants associations, small farmers and anti-Fascists under the
leadership of Peadar O'Donnell, Frank Ryan, Seán Murray, Kit
Conway and others who had lost confidence with the army council
of the IRA. All those who set up the Republican Congress were
formally expelled by the remainder of the IRA. In Dublin the
resigning IRA men reformed Connolly's Citizen Army.

I was still a practising Catholic and admired the great Fr Michael
O'Flanagan, outlawed by Maynooth College, and the Vatican I
believed, for his Republican and humanist sympathies. However my
last voluntary attendance at Mass was when there was a High Mass
at which de Valera, the head of the government, was in attendance. I
tried to follow him through the main doors of the central sanctuary

at the Pro-Cathedral but I was refused entry because I only had two pence. Unable to pay the six pence admission I was told 'You can't come in here; go to the other door – the side door.' I refused and walked down the steps saying 'If that's the price to go into the house of God then that's my last visit. The only time I have been since has been by force and through fear of reprisal.

(The New Testament's letter of St James describes this situation: 'If you show special attention to the man wearing fine clothes, and say: "There's a good seat for you" but say to the poor man: 'You stand there, or sit on the floor" haven't you discriminated, become judges with evil thoughts – you have insulted the poor.' Frank Ryan shared some of Bob's criticisms of the Church at that time: Eugene Downing remembers him as 'a Catholic, all right, but he was also in favour of social justice, and said, "If you can't reconcile the two things, there must be something wrong with your Catholicism."')

I was a delegate to the conference of the Republican Congress at the Rathmines Town Hall in 1934. It was our first conference, united under the socialist policies of James Connolly, we came together to discuss the needs of the working classes, the struggle against imperialism and the Irish capitalists. Those same Irish capitalists whose newspaper editorials had blessed British bullets, which put an end to the lives of Connolly and his associates.

While the conference was in session, Catholic Action and their Fascist supporters had assembled a hostile mob outside screaming for our blood and singing 'Faith of Our Fathers' and 'To Jesus Heart All Burning' while waiting to lynch us as we came out. The police offered no protection and we had to flee for our lives from the mob, fired by the incitement of the press and clergy. I escaped with others out the back and hid all night in the basement of a flat of a sympathiser in Stephen's Green.

A few days later while returning after lunch from my job as a presser, I was attacked by a gang outside the factory. I knew they would be waiting again when I knocked off, so I sent a message to my brother Peter, who came down with my loaded .45 revolver. With Peter, who they didn't know, walking well behind, I turned the corner into Abbey Street and spotted the gang coming out of a lane towards me armed with sticks and iron bars. I shouted to Peter who got out in the middle of the road, firing three shots over their heads. The gang scattered in all directions and we made our escape. After that, whenever I passed the corner near Capel Street where a couple of the gang lived, I'd have a hand held inside my jacket as if holding a gun, and they would sing, 'Who's Afraid of the Big Bad Wolf?' but they never tried it on again.

The Bacon Strikes were over union recognition. We'd be walking up and down in Henry Street and Moore Street in groups of a dozen or two Republican Congress activists shouting, 'Strike On Here' and 'Don't Support Scab Labour' and going into the shops. Once I had a stick for smashing up the weighing scales.

(The *Irish Press* of January 3, 1935, reports a court case where three men were charged following the smashing up of the Arran Quay branch of the Bacon Shops in support of the strike: three armed men held off the guards while eight or nine others with bars and sticks rushed into the shop. Another report, in the *Irish Press* of Tuesday 8 January, records a peaceful picket by a different element of the Republican Congress, where the picketers were charged with obstruction. They included Charlie Donnelly, Cora Hughes and Eugene Downing. Eugene considered the former's violent activity was 'the IRA sort of anarchism, doing things on their own like that, instead of trying to involve other people.')

This was the kind of organised action that I was involved in, coming from the Republican military tradition, as George Gilmore said, we 'learned our political theory in prison cells, or on the end of a Blueshirt baton.' The theory evolved out of the practice for most of us. (See note, *The Economic War and the Depression*, pp. 210–1.)

5

GETTING TO SPAIN

Meanwhile in Europe the war clouds had been gathering. Fascism was on the rampage, strengthened by its consolidation in Italy and Germany, and the formation of the Rome-Berlin-Tokyo axis. After elections were held in Spain in 1936, the *Daily Telegraph* correspondent who reported the elections wrote that 'if these elections had been held under such conditions as prevail in England, then the Popular Front would have had a far greater victory because the pressure of the Right was so tremendous everywhere that people could not, or feared, to vote freely and gave their votes to the Right to make sure of their bread and butter.'

From the beginning of 1936 I was hearing more about Spain. It was everyday news. The propaganda of the Catholic Church and the official press was 100 per cent in support of Franco's military revolt. It was a tremendous campaign, preaching at Mass and the missions about the need to support Franco, a gallant Christian gentleman, defending the Catholic Church in Spain.

Within such left-wing circles as the Republican Congress, it was of course, despite the propaganda, not so much a question of going to fight in Spain but a question of giving every aid to Republican Spain. Our response sprang out of the recognition of the danger of Fascism. We were very conscious that the Nazis had come to power in Germany in 1933 and that General O'Duffy was intending to follow in their footsteps. Although the Irish hierarchy was strongly behind Franco, it seemed to me that the bishops never condemned the Blueshirt movement. Did the Church support the Blueshirts?

Well, tacit support, that's the right word.

I thought there was a danger that Ireland would go Fascist and that was one of the motivating factors in making up my mind to go to Spain. I didn't know much about Spain but I certainly knew that my thoughts were that every bullet I fired would be against the Dublin landlords and capitalists. Furthermore I always had the habit of believing that whatever the Church said politically, the opposite was true. That was one of the reasons why I was on the side of the Spanish Republic right from the start.

I was twenty in 1936 when the Spanish War broke out on 18 July, with the revolt of the generals against the democratically elected government of the Second Republic. Franco declared that if necessary he would shoot half of Spain. All were subject to the most extreme punishments by military tribunal for the possession of arms, for participating in political meetings or conferences, for the use of print or the possession of documents or papers destined for publicity, for those who left their place of work in breach of contract and for insults or any acts of aggression against the armed forces.

It was monstrous that those in revolt were now declaring as rebels all those who had participated and won in the democratic elections. To this barbarism was added the full support of the Catholic Church. The Cardinal Archbishop of Toledo, Isidro Gomá y Tomás, declared that the war between Spaniards was a holy crusade and that Spain could not be pacified without the use of arms. The bishop of Cartagena, Monsignor Díaz Gomara, thundered, 'Blessed be the cannons if the Gospel flowers in the breaches they blow open.' Franco even claimed that the Pope would grant one hundred indulgences for every Red killed.

These satanic verses resulted in the execution of sixteen priests in San Sebastián by the Franco Fascists for the crime of 'non-rebellion'. A further 278 were imprisoned and 1,500 declared as 'undesirable'. The Archbishop of Burgos said in a sermon, 'You who bear the name of Christians, no pardon for those who destroy churches, and for the killers of holy priests, may their seed be wiped out.' Immediately following these military and episcopal orders, it was no surprise that

Republican militiamen taken prisoner at the front, and even the wounded in hospitals, were executed. Examples of massacres where the Fascist forces triumphed within the first days were Mallorca and Navarra, and after Badajoz was stormed 2,000 were shot within 24 hours.

In Málaga which was conquered by Italian and Franco troops in February 1937, more than 5,000 were executed without trial for being sympathetic to the Popular Front. Men and women, peasants and intellectuals, were shot on the beaches and against the cemetery walls by Italian mercenaries. However, in the interests of historic justice, it is well to remember that there were honest men of the Church who refused to give aid to the Fascist military revolt against the Republic. They were few, because, as in all corrupt societies, the brave and honest are always the few, but not all the military rose against the Republic and neither did all the men of the Church support Franco's crimes.

The Cardinal Archbishop of Tarragona, Francisco Vidal y Barraquer, issued episcopal documents from the beginning of the Republic calling on the people to support the legitimately elected government, and refusing to bless the cause of the Fascist generals. He was forced into exile to a small village in Switzerland where he died seven years later. Monsignor Mateo Múgica, another bishop, was also forced into exile for refusing to approve the crimes and abuses in his diocese of Vitoria, in the Basque region where the 16 Basque priests were executed, all charged with the crime of 'not having rebelled' and refusing to state from the pulpit that it was Republican planes which had destroyed their own town of Guernica, when the world knew it was German planes that had carried out this act which horrified democratic opinion everywhere. There were others but they were indeed the few. Never in the history of the Spanish Church had such barbarities been blessed by its bishops, and never in Spain had such treachery been committed against Christianity. How could the democracies of the world look on? (See note, *The Outbreak of the Civil War and the Catholic Church*, pp. 211–2.)

At the beginning of 1937 I was with Alec Digges and others

who were working for Spain here. There was some awareness among the thinking sections of the Irish population of the need to aid the Republicans in Spain but it was not easy to gather support. The Jewish sections in the South Circular Road were the only ones we could get backing from. (See note, *The Republican Congress and the War in Spain*, pp. 212–3.)

I went to see Cora Hughes in her office, thinking she was responsible for organising the Irish going out to Spain for the Republic. She told me there was nobody going now, the last group had already gone and there was no group being prepared that I could join. I think she considered I was too young. I told her, 'I'm going anyway. I'll get there under my own steam' and I did. I set out on the B&I boat to Liverpool and from there to London where I stayed at the Salvation Army in Great Peter Street in Westminster. I knew nobody so after a few weeks trying calling into jobs, I got a job as a kitchen porter like Ho Chi Minh, at Lyons Corner House in Piccadilly Circus for a couple of months, bringing down the milk and cream for twenty-four shillings a week. Luckily for me they had a bed for resting when you'd an hour or two off work. I lived just off the Edgeware Road.

When I'd saved enough money, I got my brother Peter to come with me and together we left for Jersey in the Channel Islands. It was a step towards Spain for me, where again I lived in cheap digs for two months or so. I first worked mixing guano and then I was working on the spuds and tying up tomatoes. I saved enough for the next stage to St Malo on the ferry where I got the train straight to Marseilles. Peter stayed on in Jersey. In Marseilles I could afford to stay only at the Salvation Army for two nights, so for a month I slept on park benches and under railway trucks on the siding in the daytime, it was so hot. I spoke no French at all; it was real hoboing. I was bumming my food from British ships to conserve what little money I had. The sailors were good with what they didn't need for themselves.

Every day I would go around the docks looking for information of ships plying the Spanish route. Eventually I heard of one likely to sail to Valencia. It was about 2,000 tons and was sailing under the Greek flag. With a few snacks I managed to get aboard and hid myself in a small anchor room bound for Republican Valencia. Four hours out at sea one of the crew opened the trap door to inspect the anchor chain and I was discovered, perhaps luckily because had they dropped anchor, the whirling chain would have made mincemeat of me. The ship had a German or Italian non-intervention officer aboard to see that it wasn't carrying arms or volunteers to the Republic. (See note, *The Non-Intervention Policy*, pp. 213–5.) He questioned me as regards to where I was going and what my intentions were. I told him I was going to join the International Brigades. He told me I would be arrested on arrival and deported back to be dealt with by the British Authorities. There was nowhere to lock me up so I was free to mix with the rest of the crew who were mainly sympathetic.

We arrived at Valencia on 8 July 1937. As the ship berthed I made a jump for the jetty and landed on a quay below. The captain and the non-intervention officer were shouting '*¡Policía!*' I ran up the jetty towards the main gate, out of the docks and into the main street where I was caught. I had no identity documents or passport on me. I was taken to Valencia police barracks for questioning, where it seemed the inspector, an anarchist, suspected I was German because of my fair head of hair. But he handed me over to the British Consul and left. The consul asked me the standard questions about where I was going and what my intentions were. I told him I had come to join the International Brigade, to which he replied: 'There is no such thing. They are hiding around Spain like rats.' He then told me that I would have to work my passage back to Britain and that I was liable to be arrested on arrival. (See note, *Valencia and Tory Sympathisers*, pp. 215–6.)

The British consulate was unhelpful in putting me in contact with any representative of the Republic or the International Brigade, and as I had no knowledge of Spanish at the time I was unable to make my own investigations. I had enough money to stay in a cheap boarding house and was visited by the police two nights running.

I hung around the docks all the time and discovered that a young Spaniard had deserted his ship – the SS *Calderon* – on the

McAndrews Line, a Spanish-English shipping line plying between France, Spain and Portugal. I went aboard and applied for the job and was signed as a deck boy.

On 10 July 1937, after loading our cargo of fruit and wine, we set sail for Liverpool, where I reported to the secretary of the Communist Party, Frank Bright, what had happened and my intentions to continue on the ship going back to Spain. My membership of the party in Dublin had lapsed so I rejoined in Liverpool to ensure that while sailing to and from Spain I might be able to do useful work, liaising with members of the International Brigade and bringing back propaganda to Britain. We were only a few days in Liverpool before we set sail, this time to Franco's Spain, with a load of steel plates. The first port of call was Cádiz, where, in contradiction to the claims of the English and French governments, I saw German and Italian battleships.

(Foreigners were now flocking into Spain – 'armed tourists', as Winston Churchill called them. The second expedition of Mussolini's 3000 Blackshirts and 1500 technicians arrived at Cádiz. These were all to go into action in battalions under Italian officers in the uniform of the Spanish Foreign Legion. Italian troops and pilots in Spain now totalled 14,000, according to the *Manchester Guardian*, which reported on 5 December 1936 that 2500 Italian Fascists had disembarked at Algeciras, and on 18 January 1937 that an estimated 4000 more arrived at Cádiz. They reported further on 10 March that 10,000 Italian troops arrived just eight days after their government decreed that no more volunteers should go to Spain.)

Wounded Italian and German soldiers were being taken aboard to be shipped back to their respective countries. I was delighted, I put them down as casualties from the battle of Jarama, which went on for nearly a month. That was the battle where Kit Conway had fought and died. I didn't know he was dead then. I thought, 'They're giving them hell.' Later I heard back in Liverpool and sadly read an account of his death in the first days of that battle by Jim Prendergast:

February 12 at noon. We had just swung through the
bottleneck of a valley and were beginning to deploy. I
had been told to look for a bridge, our objective. Just
then we came under direct fire. Men were hurriedly
seeking good cover among the scrub, but once we lay
down we saw that we had no view ahead.

For a while we fired from standing positions.
Suddenly Peter Daly shouted that they were advancing
on our left. I looked across. We concentrated fire on
them at 500 yards range.

But the Fascist fire, front and flank, was now pretty
heavy. Men were being hit all around. Somebody
was hit beside me. A yell for stretcher-bearers. Goff
tumbled over, his hand to his head, his face white. It
was a narrow shave; his helmet was dinged. Kit was
everywhere at once, directing fire, encouraging us all.

The fire had grown so heavy now that nobody could
tell what would happen, and fear was not felt anymore,
because it was no use feeling afraid. A Spaniard who
had got mixed up with us somehow moved over to my
side. The bush he left had been denuded by a stream
of bullets. He looked at me, laughed. We moved to the
right, to higher ground to get a better field of fire.

We took up new positions. I saw Paddy Duff
moving back, hit in the leg. Shells were exploding on
the left. Holy God! If they fall on this bare ground
we are finished! Low-flying planes scream towards
us. Now we are in for it in earnest. They pass over and
soon they are back again with our fighters at their tails.
A faint cheer from us.

Now if we quit these positions, the Fascists will
break in on the road. So here we must stay, even though
the Fascist fire is literally eating the top of the hill away.
Men from three companies are here on the hill. Things
are a bit mixed up. Kit takes command of all.

As I move up the hill, Jack Taylor, a big Cockney with whom I had one unforgettable night at Figueras, is dressing a wounded comrade. 'Hit bad?' 'Unconscious, thumbs up. I guess.' There is blood on the seat of Jack's pants. Only a flesh wound he says, and he won't go back.

I settle into a new firing position. My rifle is soon burning hot. Kit comes over. I notice his face with lanes of sweat running through the dust. He hands me a note. It is from Brigade HQ telling us that we must hold out at all costs. He tells me transmit these instructions to the section on our left flank, I look through my binoculars before I move off. The Moors are sneaking up there on the left. Oh, where are our machine-guns?

I speed away to the left, deliver the message. What's left of the others are around the White House, I am told. I get to the house, and on the way, it seems as although a thousand bees are buzzing past my face. So, it does take a man's weight in lead to kill him.

I get to the yard and shout. No reply. No noise from within. I clear the low wall and go in. Yes, they are there all right, all dead. I shiver as I move back.

I am more reckless. No fear now. Why? I do not know. Somebody calls my name. It is Pat Smith. Blood streams from his head and arm. Tom Jones of Wexford is here. Good man, Tom. Always dresses a man where he falls. A hero. He tells me that Goff and Daly are hit. I reach the hill-crest where Kit is directing fire. He is using a rifle himself and pausing every while to give instructions.

Suddenly, he shouts, his rifle spins out of his hand and he falls back. He is placed on a blanket. No stretchers now. His voice is broken with agony. 'Do your best boys, hold on!' Tears glisten in our eyes. Many are from other companies. But all remember Kit at Córdoba and Madrid. His gallant leadership then and today won them all.

Kit is taken away. I see Ken Stalker. He is the only experienced man left. I run to him and he takes over command. I see Fascist tanks rolling up the road to the right. Moors are sweeping us front and flanks. We'll never hold them now. I move to a firing position. Suddenly, I am lifted off my feet. Something terrific has hit me in the side. I cannot breathe. They are dressing me now…

In the ambulance I meet Kit. He is in terrible agony, and can talk little. Next morning they told me our great leader was dead.

Ken Stalker from Dundee was a World War I veteran, aged forty-one when he enlisted in Spain, who had fought at Lopera and Las Rozas. He was political commissar here, and was shot in the head soon afterwards, dying later that day. The news of Kit's death would not reach Ireland until 27 February when I was in London on my way to Spain. I was unaware that on my birthday, 12 February, my friend Kit had been fatally wounded.

The crew on board the SS *Calderon* were mainly from Liverpool. They had been sailing the regular route for some time and were familiar with the ports and pleasures common to most seamen. I was just twenty-one at the time and had never been further than England. As soon as we were discharged from duty my crewmates decided to go out and seek whatever entertainment they could. They quickly familiarised themselves with a respectable looking 'Casa Puta'. The women, with see-through dresses, were paraded in front of us and then took up positions sitting on our laps, picking on those they liked and enticing you to their rooms upstairs or next door.

Suddenly a group of German sailors came in. They looked around and ordered all the British sailors out. The German sailors hated the British and they roughly chucked them out and down the stairs. But because of my fair hair they must have thought I was German and one came over and spoke in German to me saying something to the effect that I was all right to stay there. I was frightened, just waiting to get a chance to bolt down the stairs. While they were arranging a sexual performance exhibition I was away like a rabbit to rejoin my comrades back at the docks.

Our next port of call was Huelva, still in Franco's territory, there were two German submarines berthed there – according to the British government there were none in Spain. Probably these were the so-called 'pirate' submarines which had already sunk eight Soviet ships bringing arms to the Spanish government. In Franco's ports there was always a German presence.

There was no contact whatsoever between us and the Germans, we kept clear of them and after a short while we sailed back to Liverpool and London. The local people didn't like the Germans. They'd come into shops and cafes, order what they wanted and throw people out. They seemed to have the run of the Franco ports. We did several trips like this, alternating between Franco and Government ports and by now I was gaining more experience of Spain and acquiring a smattering of the language. I was now liaising with the Spanish Aid Committee in Liverpool, smuggling leaflets and posters in and out of Spain and letters to and from International Brigaders when we called at Republican ports.

However our skipper, Captain Williams, began to realise what I was up to. He was infuriated to see me meet fellow British seamen who were now with the International Brigade. They were Jack Coward and Albert Coal, then in charge of torpedo boat 14 in the Spanish Republican navy. My return to Government-held Valencia was very different from my first trip there. Our captain by this time was hostile and suspicious of my activities He demanded that I should surrender anything I had so that he could censor it. This I refused to do and I even contacted the police to complain about him.

When he saw a police car come down to the ship and put a load of posters through the porthole for me to bring back, just before we set sail for England, Captain Williams threatened that I would be blacklisted on the McAndrew Shipping Line and in the industry. So I decide to jump ship on the next trip to Alicante and join my other comrades at the front. First, I decided to approach the Communist Party in London to enlist for the International Brigade.

(Chris Lance, the 'Spanish Pimpernel', used the McAndrew Line ship *Palacio* among others to smuggle out right-wing refugees from Valencia about this time.)

On my arrival in London on 29 October I went to the recruiting agency at the King Street headquarters of the Communist Party and told them that if they didn't get me into Spain to fight, I would jump ship at Alicante on the next trip. They suggested that it would be better if I went their way as I now had knowledge of Spain and the language. Within a few days a group of sixteen of us was assembled and given a weekend ticket plus £5 expenses to get to Paris. The group was jubilant on the ferry across to Dunkirk. They began drinking and singing revolutionary songs like 'The International', and it wasn't difficult to guess who they were and where they were going so I told them to shut up. They didn't listen so I tried to distance myself. I ended up by isolating myself from them. On arrival in Dunkirk two British detectives were waiting. They pulled them aside, questioned them and sent them back on the next ferry.

As I possessed a British seaman's discharge book and had by now obtained a passport, I walked up to the detectives just a few minutes before the train was to depart and asked them why I wasn't allowed to board and if I was to be prevented from continuing my journey. They asked me where I was going. I told them Paris. They asked how much money I had – I had £5 at the time – and if I thought that was enough for the weekend.

Then they asked if I was going any further. I said, 'Where's that?' They said, 'Spain.' I said 'What would I want to go there for? And in any case I have papers, so I don't need to use my passport.' The seaman's discharge book was accepted as proof of identity at ports. They let me through and I jumped on the train as it was pulling out. On my arrival at the trade union centre in the Place du Combat in Paris I reported that the other fifteen had been sent back to England.

I was given some francs and told of cafés to go to. I remained there for a few days until a group had been assembled to go across the Pyrenees.

(Eugene Downing remembers noting the different attitude of the French police in Paris, compared to the British Special Branch. Jim O'Regan from Cork, one of his group, got lost after they arrived. He went up to a gendarme, asking for the address to get to Spain. The policeman helped him, telling him how to find the clandestine recruiting offices. 'The authorities knew about it and wanted to get rid of us: "Let them go and get killed in Spain."')

We were taken by coach to Carcassonne at the foot of the Pyrenees and given a pair of *alpargatas* (light rope-soled shoes). As we went through a gap over the border, a gendarme, obviously either sympathetic or bribed, shone a light on each of us and let us pass. We were then put in the charge of a Pyrenees trapper. It was dark and we were told not to talk, not to disturb any stones and not to smoke, as there were Fascist patrols operating in the mountains to prevent volunteers from getting through. We walked all night and descended near Figueras. I believe this eventually became a route for those escaping during the Second World War. As dawn broke there, awaiting us in a hut at the bottom of the mountain was a big urn of coffee and bread prepared by sympathisers or friends of the leader.

From February 1937 on, crossing had become dangerous, so it was often done at night, sometimes in severely cold weather. It was organised by local Communist activists who had to keep an eye out for the non-intervention staff and the always watchful right-wing press.

(The mountains weren't high near the coast, about 300 metres, but steep, with smooth slopes and precipices and 'nothing but thistles to hold on to'. Gusting winds could sweep you off your feet. One route began over the cemetery wall in Cerbère where the socialist mayor was helpful but the ascent could be seen from the town. Another route from nearby Banyuls took from three to seven hours depending on your fitness, and was called 'La Route Lister' after the famous Spanish Republican general who had used it.)

6

OUR TRAINING IN SPAIN

From the hut at the bottom of the mountain we were taken to Figueras, where we were interviewed as regards what positions we would occupy or to whom we would be allocated. I was asked if I spoke any other language. I told them I learned Irish in school, if they considered that another language. 'That'll do,' they said. Then they asked if I had knowledge or experience of arms. I told them that through my membership of the IRA, I had been taught ballistics and the use of a revolver, rifle, explosives and landmines. It was enough for them to send me to the training school in Tarrazona de la Mancha, the first stop for most British volunteers.

I was in a group of fifteen volunteers from Britain and Ireland, including the young writer Laurie Lee, who had entered Spain on his own on the night of 5–6 December. We left Figueras for Albacete on 11 December with Jack Tomkins of London, who found that 'some of [us] had no political knowledge whatsoever; one or two in fact could not discriminate between Franco and the government and one person was a true Red, White and Blue – England right or wrong.' I was supervising the final stage of their trip.

Our group arrived four days later at the International Brigade base. The commissar, Constantin Dubac, reported three of them were drunk at stops en route, moaning about food. Dubac thought they were just out for adventure. Laurie Lee he thought epileptic but his conduct exemplary, willing to do his best for the revolution, politically a Communist. Irishman Paddy Tighe, he reported, was detained at Figueras for insubordination, starting fights and drinking

– an 'unconscious disrupter'.

My report on arrival was located by historian Barry McLoughlin in 1994 in the Moscow files of the Brigades:

> 545/99-29 I was appointed Military leader at Figueras, I wish to make the following report. I left London with a group of fifteen. I don't know if the number is correct. I was not the leader of the group. However we all got as far as Dunkirk. From there all were sent back except me as I had a passport. I came to Paris on my own and there reported the matter. In my estimation I put it down as neglect on the group's part and I believe one of the group was disorderly in drunkenness.
>
> From Paris I was appointed leader over a section, we had one fellow who was disorderly and un-disciplined. At Figueras this fellow was placed under arrest on the day of our departure, for misconduct and insubordination. The comrade in charge of the English at the barracks detained him and said he was not fit to become a soldier in our ranks.
>
> From Figueras I report the indiscipline and insubordination of Frederick Smith, Ernest Corbett, Thomas Booth. About Smith I think he is sorry he came out here, he was insubordinate and inciting others to join him. He says he is 'pure red, white and blue'. I advised him to alter his opinions. I will say of the whole group of English only about six of them may be loyal; the rest I class as opportunistic and adventurers.
>
> They may be all right but they need a lot of lecturing, particularly on morale as they don't know what it means. This is the best report I can give in plain words, I hope it is satisfactory. I will add that this group was a disgrace to all the other comrades (foreign) I wish you will report the matter to the Party at London.

The political commissar will certify anything here to
be true.

Fraternally yours, Comrade R. Doyle

[Overleaf Bob commented on their health:]

Also I report that comrade Laurence Lee has on two
occasions of the journey taken some kind of fits. I may
add that this comrade's conduct was excellent, that
although weak he showed his willingness to comply
with regulations.

Tarrazona de la Mancha was a small village with a huge church
hall, which commanded a view of the surrounding countryside, and
a sizeable Civil Guard barracks. Most of the land had been owned
by the Civil Guard captain and the Church. The local peasants
committee had dealt with the captain. I believe he was executed,
the priest had been removed and the church had been turned into
a cultural centre. While we were out training, the peasants would be
out with measuring tapes dividing up their newly acquired land. As
I sat down to my first meal at the British base camp at Tarrazona,
who was in front of me but Jack Coward himself, now in charge of a
land unit. Our joy was profound. Our next encounter was even more
astonishing. I was captured at the same time as he was, and later
witnessed how he managed to pass himself off as deaf and dumb
among 2000 Spanish prisoners. There was another Irishman, called
Peter Brady, with us. The food was good; we had wine, just a little,
and slept in the old Civil Guards barracks.

The training school consisted of Spanish comrades and
International Brigaders and most of the tuition was in Spanish
although we quickly learned the commands. I became a platoon
commander, taking thirty men and drilling them with wooden
rifles. I never saw a real rifle or machine gun while I was there. I also
took them out digging foxholes and showing them how to defend
themselves against attacking aircraft by crossfire. We trained with

bayonets. We had no training about how to deal with tanks. This was the early stage before we went to the front.

I was put into a training school. There were about twenty of these training groups and I used to take out one of them for drill: '*Media vuelta* [about turn] *cabeza variación derecha* (or *izquierda*) [front rank right (or left) turn] – all orders were in Spanish and the recruits didn't understand; they'd all turn in different directions. I still know all the commands in Spanish. At night-time I had a privilege; I was allowed to visit a family I'd made friends with and used to have supper with them. The fire'd be on the floor under the table at your feet to keep your legs warm – it got very cold at night.

I went back visiting the village in October 1999. The taxi driver from Albacete was very sympathetic. The church is still there but the place is built up. We had a warm reception from a couple of local peasants on the Sunday but they didn't know anything about our barracks.

While in the square looking at the magnificent huge wooden doors of the church, I remembered the evening when Paul Robeson gave us all an impromptu concert. We were told he was coming and we packed into the church, hundreds of us. It was an evening concert. Some of the songs I knew, ballads and Negro spirituals. The response was terrific. He was the only celebrity who came while I was in Tarrazona. (See note, *Paul Robeson*, p. 216.)

We also received some training from a Russian officer in civilian dress, who went under the name of Rossa. He called us together for tuition on 'How to Confront the Enemy'. He was an expert on close combat, and if we didn't show enough guts, he'd grab the rifle himself, exclaiming, 'You are volunteers; you are worth ten of the Fascists. Go into it with hatred and determination!', all the while showing us this on his features. It was a lesson well learned.

It must have been two months later, around February 1938, when news came of a draft being sent to the front on four lorries. I had received no instructions to be part of it but I wanted to go so I jumped up on the last lorry. The others on it thought I was supposed to be there. Halfway to Belchite (this was the second battle of Belchite) I was discovered and brought in front of three International Brigade officers. They asked me why I had disobeyed orders and told me that my duty was to stay in the training base and to train other volunteers who would be coming over from England. I told them I wanted to be a machine-gunner and that I needed practical experience. They then suggested that I had come here to get experience at the expense of the Spanish people, which I hotly disputed.

After being given a severe ticking off I was allowed to stay and was put in charge of a Diktorov. I'd no experience with machine guns but it was easy to learn on the way to the front. The Diktorov was a light Russian gun with tripod and an air-cooled barrel and easy to handle.

We soon came under our first baptism of fire when walking along the road beside an olive grove. There, Italian Fiat fighters came in low, strafing us and releasing small bombs or hand grenades, just flying low and throwing them out. We quickly scattered into the grove and when the planes had passed, I remember Paddy Tighe got out in the road and did an Irish jig, and we marched on in the direction of Belchite. This is where we became involved in the second battle for the town's defence.

The rest of the battalion were in a little olive grove. I took my machine gun and Johnny Lemon and Peter Brady, two other Irishmen with me, out into position, in front of the anti-tank guns, to fire on the tanks in the open country in front of us. We could see them advancing with soldiers coming behind them. Then three planes came over flying very low and started singling out the three of us. I ordered the others to retreat before we were killed out in the open. We went back about a hundred yards under the olive trees and then we were all on the move, going back to the church. The anti-tank gunners stayed.

We withdrew in order into the town as far as the church. At this point my machine gun had developed a fault and stopped working. I tossed it from me, throwing away the lock separately so it couldn't be used. Fletcher, commander of my machine gun unit, got a bullet through the hand and I took his rifle. We were about fifty yards in front of the church. The enemy's bullets were hitting the church wall behind us and exploding. They appeared to be dumdums. (See note, *Explosive Bullets*, pp. 216–7.)

The Fascist troops and tanks were getting near us. We were likely to be cut off and surrounded inside the town. I could only find a small stone for shelter, firing at the enemy who were on the hill in front. I stood up recklessly, no longer caring about my own safety, and started firing until the rifle got too hot. Even though I thought I'd be hit, it was a miracle I wasn't touched. There were several brigaders killed in this position. I could see the enemy on the move. The tanks were out of sight and we were ordered to withdraw.

Now we became involved in the last phase of the town's defence. Faced by more than one hundred tanks, the only weapons we had were rifles of different calibre ammunition, twelve light machine guns, six heavy machine guns and our anti-tank battery. The latter held out to the very end singing 'Hold Madrid for we are coming', which paraphrased the famous trade union strike ballad of the thirties known to everyone. But we weren't. After a couple of days the town fell to Italian and Moorish troops. Although we were surrounded we managed to escape having lost some very good comrades. From then on it was a continuous movement from one front to another.

In Belchite, as in most Spanish towns, the church offered us the best strategic position, the best place to make our last stand before withdrawing. Its strong fortifications were practically immune to destruction from artillery bombardment. Not that the Fascists didn't try. Their artillery pounded us relentlessly and their tanks came within close range before we were ordered to withdraw to the heights on the outskirts of the town, where we were continually bombed by Stukas.

(Later a French writer described this attack as 'serious work, the Blitzkrieg, the real thing', and said that Franco's Aragón campaign provoked a crisis in the French government. Their military response would have meant mobilising the whole French army, which they thought meant a greater risk of a European war than their deliveries of arms to the Republic had caused, so they did nothing.)

This had been my first experience of the destruction of churches that I had read so much about in the papers back in Ireland. But according to the press, particularly the Irish papers, when the Fascists attacked churches that we occupied they were defending the faith, fighting for the holy crusade declared by the Cardinal Primate of Spain, Gomá y Tomás.

We then retired about two miles from Belchite to a small height where we could barely dig even a shallow trench as the hill was too stony. You could just get your body inside it. Just then planes came over, they appeared to be German Stuka dive-bombers, and flew around where we were occupying the height. I scraped myself in on my side to one side of the trench. The bombs were screaming as they were dropping them down on us, and machine-gunning us. I dodged them moving from one side to the other of the trench as the planes flew around us. We held this position for about two days. While I was there I saw an ambulance being attacked by planes, as it went past us towards Belchite. That stopped it. (See note, *Belchite and Franco's Breakthrough*, p. 217.)

We retreated from there and were taken by lorries towards Teruel. As we passed Híjar I found a Republican tank, a Russian-made one, which had been abandoned. There was a crowd of us and finding petrol we somehow managed to get it started. We drove off towards Híjar. I got a cord and tied my arm to the front where I was sitting to stop me falling off. We could see the Fascists defending their positions. As we got near our comrades recognised us and jumped out of the trenches to come and embrace us. We came across an abandoned shop in the town which had bacon and food. I put a guard on it until the brigade came up. We got orders to leave, marching in small groups as the Fascists were close behind. Two of us were picked by Sam Wild, our battalion commander, to stay in the rear and blow up any trucks that were abandoned. I remember putting a hand grenade into the driver's seat, pulling out the pin and running behind the truck for cover as the grenade exploded.

With two others, we were moving back to a rest area when I saw a regular army officer with a squad at a bend in the road beside a pile of rifles which he told us had already been handed in. He produced a paper that he claimed was a stamped official order to us to hand in our guns to equip a unit to go up to the front to replace us. We refused, and as we were arguing with him, three enemy planes came over and started strafing us. He and his men ran for cover and we ran in the opposite direction following our battalion which had gone on ahead. When we got there, we were told by our commander Sam Wild that we'd be commended for not handing in our guns. This was apparently a POUM action to collect weapons. We'd been ordered never to hand over our guns except to our own officers. We had withdrawn towards Batea and Corbera, where reorganisation took place. The Battalion was reduced to about 150 survivors from 500 only a few days before. (See notes, *Bob's Group of Recruits*, pp. 217–8; *The POUM*, p. 218; *The Role of the International Brigades*, p. 218.)

Hold Madrid For We Are Coming

We meet today in Freedom's cause and raise our voices
     high.
Our hands are joined in unity to battle or to die.
Hold Madrid for we are coming;
Union Men/International Brigaders be strong!
Side by side we'll battle onwards
Victory will come.
Look my comrades see the scarlet
Banners raising high
Reinforcements now appearing
Victory is nigh…

7

MARCH INTO AMBUSH

We were resting for a couple of days after withdrawing towards Batea and were re-equipped. I got a new light machine-gun, a Degtiagov, a type I'd used before. The sacrifices made by the Soviet people to aid the Republican government were brought home to me later when Híjar on this Aragón front was being softened up by aerial bombardment from the Fascists. It was a bright, sunny day – so clear you could see the shining streaks of the bombs falling on the town from our vantage point on a hill overlooking it.

I was sitting down cleaning my Degtiagov machine-gun, tenderly laying the parts on the ground, when a Russian general in a big Astrakhan coat came and stood looking down at me. He began asking the interpreter questions. I wondered why he was observing me so closely and felt proud, anticipating a compliment. But I was humiliated when he said, 'Do you realise the sacrifices that have been made to get that weapon here? If necessary take your shirt off and put the parts on that to stop them getting dirty.' The Soviet Degtiagovs and Tokarevs we used were both good weapons – forerunners of the Sten gun and the Maxim heavy gun. They were water-cooled and this sometimes caused problems on the desolate heights surrounding Belchite where water was difficult to obtain. The cry would go up 'All hands to the pump; pass the piss!'

On the open plains and clear skies it was extraordinary to watch the dogfights between the Italian Fiat and Capronis and the Soviet E-15 aeroplanes, known as 'Chatos'. We were fascinated by their manoeuvrability and the incredible feats the Soviet airmen performed, despite the fact that their planes were less powerful than the German and Italian aircraft. One pilot was credited with bringing down thirty-two Fascist planes and became a Hero of the Soviet Union for his exploits in Spain and the Second World War. There were Soviet tanks too, although often they were out of action due to lack of fuel. At the rest area, we were re-formed and re-equipped for the next battle and I had my new Degtiagov.

We had been marching all night. Before the sun came up on 30 March we got orders to march again to take up secondary positions moving up through Calaceite in the direction of Alcañiz and Caspe. The battalion was marching along a road in artillery formation, two single files, one on each side of the road, with about five yards between each man. The idea was to reduce casualties if we came under fire. Johnny Lemon from Waterford was close to me and Peter Brady, whom I've mentioned before. Frank Ryan had just come up from Madrid where he'd finished his book *The History of the Fifteenth International Brigade* and had joined us going into battle. He didn't have any position of command in the battalion, although he was a captain, dressed as an officer with leggings, so he was marching back in the ranks beside us. He had no revolver or rifle. There were four of us Irish together and I thought it strange, as Frank was an officer but was with us in the ranks, even though George Fletcher was in command with Wally Tapsell as political commissar.

We heard a terrific roar of engines down in the valley below us, like a motorised column getting nearer to us. A patrol of two was sent out to investigate but never returned. Frank suggested that me and Johnny Lemon take my machine gun unit to the bend a couple of hundred yards up the road to provide cover. When my unit had passed on ahead of me and having received no further instructions, I decided to fall in with my crew next to Frank.

Suddenly we were surrounded at close quarters on both sides of the road by soldiers jumping out with guns trained on us and shouting '*!Manos Arriba!*' ('Hands Up!') Coming up the middle of the road between us, led by a tank, were motorcycles with machine-guns mounted on the handlebars. I just had time to leave my gun beside Frank and go over and look at the tank before they opened fire. I stood beside the tank, an officer was standing in the turret, it was covered in dust but I could see the Italian colour markings on it. I rushed back towards my machine-gun and shouted, 'Crikey! They're Italian!'

They opened fire over our heads at our companies behind us, shouting '*!Abajo!*' ('Get down!') to us as they fired, effectively cutting us off from the remainder of the battalion, who were retreating in the confusion. The motorcycles passed us. There was a smell of cordite, the noise of men shouting and bullets flying overhead. Frank and the others already had their hands up and I got mine up quick.

Wally Tapsell was at the side of the road. He shouted to the Fascist officer standing up in the tank turret, 'You bloody fool! Do you want to kill your own men?' Wally thought they were our own tanks. We all expected that the Lister division were ahead of us and hadn't realised that the front had broken. The officer in the tank turret opened fire with a revolver and shot him dead. It all happened so quickly. '*¡Bajo!*' ('Down!') shouted an Italian infantry officer as we crouched forward under the fire of the close range guns.

I first met Wally in Tarrazona, as political commissar for the training base. He was over thirty, and used give lectures. I will always remember him for saying, 'When you gotta dig, dig deep!' And of course we never could, the ground was so stony. He was approachable. He didn't wear officer's uniform – just dressed like everybody else. During rests on marches, Wally would tell us to put our feet up. He wasn't doctrinaire but you wouldn't describe him as a gentleman.

Like Fletcher who was in charge at Calaceite, Wally had returned from sick leave to rejoin the battalion going into action. He would have expected the tank to belong to the élite Lister Division, which was supposed to be still holding the front lines. He wasn't carrying a weapon when he was shot. I mentioned that when I wrote to his widow. (See note, *Wally Tapsell*, pp. 218–9.)

We had walked into a classic military ambush set by Mussolini's Black Arrow division. It was the day Rab Butler, the Tory secretary of the Foreign Office under Lord Halifax, stated in the House of

Commons, 'We have no proof of intervention in Spain by Germany or Italy.'

According to Carl Geiser's account, for the Italian crew in the leading tank there was a sequel: Garry McCartney from Glasgow was in the machine gun company at the rear of the battalion. Hearing gunfire up ahead, his crew set up their gun on high ground with trees. When a Fiat tank nosed around the bend, their bullets set it on fire. One of its crew was hit trying to escape and slumped over the side of the turret. Another tank came around the bend but scuttled back when it saw the first one burning. When Garry was captured and later marched past the tank, it was still burning but the body had been removed.

We were assembled and marched off with guns trained on us, and Frank said to me, 'My book comes out today.' We were convinced he'd be shot right away because although he hadn't a badge of rank, his uniform distinguished him as an officer. It was standard practice by Franco's forces that officers were shot on capture. We were marched past long lines of Italian reserves and their mechanised equipment, with squadrons of Caproni bombers and Fiat fighters passing overhead. I was amazed at the might of our enemy and felt very proud that our side had managed to hold out for so long.

Carl was captured in the same breakthrough. The Italian lieutenant who questioned him boasted, 'We have 30,000 heading for Gandesa this morning. On the road on our left there are another 30,000 coming down from Caspe, and another 30,000 on a parallel route on our right. We will take Gandesa by noon, Tortosa tonight and be down at the Mediterranean in two days. The war will be finished very soon. It has dragged on too long already.'

Carl thought of the hungry men of the Fifteenth International Brigade, not even numbering a thousand, who were trying to stop 30,000 without artillery and without tanks. Ten days later with 90,000 well-equipped troops, the Italians still had not reached the sea. In fact it took them over two weeks.

We were lined up against a barn while an Italian officer came along the line picking out likely officers. Frank looked conspicuous in an officer's uniform with leggings, boots, no hat. 'What are you?' the Italian officer asked. Frank replied 'Captain,' whereupon they demanded to know the complements of the battalion and the amount of arms, producing a map. Frank replied that under no circumstances would he give any other information than his own personal details.

While this was going on a lorry load of armed Civil Guard arrived and positioned themselves in the middle of the road in front of the prisoners. These were the backbone of Franco's internal security forces, known as 'the Executioners', so called because they operated behind Franco's front lines, responsible for his 'cleansing' operation, picking out prisoners for shooting, which is how he controlled the parts of Spain he had overrun. Having seen them as a merchant seaman in the Franco ports of Cádiz and Huelva, I thought this was the end.

We were ordered into a line against the wall. The Civil Guard was called to attention and an officer called out, 'Communists, socialists, Jews and machine-gunners, step forward.' There were no individual volunteers, including myself, who were both Communists and machine-gunners.

Without any cringing pain or panic, the more experienced men all pushed towards the front line to be shot first. If you got the bullets first you would have a clean death and there was no difference between the volunteers of the many countries amongst us. We were Jews, Communists and people of various political persuasions.

Arguments were going on between the officers of the Civil Guard and the Italians, the former seemingly wanted to shoot us there and then, while the Italians seemed to want to wait for orders from Burgos, the central seat of Franco's government. While this was going on, another prisoner was taken out and beaten for information.

The matter now seemed to be resolved, as we were ordered to move to another location, in a wired compound by a dried riverbed, where further interrogation took place. We had lived to fight another day. At one point ordinary Italian soldiers were decent to us. They took from us various Republican documents we were carrying and quietly tore them up, saying it wouldn't go well for us if their officers were to find these. Frank was again questioned and refused to comply with the demands, whereupon the Italian officer reached up from his 5 feet 4 inch height to give Frank a smart crack across the jaw. It was only the restraining influence of Johnny Lemon and myself that prevented him from lunging towards the Italian.

An American brigader, Max Parker, was captured separately and remembers joining the group. Soon an Italian officer asked, 'Who is the officer here?' A big man stood up despite the protests of the rest; they all knew the Fascists shot captured officers. He gave his name 'Frank Ryan'. Max was made interpreter at the head of the procession with Frank as they were moved off.

Frank kept shouting encouragement: remember who they were, why they were in Spain, maintain discipline. When they halted, Frank made Max insist to their escorting officer that they be given water, and they were. An Italian officer told Ryan, through Parker, that Gandesa had fallen, Frank replied that he was lying. (Gandesa didn't fall until 3 April.)

A German in Gestapo uniform came to Frank, asking why he was fighting here instead of in Ireland. Frank told him it was the same fight, and asked what he, a Gestapo agent, was doing in Spain. He told Frank he was a brave man and wished him luck.

We were also interrogated by a Francoist journalist. His account claimed: 'Most are manual workers, just one bookkeeper, one mechanical engineer and one painter. Many are pure Jewish and overall they present a sorry sight, thin and hungry looking.' This was the standard image of Brigade members being presented by Franco's press.

We were herded into cowsheds and pigsties, moved again to a disused church in Alcañiz and questioned by the Italian secret police, the 'Ovra'. Frank was taken out again by the police and told he was sentenced to death again. The Italians had asked if he was a Communist and he told them he was an Irish Republican 'but if I were a Communist I'd be proud to say so.' We were given no food or water and used the area behind the altar for all purposes.

Our fate was still undecided but our hopes were rising. After all we had committed no crimes; we were fighting for what is just and right. All international prisoners were subject to immediate execution up to then, what did the democracies care, we were now in Fascist hands. No Red Cross functioned for us; we were not prisoners of war under the Geneva Convention and most of our governments considered us criminal because we'd broken their non-intervention agreement since we had come to fight for an elected government against a revolt by the military generals.

As we marched through the gauntlet of the Black Arrows, we knew as they raised petrol cans as if to burn us, they could do with us as they wished. After twenty-four hours, we were moved again to the Palafox military barracks at Zaragoza. Next day all were still alive. The war by this time had reached a critical stage. Our captors were jubilant. We were a great prize to those who had been fed on the Fascist propaganda that we were ferocious criminals, mercenaries burning churches, murdering priests and raping nuns. It was their hesitancy that saved us from summary execution.

The battle following our capture, the Crossing of the Ebro, was the last heroic and suicidal battle in which the People's Militia and the International Brigades were to be engaged. The defenders of the Republic were no match against the unequal logistics of modern warfare.

Hitler and Mussolini were getting impatient with Franco's failure to occupy Madrid and poured in more equipment for the final offensive, which proved too much for the battleworn defenders facing an army of 100,000 Italians, the bulk of the Spanish army, 30,000 North African troops and 8,000 Germans of the Condor Legion, mainly pilots and arillery men, with American supplied petrol and transport.

Thus Franco set out to prove to the world and the hostile international press his humanitarian treatment of prisoners, while preparing for the long night of terror against the defeated Second Republic, and releasing Axis forces for the preparations for the Second World War, and the establishment of the 'New Order in Europe'. On arrival at the military barracks in Zaragoza, we noticed as we entered the small square, six of the Lister division standing to attention under the Franco flag with heads bowed facing each other. They were ordered to stand to attention until they collapsed when they would be replaced by another of the same division.

The Lister division was considered the most hard-core Republican resistance, comprising volunteers from the left, Communists, trade unionists, socialists and anti-Fascists. They were subjected to the most gruelling treatment. They were the cream of the Spanish working class and the Fascists knew it. Their commander was the famous Enrique Lister, once a quarryman. Lister had been raised in Cuba and become a trade-union activist in Havana. Then he operated as a revolutionary in La Coruña.

I felt humiliated and defenceless and faced with such inhumanity, what could we do? The world, that is the capitalist world, didn't care or didn't want to care. They reminded me of the stations of the cross and what Jesus Christ must have gone through. The Catholic officers who administered this form of torture perhaps had this in mind or had learnt it from the Inquisition. We will see how they furthered this later. Most of those men of the Lister division were to be shot or sent to one of the seven labour battalions where they died in the construction of Franco's '*Una España Grande y Libre*' – reconstructing the whole of Spain on the bones of slave labour.

Our abode for those couple of days overlooked a wire compound where the Lister prisoners were herded like cattle for slaughter. We now felt safe and wondered why we could argue with the officer on our rights to refuse to give the Fascist salute. Little did we know that the next morning we were to be lined up for interview with the world's hostile press.

Such papers as the British liberal *News Chronicle* were prohibited as was anything remotely associated with progressive opinions. The British and American press reported our treatment in glowing terms. We were given a meal with an apple for the occasion. We were never to see one again for the rest of our imprisonment. At least we were safe, our names would be published in some of the papers. The argument had gone on about our rights to refuse to use the Fascist salute and a compromise was reached to give the British military salute, but the threat that we would be shot for refusal to comply with the order quickly changed our minds. We gave the salute. Only Frank Ryan refused, stating, 'Only when a pistol is placed against my forehead,' would he obey.

Next morning we were lined up for members of the press, amongst whom was Merry Del Val, an officer and an aristocrat, who recognised Jimmy Rutherford from Edinburgh as having been captured before and released. He had been one of thirty British prisoners captured at Jarama in February 1937, and interrogated by Merry del Val. They had been seen and photographed by a *Daily Mail* reporter before they could be shot; they were freed in exchange for Fascist officers in May of that year. (See notes, *Merry Del Val*, p. 219 and *Reporters and the War in Spain*, p. 220.)

Six of them came back to Spain. Rutherford was now going under the name of Jimmy Small. He was standing beside Garry McCartney of the machine gun company, whom Val appeared to concentrate on. then he suddenly switchied to ask Jimmy if he'd been in Spain before, which Jimmy denied. He'd been released with the pre-condition that he never came back to Spain. He was to be executed three months later at the age of twenty-two in Burgos prison, on the day Frank Ryan was tried and sentenced to death by the Military Tribunal. We were now transported to the concentration camp of San Pedro de Cardeña, where we were to remain for eleven months.

(The British battalion had 140 men taken prisoner, and 150 casualties in the ambush at Calaceite, although Franco's HQ at Burgos was claiming that an entire battalion of British International brigaders had been captured, including the commander. When John Peet arrived to rejoin the remnants of the British battalion he was dismayed. 'What we in fact found was a smallish group of really rather shell-shocked people, mostly without equipment of any sort.')

8

THE CONCENTRATION CAMP

AT SAN PEDRO DE CARDEÑA

After two days at the Palafox barracks at Zaragoza, and after the departure of the foreign press, we were taken by train under heavy guard to Burgos, the central seat of Franco's rebel government. From there we were marched ten kilometres to San Pedro de Cardeña, arriving late in the evening. The camp was a sinister and forbidding looking fortress and our recurring thoughts were whether we would ever get out of it alive and what would happen if the next world war began, we were afraid we'd just be left locked up for the duration and forgotten about. Escape was constantly on our minds. The guards awaiting us, supplemented by a small group of Civil Guards in their *tricorno* hats, were commanded by a vicious sergeant by the name of Castaña, whom we promptly dubbed 'Sticky' because he couldn't pass a prisoner without lashing out with his stick. We must have looked a decrepit, dirty, unshaven and disorganised lot and we were herded with rifle butts, sticks and kicks into a barren, barn-like room.

We were on the second floor, with the new arrivals occupying the first. Our beds were straw sacks, with a single blanket to protect us from the freezing cold at night. There was one mattress between two, laid out on the ancient, dusty tiled floor; we were packed like sardines in a tin.

San Pedro was an old monastery built around the fifth century. Believed to be the burial place of El Cid, a hero of Spain's wars against the Moors, it had not been used since the 1920s because it was in an advanced stage of decay. After the fall of the north in October 1937, it was reopened as a concentration camp for processing prisoners from Asturias and the Basque Country who had escaped the firing squads. As mentioned before, their fate was to provide the slave labour to help construct Franco's '*España Grande y Libre*', the 150 prisons needed to house two million prisoners from the subjugated north and later the final conquest in 1939.

They were processed into seven labour battalions, which were constantly replenished. Many died under this brutal exploitation, most notably at Cuelgamoros where from 1940 on, the monstrous mausoleum was constructed for Franco's burial. Cuelgamoros is now better known as the tourist attraction '*Valle de los Caidos* – The Valley of the Fallen' – in the hills forty kilometres north of Madrid. The cross of the underground basilica is 153 metres high, and the total cost was one billion pesetas. Twenty thousand prisoners laboured with picks and shovels building it and dozens died there. It was inaugurated in 1959 as one more lavish prestige project in an impoverished country.

Over the doorway of San Pedro was a full-size sculpture. At the time I didn't know what it was. It depicted the monumental figure of St James-the-killer-of-Moors, driving them out of Spain in the conflict with Islam. Ironically, it was Franco who invited the Moors back again to rape and pillage in defence of the Catholic faith, promising them revenge against the Spanish government who had oppressed them for so long. It was a lesson not lost on the prisoners. The French writer François Mauriac said in 1938: 'At least the Reds, even though there were crimes committed on the side of the Republic, never compromised the name of Christ.'

(Once the original coup by the generals had failed, Franco's colonial Army of Africa with its Moors and the Spanish Foreign Legion became the conquering force turned loose on mainland Spain. They shot their way through peasant and worker militias to the gates of Madrid, with a well-earned reputation for savagery. (See note, *The Army of Africa and Franco's Moors*, p. 220–2.)

Today the area surrounding Burgos and San Pedro de Cardeña is a tourist attraction. The monastery is occupied by Cistercians monks, having been refurbished by prison labour, and houses some friendly friars. But nothing is allowed to indicate that it was once a hell-hole of Fascism's crime against humanity.

The morning after we arrived, we were given a special display of brutality. As the Spanish prisoners assembled in the patio below us for their breakfast (oily water containing a few crumbs) they were attacked with sticks and rifle butts, scattering them in all directions as they tried to form the lines the Fascists demanded.

But even in the grim atmosphere, there were lighter moments. One prisoner entered the patio with a small bird – it looked like a sparrow – on his shoulder, which would fly away when the guards began their frenzied attack and then return to its owner in the long line of prisoners. I couldn't figure out how it could find him and thought he had some magical powers over his feathered friend. After a week, things changed. Now the guards' fury was directed against the international prisoners. Reveille was sounded at 6am, with the guards rushing into our quarters with rifles and sticks, while the prisoners dodged their blows by running behind columns and hiding in alcoves. I couldn't help admiring a young Moor, a deserter from Franco's forces, who when cornered would simply curl back and take blows which we would dodge.

As we went down the two flights of stairs, the guards along with Sticky would be waiting at the bottom door to lay into us as we came out. The return journey was the same. We tried to organise ourselves to make our passage less dangerous, one entering slightly behind the other. But the Fascists didn't like this show of discipline and the unfortunate prisoners at the rear would get the worst beating. Warmer weather made our lives a little easier but the daily beatings continued. Individual assaults were carried out in a ground floor room known as the 'sala de tortura', the torture chamber. We were fed beans and a couple of sardines in the evening from a huge cauldron on the outer patio where everyone would assemble in lines. We were fed a minimum with the sergeant watching the rations.

There was always some left over, supposedly for *renganches* (seconds) even though prisoners were starving. When all were served, some prisoners would dive towards the pot when the sergeants weren't looking, and would be beaten with sticks. This was the level of demoralisation we were subjected to.

(Fellow prisoner Carl Geiser recalled that an early problem was the theft of small bread rolls. The thief was caught red-handed and the prisoners unanimously elected Frank Ryan as judge. With lookouts posted, Frank opened proceedings saying that stealing a small piece of bread might seem trivial. If it had happened in Dublin he'd be defending, not prosecuting. But here in Fascist hands, their future unknown, unity was vital, which meant they all needed to trust in one another and look out for each other. Because stealing a piece of bread threatened this unity the court was convened, not so much to punish the guilty as to strengthen their unity. The guilty one apologised. He hadn't realised he endangered everyone's welfare and he was ordered to return part of his bread roll each day until he had made restitution.)

We had to eat our food standing up in single file. One sweltering day early in July, thinking Sticky couldn't see me because I was next to the ancient wall from which a rock protruded, I decided to sit down. Three others followed suit but Sticky caught us. I could hear him tell the camp commandant that he was taking us into the *sala* for a caning. I told the others it was OK; we were just going to get a few smacks. As they marched the other prisoners off to their quarters, we were kept behind and then taken to the *sala de tortura*. I was taken in while the others remained under guard facing a white wall.

As I entered I was surrounded by sergeants, including Sticky. 'So you refused to fall in!' they screamed. Before I could answer, four of them closed in and began raining blows on my back, shouting '¡Rojo! ¡Rojo!' ('Red! Red!') and in their frenzy they sometimes missed their target and hit each other instead. I was wearing only a light khaki shirt. I managed not to scream, doubling up I protected my face and head with my hands. Two had heavy sticks, another had a heavy strap and Sticky had his favourite 'bull's penis'. I remembered the beating by the nuns and the Blueshirts in Dublin and thought this would be my last.

'What have I done to deserve this?' I thought, as my knees began to buckle and I clenched my teeth. The beating lasted ten minutes. Sweating and panting, the four called for a soldier to take me back to the others, where I had to stand at attention facing the wall until everyone had been beaten. I could hear the shouts and blows as each was taken in. Jack Flior, a short stocky South African fell to the floor under their blows and we could hear his groans and screams as they beat and kicked him. After facing the wall for about four hours we were surprised to be sent back to our comrades instead of the dungeon, the usual destination after a beating. The dungeon was on the ground floor. It had no windows, and the German prisoners were kept there. On seeing my back later, Frank Ryan ordered me to take off my shirt and walk up and down among the prisoners to show them that 'This is what Fascism is.' They were horrified by the welts and caked blood.

Shortly after, the newspaper *Diario de Burgos* reported that Jacques Doriot was visiting Spain to protest against the Soviet Union's support for the Republic and to help those International Brigaders who wanted to escape from their 'criminal Communist betrayers'.

(Doriot had begun as a Communist deputy in the French parliament, then been a follower of Trotsky before forming his neo-Fascist *Parti Populaire Français*. The PPF became openly Fascist from 1940, collaborating with the German occupation of France. At this stage it was trying to appeal to the same social classes that supported the French Communist Party, by avoiding any comment for or against Franco, but demanding strict neutrality, legal steps to prevent volunteers leaving for the brigades and making strident calls to 'rescue the volunteers still in Spain'.)

Carl Geiser remembered Doriot arriving in search of rebellious brigaders, all the French being lined up as sergeants tried to find someone to meet Doriot, who 'was here to help them'. An elderly lorry driver who had come to Spain buying oranges said he would, if he could remain in the ranks. When Doriot stood before him, tall and well-dressed, the Frenchman could barely speak. Then he said the wrong things: that he was always hungry, covered with lice, beaten daily, ever in fear for his life and despite being a civilian, he had been arrested and thrown into this camp.

The driver pleaded with Doriot to let him back to his wife and family but this was not the response Doriot wanted. He had failed to find his rebellious brigaders and, promising to do something, he left. The sergeants didn't even bother to hide their sticks and whips for Doriot's visit.

The Americans were to receive another visitor, William Carney of *The New York Times* – a known Fascist sympathiser. When they ordered the Americans to the assembly area, I was substituted for one of them. Carney demanded to know how many of us were members of the Communist Party, but the American spokesmen, Lou Ornitz and Edgar Acken, replied that we were all anti-Fascists and they didn't know how many Communists there were amongst us. When Carney expressed doubts about our claims of brutality and the atrocious living conditions and refused to visit our quarters, they turned two of us round and lifted our shirts to reveal the long red welts across our backs. Carney was taken aback. Soon we were to receive a copy of *The New York Times*, which described our treatment in glowing terms.

The assembly area contained a church, which was never opened. Any prisoner approaching it was beaten, which made us suspect that the Fascists stored ammunition there. They knew that the Republican force would never bomb their own men, as they had never bombed the civilian population. It was in the outer patio that Mass was said and we had to salute the flag and sing the Fascist anthem '*Cara al Sol*'. With the Spaniards in front of us singing, we would pretend not to know the words. Behind us, out of sight of the sergeants, a couple of characters would pirouette away to a souped-up version of 'It's a Long Way to Tipperary'.

'*Cara al Sol*' finished with the Fascist salute – the right arm extended upwards through seventy-five degrees. But the sergeants always suspected that some of us were giving the clenched fist salute instead and anyone making the slightest deviation would be punished by the stick or worse.

As an indoctrinated Catholic from the year dot, the Fascist Mass seemed to me an insult to anyone who was devout. The priest, on a specially raised platform, opened the service with the Fascist salute and '*!Viva Franco!*' When it came to the raising of the Host and the genuflection, those who didn't know the ritual were beaten down to their knees. They quickly learnt the routine.

(When Frank Ryan told his friend Fr Mulrean of a similar Fascist misuse of the Mass by the priest in Burgos jail, Fr Mulrean reported the scandal to the Papal Nuncio, the Pope's representative. He had apparently got nowhere through Spanish channels. Burgos then became one of the only prisons for defeated Republicans which didn't have Fascist clergy abusing religion.)

Lou Ornitz told how in another camp a Basque priest refused to conduct religious services praising Franco's regime and protested about the brutal treatment of prisoners. When he died of a beating, other imprisoned Basque priests arranged a secret 4am Mass for him.

Part of our indoctrination was a lecture by the Bishop of Burgos. All the Spanish prisoners, Asturians and Basques, were lined up in front of him. We stood in a couple of long lines to his left. Standing on a raised platform he addressed the congregation: '*!Españoles! !Mirad ellos, el escombro de la tierra!*' ('Fellow Spaniards, look at them, the scum of the earth!') And indeed we did look like the scum of the earth. Ragged, filthy, there couldn't have been a greater contrast than with the bishop in his Vatican robes and gold cross on his fat belly, proclaiming that we were the enemies of Christianity and the Catholic faith, in the hope that he would drive a wedge between us and the Spanish prisoners.

The camp held more than 2,000 Spanish prisoners and some 750 Internationals, the Spanish being subjected to an intense political re-education programme, which would allow them out to enlist in Franco's army if they did well. The Internationals were kept in isolation to avoid their ideologically contaminating the Spaniards. (See note, *The Spanish Bishops and the War*, pp. 222–3.)

9

PRISON LIFE AS WE ORGANISED IT

We soon established an underground committee and began to organise the 'San Pedro Institute of Higher Education' to maintain our dignity and show the Fascists our level of culture, which they despised. We grouped ourselves into different classes: maths, music, languages and so on. Having a good phonetic grasp I took Spanish. I concentrated on grammar and strengthened my knowledge by close association with Cubans. There were about six Cubans who had mainly come over to Spain in their youth. The choir, which had no musical instruments, was the pride of the camp. With the voices of the different nationalities, and an excellent tutor, it raised the morale of the prisoners.

The Americans put on a play about Hiawatha, but it didn't get much further than 'Is that your manchild, Dropping Water?' before everyone burst out laughing at the sight of the 'squaw' walking in with straw wrapped in dirty rags as the 'child'. There was more basic entertainment too: some of the Americans, who'd got hold of a candle, held farting competitions to blow it out. With the lighted candle on the floor, each challenged would get their bum as close as they dared and let go, to cries of, 'Go on, Tex!' and uproarious laughter. The smell of methane from our regular diet of beans was even worse than that of cordite when we were captured.

Mice racing was another diversion. I could feel them at night, running across my blanket. I used my tin plate to catch them, setting it at an angle against the wall next to my head, with a sardine bone as bait. When I heard a mouse, I'd slam the plate against the wall, trapping him. Next day, we would tie a long thread to their tails and lower them out of the window on to the patio to race.

But often the Fascists would burst in, confiscating the improvised chessmen that prisoners had made with such patience and risk, scattering people in all directions. Our initial shock and uncertainty had by now been much reduced. Our main fear was the impending outbreak of the Second World War. If it were to break out, the likelihood was that we'd be forgotten about while it lasted – or worse. But now we were getting confident, knowing that our names had been published in the Western press and that our friends at home were campaigning for our release.

Though we distrusted Carney, his report in the New York Times triggered the start of moves by the US State Department for our repatriation, and to increase pressure on the regime in Spain to improve conditions. This was not so for our fellow prisoners who were German anti-Fascist members of the brigades, some of whom tried to escape. They were caught, beaten unmercifully, thrown into solitary confinement and fed starvation rations. Our hearts bled for them. The dungeon they were kept in was small. Its only windows were boarded up and they were left in complete darkness. They were only allowed out once a day to relieve themselves. Several prisoners died. When they were seriously ill they were taken to a so-called hospital, run by nuns, which was part of the prison camp. We would never see them after that. The next thing we'd be told was they had died.

They made a coffin out of fish boxes and we'd be forced, although we'd have done it voluntarily, to line up while the coffin was taken to the burial ground. In all cases, irrespective of the fact that the person who'd died might be Jewish or Orthodox or Protestant, we were told that he had asked for the last sacraments.

Carl Geiser wrote that these nuns, who were also prisoners, had been at Guernica when the Germans bombed it and refused to sign statements that it had been destroyed by 'the Reds'. Stan Heinricher had been seriously wounded when he was captured, and found the sisters kindly, and they did a good job – his hospital bed was clean, his bandages washed every day. The food wasn't plentiful but well prepared and nourishing.

A month after our capture, we had a visit from a Colonel Martin, who seemed to be acting as some kind of representative of the British government. We told him of the beatings, starvation and vermin but he was only interested in knowing who in England was responsible for our recruitment. He threatened that if we didn't tell him there would be no possibility of an exchange. We refused his demands; we knew he wanted the information in order to prosecute individuals and organisations in Britain for supposedly breaching the non-intervention policy. Not one of more than a hundred British and Irish prisoners acceded to his demands. We were mainly afraid that the European war would break out. We talked of almost nothing else, knowing that war was coming. We thought we could be killed once Britain was involved, because Franco would join Hitler, and we'd be the first bumped off. The British government had forbidden its citizens to fight in Spain, warning them that any who did would receive no assistance in the event of their getting into any difficulty.

Three of the Irish – myself, Maurice Levitas, a Dublin Jew, and Jackie Lemon from Waterford – approached Frank Ryan and asked him would he declare himself British or Irish. Frank stated that he would never hide behind the Union Jack. So we declared ourselves Irish, although we knew that because of the hostility and hysteria in Ireland, our exchange might be delayed. Frank was often lying down on part of our floor; he appeared to be ill a lot of the time.

(Frank's health had collapsed in April 1936, apparently from stress and overwork. His cousin, a doctor in Liverpool, detected high blood pressure. X-rays showed an enlarged heart. His future health was thought problematic and he was to keep regular hours, rest and have a careful diet.)

We had amongst us a couple of collaborators who, when captured, quickly gave the Fascist salute. From then on they acted as agents for the Fascists within the camp. We named one of them 'Rin Tin Tin', and swore that if we returned home we would endeavour to kill them or throw them overboard. They became 'cuartaleros', prison guards, and collaborated in every way with the Fascists. They even asked to be transferred because they didn't want to mix with the Reds. One was soon sent home and supposedly wrote a pamphlet praising Franco and telling of the defeat of the Republic. A copy of this pamphlet was sent to the camp. They asked for an English prisoner to read out its contents but everyone asked denied being English saying they were Scottish, Welsh or Irish. Eventually they forced Maurice Levitas to read out the tract. Maurice, knowing the guards couldn't understand any English, read out something with quite a different interpretation. The guards, noticing how we were enjoying ourselves, put an immediate stop to it. Maurice was beaten and sent back to the ranks.

More frequent visitors were two members of the Gestapo. Dressed in civvies, they would drive up from Burgos in a Mercedes and interrogated all the international prisoners without any protest from Colonel Martin. We were not as frightened of them as the German prisoners were. When I was brought before them, they showed me several blown-up photographs – a long wooden table with empty wine bottles, spent candles, and bits of arms and other human remains. 'Look at these!' they said. 'What do you think? Terrible! You did it.'They demanded, 'Why did you come to Spain?'

'I'm an Irish Republican, I came to defend the Republican government,' I replied. 'Don't you think the Franco flag is better than the Republic's?' This I found difficult to respond to. I had no idea what either flag looked like when I left Ireland. 'Where did you have your first woman? Was she a prostitute?' Next, one of them measured me, while the other jotted down the readings: everything about me 'athletisch' ('athletic)'. Then I was photographed naked. The object was to prove that we were subhuman. Our treatment as prisoners was a deliberate strategy to demoralise us and make out that we were subhuman, and could not be normal to have come and fought in the International Brigades.

On Sunday 12 June 1938 Frank Ryan was taken away by three guards. He told us he thought he was going home and was in good form. Johnny Lemon and I gave him notes to take back to Ireland

and post. It was a sunny day. An American jeep came and Frank got into it. There were two guards and he wasn't handcuffed. We watched out of the window as he was driven out of the patio. Franco's army already had US jeeps available in Spain, before they were used in the Second World War. When the last brigaders were repatriated the only Irishman left behind was Frank Ryan. Only later did I learn that he had been taken to Burgos jail and sentenced to death. Like Johnny Lemon and Maurice Levitas, I had expected Frank to be home. We thought he'd become a TD and take the fight for social justice forward through political action in Ireland. I knew Frank for many years when we worked and fought together, in Ireland and in Spain. All during those years he never changed his principles, he was always the same man, a left Republican, an Irishman who fought consistently for democracy and against Fascism.

Later all the prisoners were taken out to a wood and filmed, with all the 'non-Aryans and Jews' placed nearest the camera. We had few clothes because they took our good clothes and boots off us when we were captured. I had no trousers, for example, and only wore a bit of a blanket around me. Photos appeared in the *Diario de Burgos*, which was shown to us in jail, with the caption 'Russians captured on the Aragón front'.

Colonel Martin came to the camp and gave us the first news of Jimmy Rutherford and Frank Ryan. He just said casually, 'Jimmy Rutherford was shot and Frank Ryan was sentenced to death, and the sentence was commuted to a life sentence.' Jimmy was twenty-two when he was executed in Burgos prison. One prisoner had a hammer and sickle tattooed on his forearm, he gouged it out and hid it with a bandage before his interview with the Gestapo. But it was a different matter with the German anti-Fascists. Many of them had previously escaped the Gestapo's clutches and some were on their wanted list. They were forced at gunpoint to sign a document stating they wished to return to the fatherland. Eleven were subsequently shipped off to Germany and butchered.

It was the same with the Sudeten Czechs. By the Munich Agreement in September [1938], Britain and France handed over the Sudeten part of Czechoslovakia to Hitler. Unaware of the implications of the Nazi occupation of the Sudeten region, they told the Gestapo that they were Czech nationals. 'Now you are German,' they were told, and their fate was sealed. (See note, *The Sudetan Germans and the Munich Agreement*, pp. 223–4.)

Six months after our arrival in San Pedro, the first week of September 1938, we were surprised when all prisoners received a khaki shirt, a pair of breeches and canvas shoes. We wondered what was happening and learned we were to receive an 'important visitor'. It turned out to be Lady Chamberlain, widow of the British Foreign secretary, Austen Chamberlain, who was the brother of the Prime Minster, Neville Chamberlain. She was accompanied by a lordly-looking type complete with monocle, cane and spats

The British and Irish were lined up for a rehearsal of '*¡Rompen filas!*' and to make sure we hadn't forgotten the Franco salute. As the retinue emerged from the commander's office, Sticky barked out '*¡Atención!*' and then '*¡Rompen filas!*' but as everyone was at ease, not a single arm was raised. He repeated the order several times but not a single one of us shouted '*¡Viva Franco!*' Sticky's face was furious with rage.

Lady Chamberlain inspected the line of prisoners, asking why they had come to Spain. Everyone replied 'To stop Fascism before it comes to England.' This is not the answer she wanted. Presumably she would have preferred someone to say, 'I was in Hyde Park one day and someone came up and asked me if I wanted to go to Spain. As I was unemployed, I joined up.'

Disgusted with the replies, she turned to her escort and said 'I say, can you pick me out an intelligent one?'

(Carl Geiser tells how the escort moved in front of Kearney, hemmed and hawed, fussed with his cravat and then asked 'Rawther ghastly, wot?' Kearney, not to be outdone, came back with 'Raaawtherr.')

But her visit brought us some comfort; we received our first bit of greens that day – three lettuce leaves with our beans, a welcome sight for all those already suffering from scurvy.

Lady Chamberlain later said she had gone to Francoist Spain to know the truth. When asked at the border by a journalist if she'd consider visiting Republican Spain, she retorted 'And why would I want to do that?'

We had now established that Colonel Martin was the British military attaché in Burgos. He confirmed that negotiations for a possible exchange were under way. We had heard that the Italians wanted five artillery men for each of the International Brigaders. We felt proud of our exchange value for each Fascist. Rossa, our Russian instructor during training, was right.

One of the Irish with us now was Jim Haughey from Lurgan who'd once gone for the priesthood. He was captured on the Ebro.

(Eugene Downing remembers him asking before the battle if there would be a priest at the front; the others had found that amusing. He had left home meaning to join the Franco side but he'd ended up happy to be on ours. He was later killed with the Canadian Air Force in 1943. A poem he wrote appeared the following month in *The Times*.)

Christmas 1938 was approaching. The beatings got less and we were even taken to a river and given a bar of soap to bathe. The river had a few deep pools, and it was our greatest treat – the prisoners, all naked, splashing around in full view of the local peasant women pounding their clothes, while our guards kept watch. Occasionally we were taken to a nearby field for delousing. It was pathetic to see the prisoners with their shirts off, cracking the fat lice which had penetrated every crevice of clothing, between thumb and finger.

Christmas that year was an historic event. The nine months of terror against us had failed to break our spirit. A number of prisoners had died under the strain but we managed to maintain our morale, despite the Fascists' attempts to demoralise us. The committee had decided to celebrate Christmas by holding a concert, and coordinate the efforts of all the groups who had been attending the various classes. We were determined to show our persecutors that we had culture and inwardly hoped that our efforts would result in a better climate and lessen the beatings. Rudi Kampf of the Heidelberg

Conservatoire of Music was nominated to provide the music and conduct the choir of eighty. I sang tenor.

The commander's initial ban on our rehearsals was lifted after it was agreed that no revolutionary songs would be performed. We were delighted and invited him and his officers to attend the performance. On Christmas Eve we were surprised to see him crossing the patio with a group of officers and men, including Sticky. We were even more delighted to see that they carried no arms or sticks.

As they came up the stairway, they were greeted by our official translator, Alex, a Russian posing as a Dutchman, who spoke seven languages. We showed our guests to the front seats, made up from our sleeping bags of straw. Filthy blankets hung on a wire comprised the curtain, decorated with several silver three-pointed stars – the International Brigade symbol with three points, representing the Popular Front uniting liberals, socialists and marxists against Fascism.

Our guests, oblivious of their significance, ignored them. The prisoners sat on similar sacks of straw, packing the room from wall to wall. The atmosphere was tense as our MC greeted the commander and his men with the words: 'We are happy that you have come to celebrate this Christmas Eve with us.' The programme was truly international: carols and folk songs from Germany, Poland, Italy, the Slavonic countries, Cuba, England and the US, and included a shortened version of *The Barber of Seville*.

The show began with eight German prisoners, who astounded our jailers with their rendition of 'Stille Nacht' and 'O Tannenbaum', after which the audience burst into a round of applause and 'Olé! Olé!' which could be heard all over San Pedro. In the grimness of our surroundings it was impossible to forget that these same Germans had suffered more than anyone from the wrath of the Fascists and the Gestapo and faced a bleak future, even death.

The Germans were followed by all the other nationalities, each making their unique contribution. *The Barber of Seville*, performed with the crudest props, brought roars of laughter. The Cubans put on a cabaret with some of them dressed as women; they minced across the improvised stage to the applause and delight of the prisoners and guests. We all wondered how they had managed to get hold of the women's clothes.

The climax of the three-hour concert was reached with Rudi Kampf and his eighty-strong choir, consisting of every nation in Europe and the USA. Absolute silence prevailed within the three-foot thick walls and the dimly lit room, as with perfect clarity the voices penetrated into the adjoining building where the Spanish prisoners were held. It was as if the singers were pouring their hearts and souls into every note, in rebellion against their inhuman treatment.

As the last notes of the 'Bell Song' rang out from the top tenor blending in with the rest of the choir, there was a stunned silence for a second. Then the whole audience rose to its feet, clapping and cheering wildly. Even our jailers stood and joined in the applause. The commander, an old professional soldier, was overheard to remark, 'And these are our prisoners who can sing like this.' He requested a further performance, promising to bring officers from Burgos, to which we readily agreed. We had broken the barrier. We had proved the superiority of our culture and philosophy against that of the German minister Goering, who is supposed to have said: 'When I hear the word culture, I reach for my gun.'

For weeks after, life became a bit easier, even Sticky relaxing the use of the stick. Things got better on the vermin front too. In the words of Carl Geiser, who played an active role in the concert, 'Many of the fleas and lice left us after each performance to establish new residences with our guests.'

10

THE EXCHANGE OF PRISONERS

(When fourteen Americans were exchanged before the British and Irish, one of the Irish who had fought with the Americans went as one of them. He was John O'Beirne, originally from Balbriggan. He was put down as 'John Berkley', a name similar to John's mother's name, Berkery. A good friend, Leo Berman, was on the list of fourteen getting out but felt bad about leaving his pal John O'Beirne, who was in his forties and suffering from a leg wound and arthritis which slowed him down. This had made him a frequent target for the sergeants.)

Leo let John take his place on the list. Both were lucky however. The prisoners left Ondarreta prison in San Sebastián on 8 October for the bridge at the border. There each had to wait until his name was called, then walk across. Fourteen names were called, including 'John Berkley', which left Leo standing there. The Red Cross staff man asked Leo his name. 'Berman, but my name was skipped.'

'Son, you are the fourteenth, hurry up and cross.'

John was held up for some time, along with nine British prisoners and some Canadians in Ondarreta where Colonel Martin left soap and money from the British Dependants Aid Committee. He arrived at Balbriggan station near Dublin, still wearing light Spanish prison clothes and *alpargatas*, but couldn't manage the four-minute walk downhill to his family home. When his brother-in-law collected him with a motorbike and sidecar, he had to lift John in. The leg wound which aggravated his arthritis healed slowly. (See note, *John O'Beirne*, p. 224.)

After eleven months, news finally came through that we were to be exchanged. We were transferred from San Pedro to San Sebastián where we were paraded round the plaza. People began to gather on the pavements in response to a loudspeaker blaring out, 'Spaniards! Come and see these criminals who came to fight against the Spanish people.'

Certainly, at that time we must have looked a pretty decrepit bunch. We were afraid that this was an incitement to get us attacked so that Franco could mount a propaganda scoop in the international press and claim it was the 'wrath of the Spanish people'. So we decided that the healthiest of among us would march at the front, heads held high, in as disciplined a fashion as we could muster. The Fascist officer in front, noticing our change of mood, ordered us to slow down in the hope that our ranks would be thrown into disarray. Suddenly people moved towards us and began pressing chocolate bars and cigarettes into our hands. The Fascists were furious and ordered us to march quickly to the prison.

(The newspaper *ABC* published in the Republic for 5 March 1939 describes a similar incident in Bilbao: 'The public, becoming aware of the prisoners from the San Pedro concentration camp, began showing their sympathy, with women even kissing and hugging them.' My pal from Tarrazona, Jack Coward, had been captured with Spanish troops when he was on the run after Calaceite. He was lucky not to be identified as a brigader, and had to pass himself off as deaf and dumb among the 2000 Spanish in San Pedro. He was released with other Spanish prisoners over the age of forty-five when the war ended, got to the northwest coast and was smuggled home from Vigo on a British ship to Liverpool. He later became prominent in the Seamen's Union.)

Ondarreta was a real jail, not like the improvised concentration camp at San Pedro. The prison no longer exists; it appears that the Fascists feared it would become a place of pilgrimage. In the surrounding region, Guipuzcoa, 70,000 were arrested and screened. We later found out that four thousand were executed here. When we were taken out for exercise we saw a firing line in the yard and one of the walls was practically cut in two with the bullet and machine gun marks. Of course we rushed over to look at them, and as we did the Fascists rushed at us with sticks to keep us moving around.

The twenty-six Basque priests here, who were held in solitary confinement, were those who refused to stand up in the pulpit and denounce 'the destruction of Guernica by Republican planes' when the world knew it was the Germans who were responsible for that genocide and destruction. My abiding memory of those priests is the sight of the last two of them, who bade us farewell with a clenched fist at their side. We couldn't salute them back but we indicated our understanding in our common language.

(There were also Basque nuns who had been at Guernica when the planes of Hitler's Condor Legion bombed and strafed it. Now two years later they were still in prison as they also refused to sign statements that it had been destroyed by 'the Reds'. Some were ill with TB and were thought likely to die there. See note, *Guernica*, p. 225.)

We remained several weeks in the prison, a frightful place, pending our exchange. Our cells were below ground with a small window level with the exercise yard. Here the Spaniards would pretend to be talking with each other while communicating with us. It was amazing how they played football in the yard with a rag ball, even though they were condemned to death. The prisoner in the cell above us, Cipriano Antonio Arce, communicated with us via a water pipe – apparently at one stage they'd planned to put water in the cells, but there were no taps. We exchanged songs and talked. He taught me '*Un Inglés Vino a Bilbao*' and I responded with familiar tunes like 'It's a Long Way to Tipperary'. '*Un Inglés Vino a Bilbao*' is still a popular Basque song today:

> *Un inglés vino a Bilbao,* (An Englishman came to Bilbao,)
> *A ver la Ría y el mar,* (To see the estuary and the sea,)
> *Pero al ver las bilbainas* (But seeing the girls of Bilbao)
> *Ya no se quiso marchar* (He didn't want to leave)

Y dijo: vale más una bilbainita (Saying: a Bilbao girl's
    worth more)
Con su cara bonita (With her pretty face)
Con su gracia y su sal (With her grace and her health)
Que todas las americanas (Than all the girls of America)
Con su inmenso caudal (In spite of all their wealth)
Con su inmenso caudal. (In spite of all their wealth.)

Then came the day when he told me he'd been visited by *el carnicero* (the butcher/executioner) and *el cura*, the priest. Next morning we heard him being taken out for execution. His last words were '*¡Viva la República!*' Such visits were normal procedure prior to execution. The priest would ask: 'Are you going to confess?' This really meant admitting you had infringed Franco's proclamation in any way. The only advantage of 'confessing' was that burial in consecrated ground was guaranteed. (See note, *Confession for Execution*, pp. 225–6.)

We were subsequently taken to Hendaya, right beside the International Bridge, where we were deloused, given a shower, a pair of dungarees and had our hair shaved. The *Manchester Guardian* reported on 6 February 1939 that sixty-seven captured British volunteers who had been exchanged for Italians, had that day marched across the international bridge at Hendaye singing 'It's a Long Way to Tipperary' as happy as schoolboys going on holidays. While waiting on the French side they sang war songs and Spanish melodies learnt in prison.

After delousing, we were taken by the Spanish Civil Guard to the borderline on the International Bridge and handed over to the French gendarmerie. We three Irish, Maurice Levitas, Johnny Lemon and I, were put on the rear of a train with a gendarme and travelled under guard to Paris, where we were taken to the Irish consul. He tried to make us sign a statement saying we would pay for our fare from Spain to Dublin; this we refused to do. He then asked us to sign on behalf of our parents so that they would foot the bill; again we refused, stating that we hadn't asked to be taken out of Spain and would be quite happy to go back to join the Republican forces. Reluctantly, he gave us a ticket to Dublin via London.

(British brigaders returning were sent bills for years afterwards by their Under-Secretary of State for Foreign affairs for £2/4s/11d but nobody paid, although one bloke, Bobby Walker, said he'd pay if the British soldiers evacuated from Dunkirk in 1940 paid their costs. But the prize for crass official behaviour went to a member of the Irish diplomatic staff in London whom Eugene Downing met on returning from Spain, having lost a leg. 'We went into the office of the Irish High Commissioner, Mr Dulanty, in Regent Street. We were sitting in reception with the young clerk staring at us with disdain. He taunted us, saying "Franco's winning!" It was the first insult we'd heard from anyone until then. We didn't answer him back but the thought did occur to me, bedad, this chap is great material for a diplomat.')

We arrived in London with only some French money at 6am, but cabbies recognised us from the other brigaders who had arrived the day before. They paid for a great breakfast for us. During our stopover we were kitted out with a new suit of clothes courtesy of the Co-op. It was with considerable satisfaction that we learned the exchange rate for prisoners was five to two; we prided ourselves that we were worth more than double Mussolini's Black Arrows.

On returning to Dublin we were met by Fr Michael O'Flanagan, the great Irish socialist Republican priest, a staunch friend of the Spanish people and the Republican movement. The Spanish Aid Committee organised a meeting at Molesworth Hall, where we made a plea on behalf of Frank Ryan, who had done more for the Irish people than any Irishman living here and the other prisoners still in captivity.

I spoke with fellow ex-prisoner from Spain, M. Morris, pointing out that Frank's exchange had been affected by the fall of Barcelona when more important Republicans had been taken prisoner, replacing him on the exchange list, also that Frank was not safe while in Franco's hands, for any news of defeat of Franco forces always produced, in our own experience, an outburst of violence against helpless

Republican prisoners, and Frank was not a popular prisoner with the authorities; he was too outspoken. The poor attendance reflected the anti-Republican hysteria that prevailed throughout Ireland during the course of the Spanish War.

The following morning I arranged to meet Fr O'Flanagan in town. He came down from the National Library where he then worked; de Valera's government had given him a job working on local history there. He had been acting chief of Sinn Féin when de Valera was imprisoned. He and Dev were both on the anti-Treaty side in the Civil War and they were still friendly.

He spoke at the Gaiety meeting during the Spanish Civil War, supporting the Basque priest, Fr Laborda, who came to Ireland to present the case for the Basque Catholics on the Republican side. Fr Laborda had said it was in no sense a religious war: where Fascism had conquered, the native Basque language and culture were banned and writers, poets and musicians had been imprisoned or shot.

Not long before he had greeted the Irish volunteers who had come home before us. He brought me along Nassau Street for something to eat in a posh restaurant, I think it was Findlaters. I said to him, 'I can't go in there.' My head was shaved from the Spanish prison camps and I looked like a convict. No one wore their heads shaved then.

He said to me, 'Take off your hat,' and I did. He looked at my head and said, 'My goodness, you should be proud of that,' adding, 'Come in and be proud of it.' We both went in, I sat down and removed my hat and we had our breakfast.

(At the start of the war when the Church and the papers were all for Franco, Fr O'Flanagan told the people here, 'They have fooled you again.' He was chairman of the Food Ship for Spain Committee, and had visited Barcelona in December 1938 before it fell. Like Frank Ryan, he said the Church was not a safe guide in political ideas. He had chaired the meeting for us coming home and he was happy to show me off. Later in 1939 the Papal Nuncio, Bishop Robinson, who also intervened for Frank Ryan with Franco, got the ban on Fr O'Flanagan saying Mass in public lifted. It had been imposed on him in 1925. He worked as a priest again in Dublin convents until he died in 1942. He still visited Republicans in prison. He was first suspended back in 1918 for speaking from Sinn Féin platforms in elections and against conscription. Even the Irish *Catholic Standard* wrote well of him when he died: 'Like Pearse he was a student and a teacher, with thought and sympathy for youth; like Tom Clarke he seemed in his person to typify the spirit of resistance to oppression... like Connolly he loved the people who work in poverty.' (See note, *Irish Church Aid*, p. 226.)

Our reception in Ireland contrasted markedly with the reception of the Blueshirts, and the contempt with which they were treated on their return. It indicated than in Ireland an understanding was beginning to develop of what the victory of Fascism in Spain really meant. The next day we were photographed on the roof of the *Irish Press*. But there was no story in the Catholic newspapers: the Pope had died – the same Pope who had backed Mussolini's obscene war against Ethiopia and whom Franco claimed had granted a hundred indulgences for every Red killed in Spain. However, our picture did appear in the pages of the Dublin *Evening Mail*, a Protestant paper.

(US journalist Vincent Sheean, who covered Europe from Mussolini's coup de état in 1922 through World War Two, shared Bob's view of what Fascism's conquest of Spain meant:

France's life depended on checking the Fascist advance, and that to present Spain to the enemy, as the non-intervention arms embargo did, was equivalent to turning over part of France...French premier Blum never saw this until it was too late, recanting in tears at the Socialist Congress of 1939 when the Spanish Republic had already fallen – preceding the fall of the French Republic by little more than a year.

Nothing but resolute action by the French government would have enabled the Spanish government to face the sinister conspiracy of its powerful, well-equipped enemies. Of all the might-have-beens of the years 1935-38, probably the bitterest is this: that it would have cost France little to defeat Fascism in Spain in 1936 and 1937. As it was, the resistance of the Spanish Republic had given the blind

French and British time – time which they had mostly wasted but otherwise would not have had at all.

When Sheean invited the exiled Spanish premier Juan Negrín to lunch in wartime Paris, they found themselves seated beside French right-wing politician Pierre Laval. 'Is that who I think it is?' asked Sheean. 'You are right,' said Negrín impassively. 'That is the man who will make the peace with Hitler.' Less than a month later these words became fact.

Under German occupation, Laval as premier became the leading collaborator, working with Doriot who had visited San Pedro. Despite the sympathy he had always shown to Franco, Laval was extradited from Spain after France's liberation from the Nazis and executed for his collaboration with the Germans. (See note, *As the Dust Settled in Spain*, pp. 226–7.)

11

THE SECOND WORLD WAR

It was impossible to obtain work in Dublin following my return from San Pedro de Cardeña in February 1939. Even qualified people like Frank Edwards, a teacher, were denied a place in any Catholic school on the orders of the bishops, and it was only the Jewish community which enabled him to earn a living by giving him a post in a Jewish school, Zion Road, then on Bloomfield Avenue off the South Circular Road in Dublin.

I gave up and made my way back to the Channel Islands where I had previously worked for a while on my way to join the International Brigade. The work was arduous and painful: drilling 18in holes into granite quarry all day with a cold chisel. I stuck that for six months until relieved by Chamberlain's declaration of war in September 1939 when jobs became more easily available. I was able to use my previous seaman's discharge papers and signed on the *Isle of Alderney*, plying between the Channel Island ports and southwest England. The fear of German invasion and occupation of the islands was uppermost in people's minds, most of all mine.

After Spain, the appeasement of the Nazis and the stasis of the 'Phoney War' (See note, *The Phoney War*, p. 227.) it was difficult to see how Britain could defend the Channel Islands. I certainly had no confidence and decided to get out and establish myself on the mainland, obtaining a job building air-raid shelters in Aldershot. In London, fellow veteran Eugene Downing remembered:

I was just doing some typing in the Brigade's office when Bob came in about something. That's the first time I met him. I got a job and I think it was £3 a week. The war was beginning to get a grip but before that it was hopeless looking for a job. University professors were cleaning out toilets at that time, German refugees, fellows offering to teach you languages. There was nothing, nothing. I'd get jobs in England and to get them in Dublin you'd have to be a relation of the archbishop or somebody, even without our Republican past, in normal times.

It was about this time that I met a Spanish girl. It was the first reunion of the survivors of the International Brigade and it was held near St Paul's Cathedral. It was a commemoration social supported by Spanish Republican sympathisers to raise support for the two million prisoners forgotten by the democracies. Lola (Dolores) had arrived in London in 1932 and worked as a domestic for the Republican consul in London. We became friends, seeing each other often, and decided to get married a few months later.

Our views on life and the Spanish War coincided but she was a practising Catholic and this created difficulties. She was an associate of the Spanish convent in Bayswater who were solid supporters of Franco. I was an atheist by now, having passed the agnostic period while in Spain. I tried to persuade Lola to marry in the registry office but she was concerned that the nuns would pass on the information to Madrid, and to Oviedo where her family was from, that not only had she married a Red but one who had actually fought against their Catholic crusade. Lola feared this would have consequences for her mother.

While I didn't agree that her mother would be in any danger, I could understand the reasons for her fears. After all, this was the height of the Fascist ferocity when two hundred were being executed in Madrid daily; the *Madrileños* were particularly terrorized for their past sins. In the circumstances we agreed on a compromise. I would go through the rituals of reconsecration but declare myself as non-religious. Her mother worked all her life for a monarchist family in Madrid who supported Franco in the belief that he was defending their religion. She acted as governess, mother and cook and brought up the eight children, two of whom became nuns. She was valued and respected by the whole family and had never taken any wages during her more than sixty years of service. She had requested that, because of her illiteracy, they should bank her wages. Her daughter Lola had been placed in the care of nuns in Oviedo in Northern Spain because of the early death of her father.

After her stay in the convent she joined her mother as a domestic in Madrid until she moved to Paris with another family, and subsequently moved to London where, like most of the Spanish domestics, she maintained a close association with the Spanish convent in Bayswater.

We agreed, in the circumstances, to put the banns up in her parish of Claverton Street, Victoria. Because I had declared myself as non-religious, the priest refused to marry us but said he'd seek out the advice of the Bishop of London. After a time he informed my fiancée that we would have to attend his vestry for tuition, which consisted of my renunciation of all those opposed to the One Holy Catholic and Apostolic Church, that I had to go to Mass and confession. He saw us individually. He told me that I was bringing this good Catholic girl into perdition but he failed to convince me. On my way out of the vestry I said to my fiancée in Spanish as she entered, 'He has tried to convince me to put it off. Now he's going to try it on you.' She replied, 'No, no, *ni hablar* – don't even think of it.'

On entering she was holding my book, Tom Paine's *Age of Reason*. On seeing the book and its title the priest exclaimed, 'My God, look what you're doing to this girl!' He was telling me that the book contained many things that I wouldn't understand that are against the Catholic religion.

I thought it was presumptuous of him to make such an assertion; it only reminded me of my formative years as I remembered questioning the catechism. The first topic was: 'Who made the world?' with the answer: 'God made the world' and the last question was: 'What means Amen?' with its answer 'So be it.' In other words the world always was and will be, so therefore it's not open to question. But I questioned that. I had a little argument with him about the book, arguing that it should be looked at on its merits and also as an enlightened classic, to which he replied, 'Yes' but that there were passages in that book whose implications I would not understand, which I thought was an insult to my intelligence.

We were married on 3 February 1940 after two visits to the priest in the vestry. I had to go to confession, the first time since I was fifteen. It was a nauseating experience; I felt unclean after experiencing the diabolical role of the Church in Spain. Was I betraying all I had fought for here in this confessional box? I couldn't think what constituted a venial sin after all these years so I said, 'Well father, I have no venial sins but if you expect me to confess to having fought against Franco in Spain, then I'm afraid that I cannot do so as I don't consider that a mortal sin.'

He replied, 'Well my son, if you are attacked by a wild beast, you have got to defend yourself.' I don't know who was the beast but he said this as he was making the Sign of the Cross over my head. That was the end, I was glad to get out. We held our reception at the Restaurant Majorca in Soho, attended by all our Spanish Republican friends. It had a real Spanish atmosphere.

Accommodation wasn't a problem then. We got a nice flat for twenty-five shillings a week overlooking Paddington Station, convenient also when my wife became pregnant, our first child being practically born in the underground station. Westbourne Court was a middle-class residence where no worker lived before the war, but as soon as the threat of bombs came the residents all skedaddled off to the country or abroad, so that the workers were able to pay the reduced rent of the vacant accommodation. We were turfed out, of course, after the war, by drastic increases in rents. I continued to work in the building trade, having now transferred to a job in Piccadilly Circus until the evacuation of Dunkirk, when I decided to go back to sea.

I signed on the *Empire Sentinel,* a captured German coaster, at the London Shipping Federation. We were ordered to proceed to Dunkirk to assist in the evacuation. On our way we received a signal from the Admiralty to change course and sink the ship at the entrance to Poole harbour, Dorset, to block any attempt by German submarines to penetrate the harbour. We were discharged from there. After loading ourselves up with souvenirs, we returned to London on leave before joining another vessel.

My next ship was a small Dutch coaster, *Motorship Express,* plying the coast of Britain. I was the only British seaman on board. We were assembled in a convoy of twenty-seven ships off Southend, our destination Plymouth. I was off duty and asleep in my bunk in the fo'castle, with my head about twelve inches from the bulkhead, when the noise of explosions woke me. I jumped out and ran up on deck but could see no one either on the deck or in the bridge. I thought it was torpedoes or that we'd struck a mine, until I looked up to see the many German planes in the 'blue skies over/The white cliffs of Dover' – the other members of the crew had taken cover.

I dived back down to my bunk as I saw a bomb from a Heinkel land on the stern of the *Island Queen,* a sister ship of the one on which I had previously served which was travelling behind us. This was being done off the cliffs of Dover by the same planes that had been terrorising the civilian population of Spain and bombing and strafing us on the battlefields. From then on we had a Hurricane – just one, all they could afford at the time – guarding us all the way to Plymouth. By the time we arrived in Plymouth Movietone News was screening *Mass Attack on Convoy* in the cinemas. I believe that Marshall Kesselring was in charge of them, the one who'd been in charge of the bombing of Guernica, and it wasn't difficult to see the relationship between that bombing in Spain and the 'Phoney' period of the war in which we were engaged – the continuity of it.

So when we got to Plymouth, I got paint and brushes from the bosun's store. I agreed with the Communist Party's leader Harry Pollitt's policy against it, especially his slogan of 'Turn the Imperialist War into a People's War,' which to me was the description of the

Phoney War period, when the strategy of the west was to turn Hitler east. I went all round the docks at night painting the slogan, and then I went to the pictures and saw the attack on our convoy on the screen, with the same Heinkels and Stukas that had bombed us in Spain, simply a rehearsal for World War Two. (See note, *The Battle of the Channel*, p. 227.)

The popular songs at that time were 'We're Going to Hang out our Washing on the Siegfried Line' and 'Roll out the Barrel', while the jolly war continued and British seamen were taking the brunt of the Nazi submarine onslaught in which thousands of them died at sea.

I didn't stay long on the MS *Express*. It was too small with only a crew of five including the captain, all Dutch. I decided my next ship would be a deep-sea sailing one and after a short leave, made my way to Liverpool to sign on at the Shipping Federation. I knew the *Rawalpindi* was a big ship and stood in the line for signing on. I was the last but one in the line when the officer closed the book, stating that that was the last of his complement. The ship sailed shortly and was sunk on the approaches of the Western Atlantic.

I took the next ship, the *Anglia* which was stationed at Gibraltar. I went on a troopship to Gibraltar and as I disembarked I looked around the harbour to see which of the big ships was mine. When I reported I was directed to the *Anglia* and to my astonishment it was a small naval yacht, my ship, much to my disgust. I now found myself in the Navy under articles T124X which meant I was subject to naval discipline, having to wear a naval uniform, etc.

The *Anglia*'s job was to patrol the Straits listening and looking out for submarines. I had signed on as an AB seaman and on hearing that the cook had not returned from leave and that the captain was going crazy looking for someone to cook, I volunteered. I had worked as a cook on special trains at Paddington, cooking for the likes of the Licensed Vinters Association with the Great Western Railways to Penzance. It was the best catering. I used to cook up on deck. The crew was delighted with my Spanish *tortillas* for breakfast. I must have learnt this skill in Spain or don't forget – I was married. They found this a relief after the greasy breakfast they claimed the other cook dished up. After a month I was promoted to Chief Petty Officer Cook. This was a happy time.

The crew's first experience of action was the bombing of the harbour by Italian Capronis. As soon as the warning siren sounded, the Spanish workers, mainly from La Linea on the Spanish side of the border, who were working on the docks, made a sudden dive for cover under the jetty, to the cheers and jeers of the British crew who called them the inferior name of *Los Calientes* (the hot ones). I made a dive for the gangway and joined the *Calientes* under the jetty. After the all-clear sounded I returned and remarked, 'If you had gone through the same suffering as these people during the last three years under Fascism, you wouldn't be so heroic.' I then went round the harbour in a rowboat and picked up the stunned fish. Most of the bombs had been dropped in the water, missing their target because of the concentrated fire of the Bofors anti-aircraft guns and the brightness of the skies.

The patrol of the yacht between the Rock and the African coast was a boring route, the same piece of coastline all day. The only diversion was a little monkey who lived aboard and spent his time swinging from stanchions all round the ship and coming into my galley to gobble up the cockroaches as I opened my cupboards. He was spotlessly clean, shitting over the side while holding onto a stanchion.

While suspicious of me as a 'Communazi' because I had fought with the Reds in Spain, the crew liked my cooking and began to see things in a different light. I developed a stomach disorder and was taken to the military hospital on the Rock. I was there for a week, during which time the army psychiatrist came around the wards to single out the 'leftwingers' and the 'dodgers' or 'slags', blokes who wanted to get out, and I was mixed up with them. (See note, *Communazi*, p. 228.)

He assured me, as I expressed my opinion on the progress of the war, that it would soon be over as we had just captured Fort Capuzzo out in the Sahara desert. He was a Lieutenant-Colonel and

I thought, what a twit, such was the mentality of the Phoney War period. The battleship *Renown* was sunk while I was there.

(On 14 June 1940, just four days after Italy entered the war, a British mobile column captured Fort Capuzzo near Tobruk by surprise but didn't try to hold it as their strategy then was to keep mobile in the face of the vastly more numerous Italian forces.)

After discharge I requested a transfer with the possibility of getting leave to see my son for the first time. I was transferred to HMS *Camito* for patrol and convoy protection duty in the Western Atlantic Approaches.

The HMS *Camito*, a former Elders & Fyffes banana and passenger ship, was one of the many merchant ships converted into auxiliary cruisers. It carried only ballast and had two outdated guns. The seamen were mostly from Liverpool. We were a mixed crew, that is, naval ratings on two shillings a day while the T124X (merchant service) were paid the higher merchant service rate, about five shillings. This caused friction between us, but as I pointed out, it was their duty to protest and fight to bring their rate up to ours, and not ours down to theirs. However, the Scousers were great and very realistic.

We slept three to four in a cabin and all carried improvised water belts for our money in case of being torpedoed. They thought up the idea that each day when we got a tot of naval rum, one of us would drink the lot in turn, so each day one of the four would be a little bit tipsy. The ship was top heavy and rolled a lot. I had now accepted the position of steward serving the officers' wardroom. One day with a rough sea and the ship rolling heavily, I had drunk my turn of the tots and had to take a gallon can of soup to the officers' mess where they were comfortably seated. I plonked the can on the table saying, 'Here's your fucking soup!' and walked out. We resented them. While we had to struggle to eat our food, they were able to sit comfortably at a table chained to the deck. We resented also that they had been supplied with a new and better type of life jacket, which was denied to us.

I was reported to the captain and brought before him and was sentenced to ten days Number Eleven (this meant running around the deck holding a rifle balanced and held away from you with one arm, and an officer watching over you). Then he stated, 'We have all your past records.' It should be remembered that Russia wasn't in the war at that point; it was still the Phoney War.

I did one or two rounds of the deck with a rifle and I said to the officer, 'Here, you hold this, I'm off.' I used to write long letters to my wife in Spanish, much to the annoyance of the officer who censored them but later on was giving lessons in Spanish to some of the officers and lower ranks It was mostly Spanish ships that we were stopping searching for arms. I was sent out to board them because I could speak a bit. For a while we patrolled the Western Approaches. Once we came across a submarine that fired a torpedo at us that missed. We saw it pass us and so we stuffed all our money in our belts, expecting to go down any time.

We had a daily mustering for emergencies but one day they were real. The alarms went and the captain ordered everyone on deck. 'We have just received a signal from Whitehall. The German battleship *Gneisenau* is attacking a convoy within our vicinity and we have been ordered to beat it to the Azores. I intend to ignore that signal and proceed to the scene of the attack.' We were about 188 miles away.

As we sailed nearer the scene, the chief gunner said to me, 'You are to sit here and not take part.' I asked him why, as my job was to hand up the powder from the magazine to the gunners. He just replied, 'Captain's orders.' On our arrival at the scene of the attack there was no sign of the *Gneisenau* or any of the convoy, only bales of cotton, upturned lifeboats and all the flotsam of the upper deck. As we picked up the dead and dying in the nets slung over the side, the doctor said in a raised voice to the other officers and ratings, 'That will show some of our fifth column.' A Liverpool deckhand turned to me, remarking, 'That was meant for you, Bob.' I replied in an equally raised voice, 'Yes, but the fifth column is more likely to be found in the wardroom than in the mess deck.' The Scousers nearby assented, showing their delight. The convoy was coming from Sierra Leone and was to be met by a British battleship, but instead the *Gneisenau* lay waiting and steamed up the centre of the convoy blasting ships. Nineteen ships out of twenty-four were sunk with few survivors.

After a few more patrols around the Western Approaches, we returned for provisions and fuel to Rossyth in Scotland. Here I was able to leave and return in naval uniform to see my wife and six-month-old son for the first time in the famous Ironbridge in Shropshire where she'd been evacuated from London. She had him baptised and named him Robert after me because I'd gone to sea and she feared I was going to be killed.

After my leave expired I was instructed to report to HMS *Mersey* in Liverpool. Here I learned that HMS *Camito* had been sunk off the Irish coast on its outward journey with the loss of all hands. My discharge book states: 'Vessel lost by enemy action; no adverse reports received.'

Having many friends in Liverpool whom I met in the anti-Fascist struggle during my earlier visits, I stayed with them instead of at HMS *Mersey*, which was only a naval base, formerly a hospital. At this time 'Lord Haw-Haw' (William Joyce) was broadcasting from Hamburg, his bellicose statements of what they, the Germans, were going to do included removing HMS *Mersey* from her anchorage, knowing well it was a base. In the course of the initial blitz on Liverpool the HMS *Mersey*, former hospital, was the recipient of a landmine.

The blitz on Liverpool was sorrowful to me having had such a close association in my earlier youth and in the struggle against Fascism. I shed tears as I walked down London Road and what looked to me like the whole of the city from the Piketown Hall down and including the docks was ablaze. I thought, 'Jesus, this is what we meant in the posters that I had brought back from Valencia earlier, "Bombs on Madrid Mean Bombs on London".' This was the shocking price for the bombs on Madrid and the fireball destruction of Guernica, the holy city of the Basques.

After further medical examination in Liverpool, it was found I had an ulcer, and I ended up having two operations for it. I was considered physically unfit for further sea services but without any explanation as to the cause or recognition of my naval services T124X. Subsequently, after an operation in a London hospital, when the lady almoner told me she would apply for a pension, she was told by naval authorities that my trouble was the result of my involvement with the Spanish War.

(Merchant sailors were officially non-combatants, serving under the peacetime ship owners for £10 a month plus £5 danger money. If the ship was sunk, the men's pay stopped from the time it went down. Crews might wait on rafts up to fifty days for rescue. Total Merchant Navy losses were later reckoned at 50,525 seamen. In 1942 1664 ships were sunk. By December just over 300,000 tons of bunker fuel remained in Britain. Churchill wrote in 1949, 'The only thing that really frightened me during the war was the U-boat peril.')

AFTER THE WAR: THE PRINT UNION

I spent the next half of the war years firewatching on the Communist Party HQ at 16 King Street, London, employed by the party. I was a regular firewatcher; all the other Communists who worked there, Harry Pollit, Peter Kerrigan, William Gallagher, had to take their turn firewatching with me. They'd be available, writing in their offices, and we were trying to stop the Fascists who were active from decorating the building outside. When that finished I got a job in the Leftwing Bookshop through the party, packing. We were doing a roaring trade with India because of the books we published. We produced more books than the Labour Party. There were too many working there, however, and we were asked to volunteer to leave; so I did.

When the war ended, my discharge from the navy in 1945 left me with the challenge of finding work. I knew there was a keen demand for labour in the printing industry as the wartime restriction on newsprint had been lifted. I contacted some comrades at the Central London branch of the print workers trade union SOGAT, now known after a merger as the GPMU, to seek their advice.

The union kept a detailed record of all full-time and casual work in the industry and in London alone had about 28,000 members. I was sent to work in the general warehouse of Her Majesty's Stationery Office based in Harrow, West London. My designated task was to work on the guillotine, the Saybold Cutter, trimming all documents before the HMSO publications could be distributed – in my case it was the London telephone directory. As soon as possible

I became active in the union, initially as a rank and file activist, contributing wherever I could.

Then one day shortly after I started, I was called into the management's office and informed I was sacked. No reason was given and I immediately contacted the warehouse shop steward, a Mr Lewington. He was astonished that any union member could be treated in such a manner and asked me: 'Have you been robbing post offices or something?' I said, 'No, of course not,' but that I suspected it was really because the bosses had been told that I had been a member of the International Brigade. With that the steward decided to hold an emergency meeting of the chapel, the traditional time-honoured name for the union branch. I was a security risk to the telephone directory. 'Could you imagine me sending all the subscribers' names to Joe Stalin!' I said to the staff.

The members needed little convincing that this was a clear case of discrimination and a strike was called which was to last six weeks – but which demonstrated how a successful resolution can be achieved when solidarity is shown. I suspect too that the employers were none too pleased by the national press coverage the strike received.

When I got home after the chapel strike vote there was an eager industrial reporter from the *Daily Mirror* waiting to question me about possible subversive activity at the Royal printers. Though I clearly explained what had happened, the front-page splash of the next morning's edition read 'Communist holds up production in Harrow'.

Though we got the desired result, SOGAT's Central London branch officials offered me another job, as an alternative to returning to Harrow, an offer I said I would go along with providing that I was given a month's pay. This was duly negotiated and with that I went to work at the Amalgamated Press, which was situated close to Blackfriars Bridge and employed 2000 workers. The work there was the same as at HMSO but a critical difference was that I was to spend eighteen years working on the trimming machines that dealt with magazines like *Women's Weekly*, and children's comics. However, at first things looked set for a re-run of the Harrow situation. I had been tipped off from one of the friendlier managers that his supervisors were already looking for ways to dismiss me at the first opportune moment.

As both an activist and Communist, I was aware that the best form of defence is to go on the offensive. During the lunch break I quite literally mounted a soapbox in the canteen and started to address my colleagues at some length. A message was sent to management that an 'emergency chapel-meeting had started', something they no doubt realised might eat into production time. Fortunately our workplace branch was a large one with a 100 per cent union membership and the company had to issue an assurance that no one was facing the sack, including yours truly. However, another much more important dispute was to be fought out at Amalgamated Press that would have implications for print workers across the country. This was the battle for the forty-hour week in 1959.

This had long been a demand from within the labour movement, but particularly within the printing industry, where even after the victory over Hitler's Fascism some fourteen years earlier, workers were putting in up to sixty hours a week in order to make a decent living – fifteen hours of that on poor overtime rates. In those days issues like pay, conditions and holiday rights were collectively negotiated between the production printers unions, the NGA and SOGAT, which included its clerical wing NATSOPA, face to face with the Newspaper Proprietors Association (NPA) and the Association of Master Printers (AMP). By the early 1950s with newsprint costs steadily falling and the demand for advertising space soaring, the press barons and their printer contractors were making a fortune yet wages remained very much shackled to long hours.

But there was an important political element to this situation. The Conservative government was keen to force wage restraint on the country and decided to have a showdown with the print workers. They had earlier in the year had a partial victory, facing down a similar demand from London's bus workers; in the end settling for a compromise forty-five-hour week.

Now they wanted to extend this policy into the private sector, and if they could influence the wages and hours worked among some of the most highly organised unions in the country, it would make the Tories' task easier. This would also seem to explain the recalcitrance of the employers to move on this. But in May 1959 they made an offer. They would agree an official working week of forty-two and a half hours, providing they could set 'efficiency demands' and redundancies, so the deal effectively paid for itself. This was totally unacceptable to the unions who immediately called an overtime ban.

In June the bosses' organisations took the initiative and instructed their members to employ workers on a day-to-day basis. That set the solidarity ball rolling, with every union giving notice of strike action that would begin on 18 June, an action that was to last for six weeks. Picket lines were set up outside the offices of printers and newspaper publishers to prevent the bussing-in of scab labour as well as to stop the supply of newsprint and ink. The Conservative Minster of Labour seemed in no particular hurry to see this dispute resolved, deciding to go on holiday on the day the strike action started.

During the strike, as a union shop steward, known in the industry as the father of the chapel, I was very much what would later have been called a 'flying picket', travelling to help organise wherever help was needed. I well remember one action with particular clarity as it could have led to my imprisonment! We had called for a mass picket outside Oldhams Press in the Long Acre area of the City of London on 25 June 1959.

The demonstration outside the plant was a noisy one, as was to be expected given the employers' intransigence, but not a violent one. However at a crucial moment, a group of officers from Bow Street Station made a clearly planned charge at our picket line. This was unsuccessful at first but as reinforcements arrived they broke through, and scuffles ensued, with several pickets being knocked to the ground.

I along with several others was pinned against a wall by officers, some wielding truncheons, who started to make arrests. At which point I noticed that one constable was falling forward and clearly in danger of being trampled by a group of his own fellow officers unless someone stepped in. Although I wasn't feeling in the best of health, having just recovered from surgery for a stomach ulcer, I stepped forward in an attempt to help him up. This was the key for two policemen to grab me by both arms, telling me I was under arrest for violent assault.

What followed down at the station didn't initially surprise me. I knew from past experience of police tactics that they would at least drum up some phoney allegation if only to maintain their arrest charge tally. So I, along with five others, was charged with riotous assembly. But for good measure, I was informed that I also faced charges of wounding and assault.

My initial reaction was 'Come off it, I've only recently come out of hospital!' That cut no ice. Our trial was set to take place at the Old Bailey, starting on Monday 9 November, and received national press coverage every day. I sat in the dock with fellow print workers John Hope, Richard Davis, Alex Fuente, Danny Bennett and Roderick Hood. At the heart of the police case was evidence presented by a procession of twenty-one police inspectors, sergeants and officers who read from notebooks their various accounts.

Many, under close cross-examination by our barrister Michael Howard, QC, proved to be completely contradictory. It was alleged that I, apparently one of the master villains of the piece, had either stood on the fallen policeman or at the very least kicked him in the head, depending on which police account was believed. Their prosecuting counsel was the appropriately named Mr John Buzzard who, as we saw it, turning fact upside-down, claimed that pickets had charged the police cordon as they tried to move pickets away from the entrance of the Oldhams Press factory.

By some good fortune, before the trial we were informed that there had been plenty of Press Association photographers who had taken pictures of our fracas and arrest. One had been arrested and only released when police realised their mistake, he went round all his colleagues in Fleet Street and gave us all the photos taken. These were to prove invaluable in debunking the police interpretation of events.

The police had been trying to help force a lorry through the picket at the entrance and you could get the time of each photo from the position of the lorry's progress. In several pictures I could clearly be seen standing with the officer I supposedly attacked. It was clear from these that there was little animosity, that I was being detained by the wall of the plant and nowhere near the scene of the so-called cordon charge incident.

In summing up to the jury of six men and three women, our barrister said that, but for these pictures, there would have been little for the jury to assess as evidence except the contradictory words of the police against those in the dock. Mr Howard concluded that if the photographs showed what they appeared to show, the prosecution's case was 'completely out of the window'.

On 20 November the ten-day trial ended when the foreman of the jury pronounced 'Not guilty' to a packed silent courtroom. After just two hours they had decided to throw out all the assault charges. Just one of us, Roderick Hood, was found guilty of obstructing the police, fined £25 and given three weeks to pay. A union whip-around soon relieved him of that unjust burden.

As for the battle for the forty-hour week, when the strike concluded only those of us working at the Amalgamated Press had not actually needed to go on strike at our own workplace and could concentrate on helping our fellow members. The reason was that we had negotiated the reduced working time three years earlier without taking industrial action. But as a result of the national dispute the other employers reached a compromise with the unions' national leaderships. This produced an agreement to a 'stepped' move towards the reduced working week; however this was accompanied by a 4.5 per cent wage rise to sweeten the deal when selling it to their members. The settlement also provided for the matter to be referred to a judicial inquiry if the forty-hour week had not been achieved by 1961. This probably served to save the Conservatives' face – on paper at least. They had singularly failed to persuade the print unions to abide by their recommendation of a 3 per cent pay norm. The forty-hour week was finally accepted by the newspaper proprietors of Fleet

Street in May 1962.

At the end of the national forty-hour week dispute I was elected to the union branch committee of SOGAT at Amalgamated Press and clearly I must have been doing a reasonable job because five years later, in 1965, I found myself elected as the most senior shop steward, the imperial father of the chapel, able to speak on behalf of all the workplace unions.

The 1960s remained a testing period for trade union leadership everywhere, although there had been a change of government in 1964, with Labour being led by Harold Wilson. Just like its Tory predecessors this government was obsessed with pay restraint and incomes policy. In 1966 Labour proposed a typical class compromise approach to workers' pay in announcing the establishment of a broad-ranging commission comprising 'experts' under the guidance of the academic Lord Donovan. His commission would gather evidence from industry, finance, trade unions and, of course, other academics, to decide what policy was best to raise productivity and incorporate the support of the unions.

The eminent body took two years to deliver a report which included a mishmash of ideas but which basically left the door open for the government to intervene and to delay strike action when desirable. This reflected the tension on the commission between groups like the Engineering Employers Federation and the Motor Manufacturers Association, who wanted strikes outlawed and hefty fines imposed, as opposed to trade union leaders like Jack Jones, and print workers SOGAT leader Richard Briginshaw who opposed any state interference in union affairs.

The outcome which resulted was a White Paper from Labour Minister Barbara Castle in 1969, called 'In Place of Strife'. While it was full of flimflam about setting up a Conciliation and Arbitration Board, whose role was to offer the wisdom of Solomon whenever a major strike was looming, there was a sting in the tail that produced total opposition across the union movement. Castle, with the full backing of Wilson, had made provision for an Industrial Relations Court that could, at any time before a strike occurred, impose a twenty-eight-day cooling-off period so that both sides had to resume talking. If at the end of that period agreement was not reached, then a fresh strike ballot had to take place.

It was blindingly obvious that this was designed to overthrow a democratic trade union decision to take industrial action and break the workers' will to fight. Within days the entire labour movement had agreed around a platform of non-compliance and to wage total opposition to the proposals. Regular national demonstrations, which saw crowds of 100,000 attend rallies in Trafalgar Square and other major city centres, were backed up by one-day strikes in selected industries. In Fleet Street there was a mass walkout of workers by staff at the *Daily Mirror*, the *Express* and even the Tory-worshipping *Daily Telegraph*.

I was happy to carry the London Central banner on that day and was amazed to see many hundreds of clerical workers taking what was their first ever industrial action. Ten weeks later, with a general election only a matter of months away, Castle and Wilson threw in the towel. The bill would be abandoned. I had parted company with Amalgamated Press some three years earlier at the age of fifty and gone to work at the Book Centre in Red Lion Square. It was in central London, in a print warehouse that both printed and distributed publications. Frankly it was a job that nobody from the SOGAT branch wanted to take. They could not supply anyone from its vacancies list and when I arrived it was clear that union membership was far from solid or organised. Within a month I was chairman of the chapel committee and in the very next union branch elections was elected as father of the chapel. My job in the warehouse was to check the orders were accurately supplied but as a fulltime union official, I was given a free hand to deal with union members and matters.

The Centre was the main processing site for the entire book trade in the country and had several feeder depots in England, Wales, Scotland and Northern Ireland. It also served as the first computerised workplace in the industry and distributed to all main high-street bookshops and into the schools of greater London. The first issue I had to deal with was a very vicious bonus scheme put in place by management several years earlier, which set performance targets that were practically impossible to achieve. With the real threat of industrial action facing the management unless proper targets became available, they relented to the point of agreeing an across-the-board wage increase.

This had a knock-on effect within the other major depots and I soon found myself travelling by plane to all the major cities to negotiate a similar deal. It worked to such an extent that during the great strike in Glasgow, we were the only company allowed exemption; the management made a statement to the *Glasgow Herald* that we already enjoyed the strikers demands.

The next challenging situation I had to deal with involved a union recognition problem involving a self-styled millionaire 'socialist' by the name of Robert Maxwell. This was in 1970 and by that time Maxwell had characteristically wangled a deal with Oxford Council, persuading them to sell him an apparently dilapidated mansion in Oxford called Headington Hall for a song. They may have been taken in by this would-be publishing magnate who at that time was eager to be selected as the Labour Party candidate for Slough. As far as I was concerned, he was the class enemy.

At that time the Book Centre was negotiating with Maxwell to handle his distribution and the computerised back-up facility that he would need. The Centre's management had decided to open up a brand new warehouse building in Southport from scratch, to house and distribute his titles. One of the attractions, no doubt, was that some non-union labour was inevitable given the shortage of labour in the area at that time.

Not coincidentally, I decided it would benefit me and the union if I took a brief holiday up there and tried to organise a workplace branch. The Liverpool Branch had made no progress at membership. I wrote to Maxwell at Oxford to take advantage of his intentions of his putting himself forward as the official Labour candidate for Slough. Up to this time Maxwell had refused even to meet with Bill Keys, the London Central Branch Secretary, or indeed anyone else in relation to union concerns.

In the letter I stated that at all his platforms to meet the people, I would be there with a loud hailer and my own platform and would carry out the biggest campaign ever to expose him as anti-trade unionist, refusing to have his workers at Southport join a union. After a few weeks the Book Centre director got a phone call from Maxwell asking 'to speak to Doyle'. He said he'd meet me at Oxford, suggesting a date after the election. I said, 'There's no good trying that one with me. I will see you before the election.' So I saw him before the election. I got the national organiser to come with me and we drove down to Oxford to meet Maxwell in the office based at his residence.

He started calling me 'comrade', so I reminded him that he could forget the comradeship and that we represented two different sides in the argument. I continued to put forward my policy as regards the workers at Southport, and while he did not accept all of them, I must honestly say he did not put up any objections to my proposals. In 1989 when *The Last Parade* TV documentary of our veterans trip to Barcelona was being shown, I wrote to him asking for publicity, pointing out the *Mirror*'s one-time support for the Spanish Republic and reminding him of the stint he himself once spent in a concentration camp, but no reply came.

As one of 150 warehouse workers, I and the others were lucky to work more than two days a week. When there was no work the manager came and made us stand, to display his control. Since the war this had been brought about by fierce competition and monopolies, swallowing up other printing groups. There were mixed feelings when we were taken over: was this greater security or a threat to our jobs? The fears of many, including myself, were justified by rationalising and automation. Magazines were merged, even one with a circulation of over 800,000. Our sole interest then was getting paid and getting home. We felt frustrated, insecure. The old craft careers were gone and unskilled work remained.

I had given up being father of the chapel and my job was unskilled: bundling and counting magazines or trimming –

monotonous work, but because of my union work I'd had to be passed over for promotion since I began there eighteen years ago, when we had over twice as many employed. There used be almost endless overtime, double our current £20 week's wages, but most of that work had been relocated or was done by new technology. The result was that we had a quarter of our previous work and no confidence in our future.

Only our union strength in SOGAT, where I was on the London Central committee, maintained our position. Transfers offered to other London plants might mean just transferring redundancy which, despite generous compensation, wasn't a solution. I was involved in the negotiations when the first periodicals were transferred out of London, and we negotiated the formula: no redundancies without consultation, staff were to be run down through natural wastage. But new technology such as web-offset eliminated jobs, allowing super profits and decentralised production. Few workers on higher wages meant scrapping half the jobs, and no places for new entrants. It meant a rise in national unemployment.

So the print trade then was over-staffed as workers used the unions to hold jobs in the face of developments we could not control. Economists and the media called us lazy and greedy, just aiming at restrictive practices. Only a drastic cut in hours per week and longer holidays offered a solution. Accepting the employers' view would allow scientific advances to create unemployment instead of improvements for everyone in our society.

So I supported keeping staff at pre-automation levels, ridiculous as it seemed. The waste of manpower was shocking but without a lead from government, unions were forced into conservative positions. Workers like me should have trained for new skills without losing pay or security, but just increasing unemployment, hoping we could move to new industries, was a joke. Where could we get the skills? How did a middle-aged worker with dependants start again on a training allowance? Employers could take advantage of these contradictions in government policy. Workers felt they were trapped, with no control of conditions, in a business empire making millions but using its power to spread ideas that directed them away from any real solution to his problems, they were forced into becoming indifferent to all but pay.

Doing such undemanding, repetitive work doesn't develop creative outside interests. It has a brutalising effect. Racism, anti-Semitism and intolerance were common. Most didn't read their own union reports and many voted Tory. When I tried to describe possible socialist alternatives, they were unable or unwilling to see anything other than their present lifestyles. All you could discuss with most of them was horses or football. The dependence and insecurity made printers militant on wages and jobs, causing the Saturday night anomaly in my section where we had the opportunity to do a night in Fleet Street's Sunday papers on a rota. Since the bundling was increasingly automated, hundreds did nothing but get over £12 for one night. Management could pay this as they were free to install new technology and lose staff through natural wastage, yet make super profits

For a few years my union role for a number of plants meant preparing overtime and staffing lists for machines, which I considered management work. Life was a constant battle for me and the local manager on trivial issues – defending staff's right to play cards when there was no work – in a demoralising situation of insecurity for us and him. I had to make unpopular decisions, amalgamating three chapels in the same building into one, which strengthened us. I had to resign, although I'm sure the members started to understand my concerns afterwards.

I'd taken part in negotiating when senior management threatened to close us unless the factory in London was profitable. It had obsolete machines and bad management but these weren't the workers' responsibility, so I sought the best increases and fringe benefits in return for allowing web-offset and the like. It meant £6 a week more for the unskilled members, on top of their £14.75. We also got sick pay for them and other small gains like outpatient attendance on half-pay. We had to forgo shop-stewards rights to negotiate on individual wages and benefits but kept their right to carry on otherwise. We gave interchangeability of mainly unskilled labour and allowed new technology to be run on the agreed staffing levels until agreement had been negotiated.

Management seemed more interested in closing us down: we had lost equipment and contracts had been sent abroad. Work was speeded up on the remaining machines, which were more complicated for older staff. Management aimed to reduce numbers if they re-equipped. Displaced workers were standing around potentially redundant, while employers blamed government economic policy – which they supported in their editorials. Compensation was pointless when now there was no other work outside. The workers could have run our factory – we didn't need the management – although the owners' monopoly would rather have closed half their factories than hand one over. It was a political issue.

But while I advocated socialist policies, the union policy was to keep politics out of their affairs, something dear to the heart of Tories. When Labour proposed a wage freeze, I sought a government printing operation to break the growing press monopolies. Only a political solution could save us but many unions adopted a craft-based outlook instead of one industrial union approach. It was the government wage policy that introduced politics to the shop floor.

13

RETURN TO SPAIN

The first time I returned to Spain was on a motorbike. We were still living in Maida Vale but we moved out of there in 1950. It must have been around 1948 or even earlier. I wanted to revisit the same territory where I'd been held in prison in San Sebastián so I crossed over the frontier nearest there. I was quite scared of the customs officers and the fact that if they would have my records anywhere, it would be at the frontier. If I were caught the consequences would have been severe because when we were being released from the prison camp we had to promise that we would never return to Spain.

I put my passport on the desk but they didn't hesitate in letting me through – they didn't have anything on me. At that time the police had to have knowledge of whether you were on a motorbike or in a car and had to report where you were going. I got past and I stayed in a small hotel and decided to go north, I headed to Asturias. You couldn't go to a village two miles away without going through controls and there were chains across the road – at one stage I nearly crashed into them. I eventually got to Asturias anyway. I loved Spain.

On the way, it was a Sunday, I ran out of petrol which was a very scarce commodity and you had to get vouchers at the bank at that time or buy it on the black market outside of bank hours. I didn't know the correct phrase so I went up to a copper on the street and asked him, '¿*Donde está el mercado negro?*' ('Where is the black market?') – 'You mean *estraperlo*,' he answered and pointed, 'Over there.' I wheeled the bike over and asked for petrol. The guy said it would cost so much and he filled it up – two gallons or so. The next day I went to the bank to get the petrol coupons. The clerk asked me some general questions and it came up that I'd bought some petrol the day before. She asked where I'd bought it. I said, '*Estraperlo*' and she quickly hushed me up, gave me the coupons and told me not to mention that word again. (See note, *Estraperlo*, p. 228.)

I did two trips back to Spain on the motorbike, one in 1948 and again in 1951 and I took two different people. There were hardly any cars in Spain then and what cars they had were old and in need of repairs. I would take cellulose paint and spare parts for cars to give to Antonio, who was married to Matilde, a cousin of my wife Lola. We used to take loads of stuff, coffee and the like – things they couldn't get in Spain then. Once I took a micrometer for a chap who worked in a factory who had lost his – micrometers were very hard to get. (See note, *Hardship in Post-war Spain*, pp. 228–9.)

My sister-in-law, Josefa López, came to live with us in London in 1946. In 1950 Josefa took my sons Robert and Julian to Spain on holiday. It was a long journey. She travelled by train to the port, then boat, then train to Paris. A race to the other side of Paris, then the long night train to Irún, change at Hendaye, then train to San Sebastián and from there on to Bilbao. Josefa's aunt in Bilbao gave them a bad reception so she had to continue on to Oviedo She had travelled for two days and two nights. She enjoyed retelling an incident at customs on her way back: there was a very long queue, which was normal at that time when everyone was under suspicion. They went through her suitcase. They were convinced they had found something significant in my son Robert's trousers and excitedly examined it, pulling it this way and that. In the end, a stone fell out of the pocket and the whole queue laughed.

One of our first trips back to Spain as a family was in a new Ford Popular, which had just come on the market. All four of us went on the holiday. We travelled north from Madrid, having left the visit to San Pedro where I'd been imprisoned towards the end. I had gone back once before on my own on the motorbike. It was very scary but now they were spending about fifty million pesetas refurbishing it as a monastery, although it hadn't been one since the 1920s I think.

It was my idea to visit with the family and as we approached the monastery I warned my sons Robert and Julian not to say or do anything that would draw attention to us in any way. I was still listed as a *persona non grata*, a prisoner who was released and expelled from Spain. Franco's regime was still as harsh as ever. We parked up in the grounds and came under the gateway with the big statue of *El Cid Campeador* (El Cid on a prancing horse) and approached the monastery as respectful tourists. There were two Jesuits at the outer door, while another priest came down and opened it.

They hadn't started doing the place up, so we didn't even get inside the big massive wooden doors. These were the same doors that were always locked, to stop us gazing at the outside. We were standing there in the *Cuerpo de Guardia,* a courtyard where I was beaten in prison time. I told my sons about this as we stood at the door, lying open with the great key still in the lock. My wife and I had a friendly chat with the prior before leaving; we went back to the car and drove off.

About two or three miles away I felt a touch on my back from my son Julian. 'Look what I've got!' and produced the key. It was Robert who had liberated it. I said, 'Oh Crikey, let's get out of here quick!' I was afraid the officials might have noted the registration. They would have known it was an English car, and this was at the height of Franco's power. I could've had my wartime record brought to light. So I drove all night to get over the border into France before the police could start looking for us.

We gave it afterwards to my fellow prisoner Maurice Levitas although it's back now as an heirloom with my granddaughter Margarita. The next time I went there the twenty-foot doors had been replaced. Robert now says he's ashamed of his action. He says it was historical; the key was much older than the Civil War. He feels that key was part of Spain's heritage.

Another time I took them to see the prison in San Sebastián. There I took Robert and Julian for a swim. Detectives watching the beach arrested us because Robert and Julian were wearing swimming togs above the knee. They also forbade dancing at that time which involved contact between men and women in the villages; waltzes for instance weren't allowed. I went to one of the villages and danced. Someone was arrested afterwards – the police were always there. Arrests at village dances were commonplace. At the time, only men went to the *bodegas*. Now women go; it's another Spain – a different life.

(At this time boxing was banned from newsreels as it meant showing half-naked men, a young Argentinian woman was fined for wearing trousers in downtown Madrid, and on the Catalan coast the ladies of Acción Católica threw stones at tourists in shorts.)

Just before this trip another brigader, a Canadian I think, brought his wife, or his wife and family, and they'd all been found shot. It was all put down to raiders or thieves. This was the Fascist government's way of dealing with it. They knew there would be a scandal if they'd actually arrested them.

(Author Gerald Brenan was told how people suspected of underground activity used to be arrested and court martialled, which had led to controversy abroad and intervention by ambassadors. So suspects at this time were either kept in prison without trial or taken to mountain districts where police rule was absolute and left dead by the roadside. When the bodies were discovered, they were called 'Reds, shot while trying to escape'. Since May 1947, when the Civil Guard was given total freedom in certain areas, this was the usual method of getting rid of troublemakers. The regime's armed raids and executions of 'terrorists' continued until the end of 1947, when the main underground leadership withdrew the last guerrillas to France. From then on the struggle of the opposition was through urban social movements. The last wartime anarchist guerrilla, Sabate, was killed on 5 January 1960 after twenty-four years spent fighting, in the Catalan village of San Celoni, while wounded and attempting to reach Barcelona. The official instruction in these cases remained 'No prisoners to be taken!')

In 1957 the whole family including some friends went back in a Dormobile. We took the son of the manager of a Japanese bank with us and he paid his share of the costs. When we got to Oviedo, the capital of Asturias, my wife Lola's relatives had made a collection 'for the poor children of Japan'. We told them they should distribute it among the people of Asturias; this particular Japanese family were one of the richest you could meet.

We would camp at roadsides in between visits to various family and friends' houses. We stopped off at the village of Aranzana de Abajo. Lola was very close to Victorina, a girl from this village. We lived in the same house in Willesden with her and her Spanish husband. I had stayed at the village, which was four kilometres south of Nájera in Rioja, on one of my earliest visits back to Spain. I got to know everyone there. They always gave me a great reception, knowing who I was, although we never talked openly about it. When we wrote to each other we were careful to use coded expressions because the Spanish censor opened letters. I never talked about fighting on the Republican side. We mostly talked about conditions in England and in Spain.

Robert, my son, remembers being driven by car up to a nearby dam. It was a kind of homage. They told us how the Fascists came through this ordinary village and took loads of people up and threw them off the dam. Once the Fascists took over, then the purges began. People would be denounced; sometimes they were political, sometimes they weren't.

It was often a case of people having axes to grind. They wanted other people's land – that kind of thing. Once they were fingered, that was it. In these villages practically everyone was labelled, there were Fascists and there were Communists and they would denounce each other, but certain characters survived, as my son Robert said, 'Either because they were popular or funny.' I remember visiting the dam on another sad occasion when a young bloke from Aranzana was killed by a lorry there. I don't mind saying that I cried. He was very close to me and he knew I was in the Brigade.

Whenever I stayed in Aranzana we would always go up to San Vicente de la Sonsierra, the highest point overlooking the Ebro and a wine-growing area. The land is very fertile; the onions grown here were enormous. A lot of the contacts I made in Aranzana were through Victor, a relative of the family I stayed with in Aranzana. He was the secretary of the Communist Party although he couldn't read or write. Throughout Franco's era Victor never shut up. He lived with a woman whose husband was one of forty-five shot during the purges in San Vicente. They never married. He was denounced regularly from the pulpit but he never stopped. He started the co-op in his village in the later Franco years. The local Fascists opposed him but he overcame that and now in harvest time you could see the tractors going in to the co-op packed with grapes. The Fascists brought theirs too.

A woman who used to distribute milk from house to house located the bodies of most of the forty-five villagers shot by Fascists in San Vicente. She found the spots where they had been dumped. They were buried in different places, wherever they had been shot. She got others in the village together and they brought the bodies back to the village cemetery and buried them in one common grave, placing a big monument with the names of the thirty-seven they managed to find.

Victor brought us to another village where people who fought against Franco were rounded up and brought to the cemetery and shot. He showed us where the priest sat at a table with two candles, and before each was shot he asked them two questions. Some of them were scared and they tried to save themselves. They asked for forgiveness, thinking that would save them. They were all shot anyway but the ones who asked for forgiveness were buried in consecrated ground and the ones who refused were buried outside the cemetery, in a place for heathens and criminals. While we were there Victor said, 'Look, we're walking on those graves now.' The ground had sunk. A bloke nearby called out, 'Look where you're walking, don't walk there.' Another said, 'Don't say that to him; he can walk anywhere.' This was because I had fought in the International Brigade.

There was a book done by the widows of Asturias which I was given on one of my journeys. It contains the names of all those shot by the Fascists, their ages, occupations, etc. It mentions one Fascist in Aranzana with relatives within the village who hadn't got anyone shot because he didn't want to be boycotted. It also mentions that Franco had said he would have to shoot enough, to make sure there was no more possibility of a strike or vote. I consider this period in Spain to have been another Inquisition.

One day during this trip we were driving along in the Dormobile and we were flagged down by the Civil Guard. At that time they were heavily armed and always walked around in pairs. One would have a heavy submachine gun and the other a rifle. They were very frightening, particularly for the children. Remembering the experience of the other Brigader and his family I was convinced they were going to do something to us. In the end it turned out that all they wanted was a lift down the road.

However Spain was beginning to loosen up a bit. Tourism was becoming important and the dress laws had been relaxed to a certain extent. There was still a lot of repression but one felt safer. We weren't so frightened of ending up in prison or being shot but the police were everywhere, around every corner.

(Repression by Franco's regime continued for nearly forty years. Its severity shocked even Himmler when he visited Spain after the Civil War and caused some of Franco's own generals to attack it publicly. [See note, *The Second Inquisition*, pp. 229–231 for fuller details.])

14

WITH THE SPANISH UNDERGROUND UNIONS

Usually on trips when I went without my family I would bring money to the families of prisoners or take some political leaflets to distribute. On one occasion I had them sent on ahead by post to Madrid. They were held up at the Post Office and I had to get out of Spain quickly. Occasionally I would go with Juan Moreno who fled to London after the Civil War. I remember we had a leaflet that was done by the anarchists/Trotskyists which had the wrong date of a demonstration on it. We had to change it to the second of May and worked in Juan's brother's house in Madrid. Their father was kicked and beaten up by the police.

Subsequently we were distributing the leaflets – our means of distribution without being seen was to throw them out of the car window when we manoeuvred it between buses or between a bus and a tram. One time we went to Franco's area, El Pardo, and I stopped the car and pretended to be fiddling around with the engine. A bus came along, I dropped all the leaflets down through the window and revved off quickly before the people sitting on the footpath could see me. Sometimes we'd do the crowd after a football match. Anyone caught would be arrested without fail.

On another occasion I nearly crashed into a wall. I had four Spaniards with me and we were in the part next to Franco's area when the police saw me. I was panicking and I said to the others, 'Don't say anything – let me do the talking.' The police said to me '¿Qué pasa? ¿Hay algo?' ('What's going on here?') and in a mixture of English and bad Spanish I pretended I didn't understand. They asked again if something was wrong and I said that I had to let the car cool down. We got away with it. The car was stuffed with leaflets. The leaflet in question was calling for a boycott of public transport. Even nuns and priests were taking part. People were all walking, demonstrating. Throughout the city the whole police force were out in strength, trying to find how these leaflets were getting around.

Once when two blokes were arrested giving out leaflets in a fish lorry, I transferred a load of them from one person to another activist on the other side of Madrid. I was contacted to go around at night in my car. I told them we'd arrange to leave the big bundle of leaflets in a café with a sympathiser. I planned it out: we'd get between two trams, put the leaflets out and let them blow away. We nearly got caught one day. There were four of us. I didn't know the way and relied on someone giving me instructions. I drove into a dead end, just missing a wall.

Another time in Madrid I stopped on the tramlines and a tram came up and sliced the car along. It didn't cut it, but it damaged it, enough for me to go to court but I didn't dare do anything about it. It would have come out who I was. Another time a bloke got arrested, (he was in danger living next door to a policeman), when I'd brought loads of leaflets, printed in Moscow on the agricultural question.

(In 1974 the *Times* correspondent wrote that in this pamphleteer's heyday, thousands of Spaniards were bombarded with illegal political tracts, (mostly Communist-inspired) petitions, trial summaries, mildly pornographic reports, poems and cartoons that could never be legally published. Most were delivered by mail with false return addresses, circulated by hand or showered at factories, colleges or busy intersections, despite the almost daily announcements of police capturing those who were producing it.

It was a time of paper shortage and the pamphlets which were printed on only one side of a sheet were in great demand. The most active propagandists painted slogans by night, forcing police to use a special squad of slogan 'X-ers', covering countless buildings with black squares and Xes. Spaniards had created a new type of crossword, inventing possible word combinations to fit.)

I organised a large demonstration at the Spanish embassy in London in protest at their treatment of Julian Grimau, with the slogan 'Julian Grimau, you will not be forgotten!' People all over the world demonstrated their outrage at his fate. His crime was that he fought for the Republic during the war. I went later to the spot in Madrid where he had fallen out of the window. I couldn't go too near. This was 1963, the year after he was tortured and killed. Grimau had been in the counter-intelligence during the war, chasing Franco's spies in Madrid. He was sent back in 1961 by the Communist Party to work with the clandestine organisations, after it had been announced that there would be no further death sentences arising from the war.

Caught in November 1962, as a senior Communist official he was tortured, then thrown from a window in the Security HQ by the torturers to conceal the evidence. Despite his injuries he was tried in April by court martial and condemned to death for 'military rebellion', which meant fighting against Franco in the war. Grimau's medical report showed his face was shattered, the frontal bone collapsed, the jaw misshapen, fractures in both wrists and arms and his spine affected. Our veterans' association, the IBA (International Brigade Association), sent a barrister who met both Fraga Iribarne, Minister of Information, and the judge enquiring into his fall from the window.

(There was a wave of protests throughout Europe and America, Pleas for clemency for Grimau were made by church figures all over the world, by Harold Wilson, the German Premier and by Queen Elizabeth but Franco was unmoved. Grimau was executed by firing squad on 20 April 1963. It was 'the last execution of the Civil War', as his widow Angela expressed it on hearing the news. His death wiped out years of effort to improve the regime's image outside Spain.)

When I went back in the mid-nineties to Lola's cousin Matilde with Wally Togwell, another Brigader, we arrived late at night and were watching the news on television. It showed Camacho, the leader of the Communist unions, who'd been in jail. She spat on the floor. I was talking away in Spanish and didn't say anything and Wally didn't

Bob and Lola on their wedding day, 1940.

Bob in London reading his own Communist Party election leaflet.

British Battalion banner displayed in Barcelona, 1988.

Poster '*Para Amnistio Internacaional*' donated by Rafael Alberti (1902–99),
poet and Republican supporter.

Bob (in top-hat) at Poll Tax demo, 3 April 1990.
Tony Benn is on the right.

Bob meets President Mary Robinson at the unveiling of the
Liberty Hall memorial, May Day 1991. (Photo: Tommy Clancy)

Memorial to the International Brigade unveiled by Lord Mayor of Dublin Councillor Michael Donnelly on May Day 1991.

International Brigade veterans at the unveiling of the Liberty Hall memorial, May Day 1991. Left to right: Julius Margolin, Bob, Sam Walters, (Eric Fleming), François Mazou, Bill Van Felix, Michael Economides, Dave Goodman. Sean Edwards holds the banner dedicated by Fr O'Flanagan in the 1940s.

Bob with volunteers from the AABI, the Madrid friends of the International Brigades, at the launch of his memoir, *Un Rebelde Sin Pausa*, in Madrid on 10 December 2002.

Bob signs copies of his memoir in Spanish, *Un Rebelde Sin Pausa*, at the launch in Madrid on 10 December 2002.

Bob with Geraline Abrahams (daughter of a brigader), Bob's granddaughter Margarita and Manus O'Riordan, son of Michael O'Riordan, at the launch of Michael's *Connolly Column* in Liberty Hall on 16 March 2005.

Bob with US veteran Jack Bjoze in New York.

Bob revisits County Wicklow with Jane (from Barcelona) and Harry Owens.

Plaque to the memory of Kit Conway (1897–1937) unveiled
in his home village of Burncourt, County Tipperary, on 16 June 2005.

Eugene Downing (1913–2003).

Bob with Michael O'Riordan (1917–2006) at the launch of Michael's memoir, *Connolly Column*, in Liberty Hall on 16 March 2005. (Photo: Tommy Clancy)

speak a word. I said to him, 'Don't unpack your stuff. We're going first thing in the morning.' We got up early – about 6 am – and left. I couldn't stick it. My son Robert thinks that most of our family there are quite reactionary. We don't have much contact – and they didn't treat Lola or Josefa very well.

(Wally Togwell was a friend of Bob's from the Brigades. He toured Spain with Bob for a month in 1980, visiting his contacts from the time of Franco's regime. After Asturias and Bilbao they went to the Logroño area above the Ebro, to the pueblo of San Vicente de la Sierra 'to visit and stay with an old peasant who had remained loyal to the Republic, and had been beaten and tortured by Guardia Civil: a lovely old man and made of steel.

'From here we travelled to various villages within this lovely district of wine country. On our arrival in Madrid people turned their children out of their beds to allow us to stay. For the whole of the month that we toured Spain we did not have to pay for bed and breakfast or even meals during that time.

'It was good to have a friend named Bob Doyle. Again our reception was of royal character. We visited Camacho, the leader of the Communist unions at his headquarters and I have the statue of the *Comisiones Obreras* (Workers Committees) plus mementoes including a metal ashtray that Camacho was using – and cleaned for me – that depicts the unions fighting for pensioners!

'The amigos of Bob in Madrid included Executive Committee members of the Communist Party of Spain, and we were allowed into the VIP enclosure at their sixtieth anniversary festival in Madrid's Casa de Campo park. We met Carrillo, then secretary of the party and presented him with a commemorative magazine of the International Brigades. Oh yes, I know Bob Doyle! We travelled in my car, a Cortina, and nearly ruined it but a month in Spain with Bob in 1980 was another experience never to be forgotten.')

We decided that *La Abuela*, Lola's ageing mother, who continued to work as a servant to a wealthy family, should come and live with us when we moved to Neasden in 1960. I went on my own on that occasion to bring her. I drove there but commissioned a plane to fly at a low altitude for the return journey because she was suffering from a heart condition. I took some leaflets to both Madrid and Aranzana de Abajo before I picked her up.

I was coming from Aranzana then and had the leaflets with me for Madrid, when a Civil Guard with his rifle stopped me. I thought I was caught. He said he wanted to go to the next village, about forty miles away. His relative was ill. I told him to get in and he placed the rifle at the back of the car on top of the leaflets. (See note, *The Guardia Civil*, pp. 231–2.)

We chatted away and he asked how I was getting on, how I managed to have a car – very few owned cars there then. I told him what wages I got and he said, 'Good Lord! we don't get anything like that; we get about four thousand pesetas a month.' Robert says it wasn't until he visited third-world countries in the 1980s that he realised how backward Spain was then. It wasn't as advanced as Tanzania is today. (See note, *The Years of Repression in Spain*, pp. 232–4.)

15

ORGANISING FOR SOME OTHER GREAT CAUSES

My involvement in politics did not stop with the Spanish Civil War – over the years I got involved in many struggles. I never missed a demonstration. One of the earliest was a housing campaign in 1945. Rita Webb, a small red-haired Jewish actress, pulled off a stunt with a donkey. We made a placard for the donkey and hung it round its neck saying 'I don't need a house.' It never made the papers but the main slogan for the housing campaign was 'Up Churchill, down with the Tories'. The success of the campaign was instrumental in getting Churchill out.

I remember when they were voting to introduce the NHS – it must have been around 1946 – there was an awful lot of opposition among the doctors around where we were living in Maida Vale. All along Maida Vale there were placards, beautifully made, with 'NO to the NHS' written on them. I was all for the NHS and would go out on my motorbike every evening, sometimes with my sons, and pick them all up, loading them into my side-car. We'd a basement flat at the time and there was a room like a wine cellar. It was chock-a-block with these placards.

Racism is something I have been fighting against all my life. I suppose one of the earliest examples of racism I can think of was Mosley's lot in London's East End. I was proud to be there at Cable Street helping the Jewish people who were under attack at that time. There were lots of East End Jews who fought for the Republic in Spain. Mosley had a bit of a revival after the war.

One of my main political activities was public speaking. Street-corner meetings were the normal thing at one time during the 1950s and 60s. I had my own wooden platform that folded down into a sort of suitcase. On Sundays I would often go to Hyde Park Corner, sometimes speaking on a Communist Party platform but more often for the Connolly Association when I had a big Irish flag attached to my platform. I made friends with many speakers from the colonies, and would speak as a guest on their platforms.

I had many hecklers and when a Corkman asked me: 'Aroo a Communist?', my answer was to speak of Dr Noël Browne's campaign for school meals for the children of Dublin, and the clergy condemning him for this. 'I'm the kind of Communist he is.' I became a Communist at an early age, not a convinced one but enough.

I used to share a platform with another bloke. We'd set fire to a newspaper to attract a crowd and then say, 'That's what I think of the capitalist press!' I'd have a selection of newspapers with me, and I'd discuss various articles, being witty and quick. My son Robert remembers crowds of 600 or more.

In 1974, I spent two weeks in Portugal visiting the left-wing and union organisations which had just emerged with the overthrow of the Salazar dictatorship which had been ruling since 1928.

25 April 1974 was a glorious day in the history of the Portuguese working class and all democrats in that country. On that day the workers and intellectuals and the progressive elements in the armed forces came out on the streets to signal the end of the Fascist state and the immediate declaration of a popular democracy. Soldiers of the Armed Forces Movement refused to perform their normal duty of defending capitalism, and placed carnations in the barrels of their guns as symbols of their solidarity with the people.

Imagine the emotions of those who suffered the tortures of the DGS/PIDE, the notorious secret police, and the relatives of the many murdered by them when they witnessed such a transformation. Amidst the crescendo of the popular slogan 'A people united can never be defeated', there were tears of sorrow and joy. Sorrow for those who lost and those unaccounted for by the hideous activities of the PIDE and joy for the new-found freedom. Six days after the overthrow of the dictatorship came May Day, which we normally take for granted in England. To the Portuguese it is now a historic day. Hundreds of thousands poured into the streets of Lisbon, joined by the Armed Forces Movement and accompanied by a naval band.

The climax was traumatic. Democracy started to flourish immediately. How did this come about after the long period of Fascism? It was like a flower needing water and perhaps the carnation is the symbol of survival over Fascist pollution. Since the inception of the Corporate (or Fascist) State over forty-eight years ago, the Communist Party and other anti-Fascist forces had conducted resistance on many fronts. Coupled with the heroic struggle of the colonial peoples under the liberation movements, was the struggle of the workers in the trade unions.

While the unions endeavoured to fight for better wages, shorter hours and more holidays, the real objective of the left was to bring about the ending of Fascism and a democratic state. Though the unions remained passive and accepted the patronage of the corporate laws, they were a welcome alternative to the vertical labour system which was ruled from above. But when their opposition or demands became a threat to the business interests represented by Salazar and his successor Caetano, the secret police intervened.

As with the development of football, the British pride themselves on the historic role we played in the formative years of trade unionism. But despite the terrible adversities of the Portuguese trade-union movement, we could teach them nothing. They achieved everything the hard way and were in the process of building up a united movement. Not only were they determined to win better conditions for the workers, but strongly to identify the trade-union struggle with the political one to win a just socialist society. While the slogan of the stooge unions of Fascism was 'Work and Joy', the slogan now was 'Unity for Strength against Fascism and common advance for Socialism'.

Despite the apparent strength of the unions they were vulnerable to the machinations of the multinational companies and other reactionary forces. With their division of labour on a supranational basis, the multinationals can now afford to close down factories without any loss of profit. This was being done in Portugal where they considered that their interests were threatened by progressive government. Some factories which closed were taken over by the workers but this was not always practical in the immediate circumstances because of the multinationals' control of raw materials in different countries.

Preparations for the election of the first democratic government were getting under way. Offices of the flourishing anti-Fascist forces were a hive of activity but there was a reluctance to agree to a date for the elections because of the continued influence of former Fascists in the administration. In Barreiro, the big working class area containing the largest monopoly known as the CUF, the offices of the Communist Party and other democratic organisations were open day and night for the enrolment of members. It was mainly the youth who were joining. The aftermath of Fascism and the ensuing confusion created a breeding ground for both ultra-left activities and Fascist distortions.

The right wing, under the guise of 'Centrism' or some other democratic label, proclaimed 'Communism is worse than Fascism'. The ultra-left proclaimed 'No Revision; Revolution Now!" and devoted its time to attacking the Communist Party, seeking to bring about direct confrontation with the army and therefore playing into the hands of the former police agents. In contrast, the watchword of the democratic left was 'Beware of Provocation and Confrontation.'

Women had played an integral part in the struggle against Fascism and they continued to do so. They organised not only on behalf of their jailed husbands and relatives but in every aspect of social life. Demanding crèches, clinics, equal rights and education, they were often to become the victims of the Fascist torturers as in the case of Catherina Eufemia. A peasant girl who organised a strike of farm workers, she was denounced by the large farm owners, taken to the next village, shot and buried by the PIDE. A park in Barreiro previously called Salazar Park now commemorates her name.

Only a few months before the overthrow of the dictatorship, the Duke of Edinburgh visited Portugal to pay his respects and cement the claim of Portugal to be Britain's oldest and most loyal ally. His visit received the full blast of publicity in our capitalist press, the same press which throughout forty-eight years of Fascism, kept silent over the resistance of the Portuguese people. (Apart from the noble assistance of the *Morning Star* in the publicising of the struggle against Fascism, little was done by the official labour movement.)

Now that the trade unions were free and independent they needed our help and solidarity, which can best be expressed not necessarily by independent delegations, but in the form of vigilance and support from the international trade-union movement. A representative delegation from the TUC was the greatest contribution we could have made in the difficult times confronting the Portuguese people in their struggle for a democratic Portugal. (See notes, *Portugal.* pp. 234–5 and *Spain's Army in Changing Times*, p. 235.)

16

PHYLLIS GREEN – MARCHING TIMES WITH BOB

These are but a few of the good times I had on the streets of London with Bob and his banners. Bob's Army we were called, a handful of us from west London. Saturday morning you have to get up. You hear the motorbike. You know it's Bob. Up and out, it's another march. One day Bob drags me off to Heathrow, a big Anti-Fascist demo. We were all on the tube. Bob is giving out orders: where we stand, what we should do, when we push. I never let on, but I was thinking, 'Who is this Le Pen?'

Bob was never afraid to be out there on the streets. He was always out in front with his banner: Anti-Racist, Printers, Miners, P&O Ferries, NHS, Dockers, Steel Workers. You name it, Bob was there. At the big miners' march in London I was with Bob somewhere in the middle. Up ahead of us the police waded into the miners. Bob handed me the banner and pushed me into a doorway, telling me to stay put. Bob made his way up front and stood shoulder to shoulder with the miners against the police. He got a few bangs off the police truncheons that day.

Every night Bob was at Wapping for the printers' strike. One night Bob was over with the *Morning Star* crowd. The vans with the papers started to power out; everyone rushed forward. The police charged. They gave Bob a bad beating that night. Then the bastards tore up his trade union banner. During the P&O ferry strike we all headed for Dover. It wasn't a big march. There were more police than us, a bad sign. It was a tense march; I was afraid. The people of Kent were angry with Maggie T. Bob never flinched that day. Out with the banner, fall in line and we marched straight to the docks. That was a good day.

I recall a big anti-racist march somewhere in east London, I think. It was a long march on a hot day. When we got to Bethnal Green a few young lads started jeering, pushing and shoving – they might have been National Front. Bob had his International Brigade flag with him. As we passed by the wind caught the flag and it flew high. I was proud to march behind Bob Doyle that day.

Another big march, this time against the poll tax. We were all so excited. It was great. Bob had us all in London at about 8 am, some of us in the park to join the march, some of us in Trafalgar Square with the banner. Bob was in good form. That day one thing led to another. The police charged us with batons, hitting men, women and children, anything that moved. I headed for the tube and got home and turned on the news and there was Bob. South Africa House was on fire; there were cars on fire, running battles with marchers and police. Bob never ran and stood firm with his banner.

Another good laugh was the battle to sell *An Phoblacht*, the Sinn Féin paper, in Harlesden. Bob used to pick up the papers from Little Tommy and head off for Harlesden on his motorbike to do his round. Then Big Jimmy went to do his round in Harlesden; he couldn't sell any papers. Every decent Irishman had bought his paper from Bob. Poor Jim had to give up Harlesden. He laughs about it to this day. Bob is one in a million.

He fought all his life for people's rights and justice. He said to me one day, 'Anywhere you see or hear racism you must stamp on it, kick it, shout, scream do something to put it down.'

(Nicaragua – Another Struggle like the Spanish Civil War

Everywhere Bob and comrades like Mick O'Riordan were invited to speak during the 1980s, they teminded listeners that the same principles which brought them to Spain were now at stake in the fight of that small Central American country for independence and social justice.

At the end of the 1970s Nicaraguans overthrew the US-backed

dictator, Somoza. The winning Sandinistas led a government that undertook land reform and developed a nationwide literacy campaign among other hugely popular policies. The US, under Reagan and George Bush senior, had the CIA recruit the ex-dictator's forces to sabotage Nicaragua with deadly attacks on civilians, health centres, cooperatives, teachers and volunteers in rural areas – exactly what Bush junior as president would later call 'terrorism'.

When the US Congress cut off funding, Reagan's White House team ran covert arms sales to their previous arch enemy, the Iranian fundamentalists, to finance their Contra campaign. They also recruited indigenous tribes in neighbouring countries like Costa Rica. Thousands of volunteers from Europe and North America went to support Nicaragua's Sandinista revolution in 'Coffee Brigades', replacing coffee-pickers who were on military duties.

Bob saved £800 from his fundraising for Barcelona in 1988 towards an ambulance for Nicaragua. He wanted his veterans association to add £200 and bring it up to the thousand, to help the International-Brigades-sponsored ambulances already in Nicaragua. They replied that their funds were for preserving the archives and banner, so Bob and Walter Greenhalgh presented their £800 to the Nicaraguan ambassador themselves.

When Adolfo Calero, one of the top Contra leaders, was invited to Britain by the Thatcher government, Bob made his own sign, as always – 'No Contras Here' – and headed out to Heathrow to greet him. This CIA-created war of the Contras was perhaps the most significant difference of opinion between the UK brigaders association and the group of activist veterans led by Bob. Nicaragua, for them, as for the US veterans, was virtually a replay of the Spanish Civil War: a popularly supported left-wing government being attacked by the old business and land-owning classes, supported by outside powers and using extreme brutality against their enemies among the poor and the government's defenders.)

HARRY TAKES UP THE STORY...

17

HARRY MEETS BOB AT DUBLIN'S COMMEMORATION

I first met Bob through a series of unplanned events. What has become a friendship of twenty years began in a very simple way.

Eilís Ryan, Frank Ryan's sister, was closing the door of her room in the retirement home after our first meeting at Christmas 1985. Small and chirpy with her glasses perched on the end of her nose, she kept a photo of her brother Frank on her chest of drawers. I was held for a moment by her change of tone, 'You know, Harry, I'm really dreading next year.'

'Why?'

'It's the fiftieth anniversary of the Spanish Civil War. They'll be resurrecting all the attacks and rumours about Frank again.'

We said goodbye, leaving me thoughtful all the way home. It was wrong that those we felt proud of could bring worry to their next of kin. Eilís had done all she could for her brother Frank in his prison years and was the one who'd guarded his memory since. I'd come to tell her that Fr Mulrean, her old friend in Madrid, had died. He was the one who went to the Papal Nuncio in Spain and got the Fascist priest removed from Burgos jail when Frank was under death sentence there, at the end of the war, when the repression was at its worst. He never seemed to have been made even a parish priest.

When I first heard of him in 1969 from Mick Lillis at the Irish Embassy, Mick had stressed his decency and undisclosed poverty. Fr Mulrean refused to accept the state pay for clergy in Spain, and had to live on providence, whatever he got in donations for Masses, baptisms and the like. Since Franco was paying the clergy, what the

Spanish put in the collection on Sundays wouldn't feed a mouse. If I was coming out any time, Mick said, I could bring him tea, sausages and any other goodies from home.

I found him welcoming and generous with any food and contacts he had. While he'd served O'Duffy's men as padre when they came out, he'd no Blueshirt sympathies. With the ongoing Northern Ireland troubles, he was always glad of Irish papers. He'd read them in silence then throw them down, roaring, 'Fine Gael! Always playing England's game!' He had stories of Frank and many others from the war years, and blamed the current police brutality on the Gestapo's having trained them for Franco as the Civil War ended.

I think to myself: there has to be a way to celebrate these heroes. I can't be the only one today who wants to honour the Irish who fought Franco, and I know we're not in a minority any more. I sketch out a programme in my mind for the event: some veterans of the Brigades, historians, poets and ballad singers and finally the Irish in the Third World today – the Nicaraguan Coffee Brigades, Irish clergy from Central America where El Salvador and Nicaragua are repeating the suffering of Spain's Civil War. There's no money to fund it. But who cares: these things work themselves out.

Terry Quinlan, the retiring general secretary of my union, the Post Office Workers, had a brother who died at Jarama in 1937. There's Seán Cronin, *Irish Times* Washington correspondent who wrote the book on Frank Ryan and then we've Eilís herself – all as patrons. 'Why do you need patrons?' asks a Trotskyist friend. Because I'm not a member of any party, I can't just do this in my own name. Now for the Irish Communist Party, where Mick O'Riordan, a Brigade veteran, has the addresses of two others, Peter O'Connor and Bob Doyle, who co-signed a recent letter in *The Irish Times*.

I get this guy Bob Doyle on the phone in London. He'll come and speak, great, but where will he stay? There's no money for a hotel. 'Would you like to stay in our place?'

'Yes, that sounds fine.'

Well, I don't know him yet but he's keen, and that's encouraging. I hire Buswell's Hotel, right in front of the main entrance to the Dáil.

The message has to be loud and clear: we're not off down any side street; we're not restricted to trade union halls; we are celebrating the true national tradition of our people here.

Off to Oisín Breathnach the artist. We need a classy poster which I start getting into pubs, bookshops, libraries. This is all very different from my previous experience flyposting Dublin streets at night for strikes and other union activity. Near Trinity College I hear Spanish teenagers exclaim, 'Imagine, it's about the Irish and our Civil War!'

Bob turns up at our house, a trim sprightly man in dark suit and black beret, full of ideas for all the publicity we need: Bob, I find, is a genius for media and publicity. I get a call at work in the telephone exchange: Mick is insisting there's to be no Mass for this event. Those Irish bishops back in the thirties had condemned them all going to Spain and there's never been a retraction. He's insisting the Church must have no role in this, asking if I'm clear about that?

I am, and there is a Mass arranged but it's not on the poster. The Dominicans at St Saviour's have an elderly priest, Fr Tom Walsh, who was in the IRA as a youth with Frank Ryan. In 1926 he was part of a jailbreak team on Mountjoy prison that rescued nineteen Republicans. Their Fr Austin, who christened the children of Mick's daughter and was sometimes rewarded with a bottle of rum by Mick (Cuban rum, one has one's principles!) is happy to have the 10.30 Mass that morning celebrated 'for the Irish who died for the Spanish Republic', as our poster says. That afternoon Buswell's main room is filling long before the time to start.

Ronnie Drew has already met me outside with a tape of him singing 'O'Duffy's Ironsides' in case he doesn't get back to town in time to perform it live. I recognise it as another of the anti-Fascist ballads by Somhairle Mac Alastair, the cover name for Diarmuid MacGoille Phádraig who ran the Cathedral Bookshop at the side of the Pro-Cathedral – an old IRA man who was interned during the Second World War with Mick O'Riordan. We finally get the meeting going, packed to the rafters, press and TV reporters covering it and Spanish teenagers sprinkled through the crowd.

Mick, in statesmanly fashion, opens the meeting by reading out the list of all the Irish who'd died there for the Republic, in a struggle to break up the medieval social system in Spain. Pádraig Ó Snodaigh covers Connolly and the Citizen Army, Ireland (and the world's) first workers' army. Michael Farrell explains the situation which produced the Blueshirts: the trauma of post-Civil War Ireland in the years of the Great Depression, and the middle-class shock when de Valera came to power – 'As if today in Northern Ireland the reins of power were held by Sinn Féin in government. What would the RUC reaction be?' – a vivid analogy in 1986.

Peter O'Connor reads the diary he kept in the trenches in Spain. He doesn't seem to notice the total silence in the crowded room when he comes to the words: 'I realise I am now the only Irishman left in the front line.' At times the emotion is palpable. At one point a craggy face in the crowd, a man's silent tears as the young of fifty years ago are brought back in the words of their comrades. We run out of time for Fr Hudson, back from Nicaragua, who has to leave before speaking.

Bob is nervous in public, reading from his hand-written notes, not as effective here as he is in small groups. But he puts across the anger many of his generation felt at the clerical attitude to their fight for justice and for the poor, when he felt the Church was in a war against Christianity. He saw 'today's Latin American priests of the liberation theology as following in the steps of the Spanish priests who were killed for opposing Fascism. The Basque clergy whom Franco executed epitomised the best traditions which the Irish people cherish, and which are still continued in our day by many Christians who are in the forefront of the struggle against injustice and oppression in Latin America and South Africa.'

He reminded us of Franco's 192,000 post-war executions and warned that Thatcher was 'copying a lot from Spanish Fascism's anti-labour laws. In Spain I feel the threat to democracy now comes from terrorist fronts used by elements of the Civil Guard and other security agencies, while Spanish Premier González is using the situation to excuse his right-wing policies and supporting Reagan's bombing of Libya.'

Professor O'Neill from Galway explained how de Valera's policy of neutrality grew from his experience of the League of Nations' failure to enforce sanctions against Italy when it invaded Ethiopia, the only black member state. He explained Dev's condemnation of the great powers' cynical toleration of Mussolini's crime as a lesson to all small states. Being neutral wouldn't guarantee remaining outside future conflicts between them. But becoming involved in any alliance meant that war will only be declared in the interests of the great power controlling that alliance. Therefore neutrality was the only sensible policy.

Dev's first implementation of this new Irish policy would be during the Spanish Civil War when an Irish captain on a British naval patrol was the first of what in our day became the thousands of Irish defence force personnel to serve the United Nations. Ironically this naval patrol was to hinder the Spanish Republic's access to arms but have no effect on Hitler and Mussolini's supplies to Franco. They too were part of the patrols, supposedly preventing arms from reaching either side in Spain.

Oisín Breathnach spoke on the San Patricio unit who fought for Mexico against the US in 1848, Dr Bowyer Bell on the foreign intervention in Spain, Anthony Coughlan on Spain today, and its difficulties in remaining neutral vis-à-vis NATO, after years of Franco's isolation.

After the poet Michael Smith had presented Charlie Donnelly, and Pearse Hutchinson's tragic poems on the Civil War from Latin America, the evening wound down, with singing and drinking. Ronnie Drew made it back and played for us. Mick O'Riordan was holding forth in fine form. Bob was amazed at this response to him and his comrades in his native Dublin. Eilís slipped a contribution to the costs into my hand. She'd never know this was really all inspired by her anyway.

The newspapers referred to it as probably the longest political meeting held in Dublin, lasting over six-and-a-half hours. Bob had two interviews on national radio, which helped cover his travel expenses. Eventually he and I got home and soon afterwards he popped off to stay with friends in the Green Party he'd just met, before making me promise to join him in Madrid for November's celebrations of the founding of the Brigades. Well, if Bob Doyle's going and it's anything like Buswell's Hotel this Sunday, it's sure to be unforgettable.

That same year Bob was a guest speaker with Ken Livingstone up at Derry's Bloody Sunday commemoration for the thirteen marchers shot dead by the Parachute Regiment in January 1972.

Speaking first, Bob, reminded the audience of the earlier Bloody Sunday during the Irish War of Independence when British forces had shot more than seventy at a match in Dublin's Croke Park, killing twelve. Both were the cruel acts of the aggressor, but the huge crowd present was living testimony that imperialism would be removed from Ireland by the united efforts of the peoples North and South of the border.

As Greater London Council leader, Ken got a warm welcome. Saying he was proud to be on the march, he apologised 'on behalf of the decent ordinary members of the Labour Party for the regime of thuggery, murder and torture' that had been continued under Labour's minister Roy Mason: 'a mark of shame we'll never expunge'. No socialist party could impose repression on another nation and hope to achieve social progress in its own country. In Britain there was widespread ignorance about Ireland but when politicians justified keeping the North, they didn't speak for the British people. Every poll for the past decade showed two-to-one in favour of withdrawing. He looked forward to the day he'd come back from a socialist Britain to a free united socialist Ireland.

(Only six weeks before these killings, on 20 December 1971, Lt General Sir Harry Tuzo had reassured Catholics, 'You have nothing to fear from the army.' After his soldiers had shot the marchers, Lord Balniel as junior defence minister claimed, 'In each case soldiers aimed shots at men identified as gunmen or bombers.' At the Saville Tribunal set up by the Blair government, it was accepted that the dead and wounded were innocent.)

I make the fiftieth anniversary event in Madrid and meet Bob with his fellow veterans. One day sitting in the audience at the Palacio de Congresos I'm asked to interpret for the American delegate. Lennie Levinson begins quoting President Reagan, which gets everyone's attention. He goes on to correct Reagan's statement comparing the Brigaders in the Lincolns to the Contras in Nicaragua:

'The CIA's Contras aren't like the Abraham Lincoln battalion who had to leave despite their government's embargo: the Contras have the US government's blessing. The Brigaders were volunteers, the Contras are recruited for $7 a day and finally the Brigades were defending an elected government from armed right-wing attacks, but the Contras are the armed right-wing attacking Nicaragua's elected Sandinista government.'

It'll be a while before I realise that, thanks to following Bob Doyle out here, I'll be press-ganged into years of campaigns and events from now on, most of them run by Bob himself. He introduces me to some of his many friends. Their accounts are so vivid it's hard to believe they're talking of a war that was half a century ago.

With a pal who lives in Madrid I meet Bob and other veterans after their final banquet and we all head off to a disco nearby. We slip off and let them carouse through what's left of the night. These guys are livelier than we are. Forget about whenever they were born – how do they do it? As for the way they attract the girls, it's just one of life's great mysteries.

18

ORGANISING WITH BOB FOR BARCELONA

I thought that was surely the end of such events but in the summer of 1988 Bob is back with a new one: the Lincoln Brigade veterans have commissioned a bronze statue of David and Goliath. Barcelona has provided a site on the old road out to the French border, and it is to be unveiled in October to mark the fiftieth anniversary of the Brigade's historic farewell parade in that city. Can I get a crowd to come from Ireland? I ask about support from the UK. None: the veterans' organisation there weren't in agreement, 'But everyone else is,' Bob quickly assures me. I could feel he was on a roll.

I was then a delegate to the Dublin Council of Trade Unions, and with the support of Chris Hudson from our Post Office Workers Union, the Trades Council agrees to back the event. Once more I find that the people who respond best are from the Northern Ireland media. They call back; they want more details. How about an interview? For weeks there were almost no bookings. Then the travel agency cancelled the flight but didn't bother to tell me. This was going to be sticky. I start phoning firms again and end up with Joe Walsh, boss of JWT Travel, who usually does Lourdes rather than old Republican events but he offered the same £149 price. The snag is that I had to take half the plane. We'd need at least £1,500 in bookings. I accepted with fingers crossed.

In the last few days things started to move quickly. Then suddenly the flight was sold out. Bob was on the phone every few days with more ideas. He was running a Spanish musical evening in London to raise funds. He even got large colour posters printed for 'The

Anniversary Social with Artery Band, Tapas and Flamencos in the Emerald Centre, Hammersmith'. A few would fly from the UK and an entire busload were coming from the midlands. But with his own veterans' association giving the whole event the cold shoulder, many who might have come just wouldn't be there.

At the airport I meet most of the nearly hundred Irish for the first time. Barcelona was wonderful, and revealing: we ended up singing old Spanish songs to locals who didn't know the airs of their own folk music. The Derry group with us sang ballads about the Northern troubles and about the miners strike for some young English lads who joined the crowd in our pub. Paddy McAllister, a veteran from Belfast, ended nights down in Salou standing on café tables singing out Spanish Republican airs – and that was just him warming up.

At one stage Bob and I finally had a happy moment together. We were both overjoyed at the Irish turnout and at the wonderful celebration that the Americans and Cataluña's coordinator of Republican veterans arranged for us all. I met more of these remarkable veterans: Walter Greenhalgh, John Taylor and from the USA Carl Geiser whose book on the prison experiences of captured brigaders is a treasure of lessons in history and people. And we Irish were the third largest group here, thanks to Bob.

We had a special reception with *Comisiones Obreras* and their rival, UGT, the two main Spanish unions, since we had many leading figures from Irish unions with us. The hard facts of today's working class life in Spain were explained by our hosts. What we were hearing was the first rumblings of the long-dreamt-of 'UHP', the united general strike, the great goal of Spanish workers' organisations during Franco's time.

It would soon be held against the current Spanish socialist government, led by some of the socialist trade unionists we had been speaking to in Barcelona.

(On 14 December 1988 it happened: the first general strike since before the Civil War. Long struggled for at great cost during Franco's forty years but never achieved, now the hoped for three-million target of strikers was surpassed. Eight million walked off the

job for better pay and more jobs for young people. Madrid, said the
Guardian, was quieter than on a Sunday. TV and the main papers
were out, even soccer matches were off. Spain had then the highest
growth rate and the highest unemployment in Europe, with half of
the workers under twenty-five, only one third of whom got the dole.)

The unveiling ceremony was held late in the morning, in the
working class suburb of El Carmel. Crowds of veterans and relatives,
Spanish Republicans and supporters from many lands watched
as the mayor unveiled the statue, an enormous modern version of
David and Goliath. It was the gift of the American veterans of the
Lincoln Battalion and the Spanish Civil War Society. The sponsors
included Woody Allen, Norman Mailer, Gregory Peck, Pete Seeger
and Leonard Bernstein.

As we reached the brow of the hill we saw the colourful throng
below us, the band and the banners waving. One of them was our
own Starry Plough, the Irish Citizen Army flag brought out by John
Kane and friends from the Irish Transport Union. It was the only
such flag there apart from unofficial Republican banners brought by
English students.

Brigadistas spoke, their common theme that no one people
can remain free unless they are willing to fight for the freedom of
another people also. Only their heroine, La Pasionaria, was absent,
too frail at ninety-three to make the journey.

The trip was so popular that even the critical leadership of Bob's
UK association were there. I found this out when I was told on the
Saturday morning by local organisers that Bob wouldn't be speaking,
as agreed and as printed on the programme, that afternoon at the
university seminar. Instead there'd be a British speaker, one of just
two veterans representing the UK association. It looked as if there
had been a meeting we weren't told about.

We had a huge banquet arranged by the Coordinadora, the
organisers of the commemoration. There had been concerts with
top Spanish folk singers, the dramatic bronze monument had
been unveiled, there was even a reception in the historic Catalan
Generalitat. Three of us got mugged but nobody was hurt except

maybe one or two muggers, and the mad happy Irish throng of lefties, Republicans, greens, pacifists and assorted followers headed home.

Bob and Wally Togwell stayed for a meeting at which the local Communist Party made a presentation to them for the wonderful support, which may have been a better tribute than speaking at the university would have been.

The film which Gerry Gregg made on the trip, featuring Bob's campaign for this commemoration and his time with us in Barcelona, was later shown on RTÉ.

The Last Parade is an account to tape and keep. While Bob had hoped the weekend's activities would help to arouse local interest in the hidden history of the Franco years, there had been a total ban on any use of the old Republican flag or colours. I had read in recent news reports that this Spanish government had ignored court rulings in favour of granting full military pensions to veterans of the Republican Army, whose average age was then over seventy. Some things never changed with democracy.

A left-wing Spanish commentator noted the ban on the veterans once more parading, the mayor's speech with the refrain 'Forget the past' and the last minute official reception which left many elderly veterans excluded. 'What should have been a public homage became a gathering of elderly volunteers whose history would have taught us all something, but which we were never allowed to hear.'

Was that it? Not quite. It turned out that one of the veterans I didn't meet had been impressed by the turnout and wanted Bob's help with another project. I was about to get to know François Mazou and hear a lot about the battle of Jarama, and the town of Morata de Tajuña. Meantime there was going to be a memorial in Dublin at last. But before either of these, Bob had one more visit to pay to Madrid, to pay a debt he owed to a heroine of the Spanish Republic's fight for survival.

19

LA PASIONARIA'S FUNERAL IN MADRID

Dolores Ibarruri, La Pasionaria, was the most important symbolic figure of the Republic, especially to the International Brigaders. The eighth of eleven children, married off to a miner, she became active against the savage repression which followed the crushing of the 1934 rising of workers and miners in her native Asturias. She was elected to the Cortes in 1936 and returned to Spain in May 1977, the last Spanish Communist leader to do so. She campaigned energetically in the June elections that year and was elected again for her native Asturias. The first democratically elected Cortes since 1936 chose her as president when it met. She died on 12 November 1989.

Bob and Mick O'Riordan flew out and met in Madrid for one of the great funerals of the century. She had lain in state for three days. On the day of the funeral crowds of hundreds of thousands of people overflowed pavements on to the streets. In the distance were shouts of '¡Viva Dolores!' The magisterial phrases of their great Civil War poet Rafael Alberti contrasted with the lines of simple poems called out from the crowds as the coffin passed them by on the day they ran out of metaphors in Madrid.

At four in the afternoon the Party committee and press cars steered through the overflowing rivers of people, as slowly the flags led the way. It was a living canvas, and the press noted above them the Republican tricolour, with the legend '1936-39 International Brigades, Spain', borne by Bob, the banner made at home in Neasden by his wife Lola for the funeral of her fellow Asturiana.

He was walking beside Mick O'Riordan: two Irishmen who

had felt as she had – 'if the Spanish people were to be crushed…', all marching together to the Plaza de Colón. The film directors, the old politicos, socialist rivals and well-known figures from the arts, sang 'The International' with their clenched fists raised.

Tomás Borges, the Sandinista minister from Nicaragua, was in uniform, his presence recalling the current struggles against imperialism in Central America, echoed by the news now beginning to come through on radios of the six dead Spanish Jesuits who worked with the poor of El Salvador, massacred by the military there. Bob saw them and priests of liberation theology as, 'true disciples of Christ, who follow in the footsteps of those courageous priests in Spain who made the supreme sacrifice in defiance of the Catholic Fascists and the Vatican's condemnation of their struggle against the abominable injustices and prostitution of the name of Jesus. That is the religion I follow.'

The smooth technocrats of the ruling socialist government were invisible, lost in the sea of flags and the shouts '¡No Pasarán!' As the cortège passed the headquarters of Spain's new party of the right, the Partido Popular, one could hear the elegant applause from party staff, from beneath their symbol of a blue seagull.

Finally words from Julio Anguita, the Communist Party leader, in a grey suit and black tie – a brief speech, contained, hardly emotional until in his last paragraph you could hear an almost imperceptible break in his voice. He denied the myth, 'You have not been just an idea. You have been, and are, the stock of human flesh, whole overflowed and generous…you belong to all, to those who raise the clenched fist and those who cross themselves.' In Madrid that day, it was the final day of the Popular Front.

Bob described his day: 'What a momentous and emotional occasion! The Brigaders and all the sympathisers at home were well represented by Mick and myself with Lola's beautiful flag, made especially for the occasion. We were asked to take it to the front of the foreign delegations who proudly marched along with it to the choruses of '¡No Pasarán!' and '¡Viva las Brigadas Internacionales!' People were breaking ranks to kiss the flag.

Pasionaria: Why She and Madrid Meant So Much to Bob

Pasionaria had been a symbol of Republican resistance throughout the war, having broadcast on behalf of the Communist Party after the generals revolted in July 1936. Taking the famous slogan of the French Marshal Pétain in the First World War, she launched the call '*No Pasarán!*' that became the Republic's battle cry.

At the end of October, Colonel Cisneros, who commanded the Republican airforce, had told an English war correspondent that the Republic's last fighter would take off the following morning. On 4 November, Varela, a Franco general, told the foreign press, 'Madrid will fall this week.' Their Army of Africa reached it on the sixth and had laid siege by the night of seventh.

The government fled to Valencia, civilians dug trenches, unions organised militias as Franco's troops fought their way through outlying suburbs. Henry Buckley of the *Daily Telegraph* saw hundreds of citizens going to the front without uniforms, rifles in hand and two dozen bullets in their pockets. Some rifles were so old they were more dangerous to their users than those targeted. Many of these men had never handled a gun before. These were nameless heroes, building workers, taxi drivers, transport staff, salesmen, who would never be known to history although they were laying down their lives in defence of their city. They fought without medical services or organised feeding, at times even without orders, without any officers in broad stretches of their front. Yet they were holding up the advance of the best soldiers in the Spanish army, the famed Tercios, the hardened Moors, the zealous Carlists from Navarre.

A telegram arrived addressed to 'His Excellency, Generalissimo Franco, War Ministry, Madrid,' from a Central American state. (It was returned 'unknown at this address'.) That night the enemy hadn't broken through, and Madrid's *milicianos* cheered, tired and afraid but fighting still, while the world waited for the end.

Early on Sunday morning columns of trained men, in matching uniforms, came marching up to the front, causing panic – who but Franco had real regiments? Yet these came from within the city. In 1994 an elderly Madrileño described how, as a child, he'd stood with his parents in a doorway of the half-destroyed streets of their Argüelles neighbourhood, as the column singing the 'International' came closer, and the crowds burst out cheering '*Los rusos, los rusos* – for who else but Russia would have sent them soldiers?'

It was the first of the International Brigades, with many German anti-Fascist refugees in the ranks of '*los rusos*'. That night Madrid talked of how 'our Germans' had stood up to the 'Other Germans', had fought to the death but not retreated. Pasionaria's great cry '*¡No pasarán!*' was theirs too, and became Madrid's.

The radio broadcast an appeal by Fernando Valera, a Republican deputy: 'Here in Madrid is the universal frontier that separates liberty and slavery... It is fighting for Spain, for humanity, for justice and with the mantle of its blood it shelters all human beings.'

There were Russian tanks and aircraft, not enough but some. Civilians took their place in trenches, waiting for scarce rifles from dead militia. They had fruit cans filled with dynamite. Everywhere people built barricade. You could take the tram: 'To the front, five centimos', conductors called out, as a tram full of barbers went, wearing their white smocks, their combs still in their pockets.

The defenders lived on food brought up by civilians: wine, bread, stews, paella. Three-engine Junkers 52 bombed them and Franco announced that the bombardment 'will be continued until Madrid surrenders. Madrid will have to be destroyed, district by district, no matter how much I regret it.'

To a whole generation, the word 'Madrid' came to symbolise a people taking arms and standing almost alone against the tide of Fascism which was sweeping over Europe. The photos of children killed by German bombers, the rallying of idealists and trade unionists from around the world in the Communist-organised International Brigades, made Madrid's trenches the frontlines of democracy. Workers handled rifles sent by Mexico. In the Casa de Campo were German, French, British, Irish and Polish volunteers fighting and dying for them, in the Parque del Oueste the Basque unit was digging in. Anarchists from Cataluña had come. Overhead flew snub-nosed Russian fighters.

La Pasionaria often helped to dig trenches to defend Madrid. She stopped panic retreats. When the government fled Madrid, she remained, addressing a mass meeting one kilometre from the front. She was deeply moved by the arrival of the first units of the International Brigades, telling them that to fight for Spain was to fight for freedom and peace for the whole world. Devoted to the rank-and-file soldiers, her arrival always lifted their spirits. She raised hell about the quality of their food. Ex-Communist Franz Borkenau remembers her speaking to a crowd of 50,000 at Valencia that August: 'Simple, self-sacrificing faith – lack of conceit. Dressed in black, without the slightest attempt to make herself look pleasant, she speaks simply, directly, without rhetoric, without caring for theatrical effects…the masses worship her, not for her intellect, but as a sort of saint who is to lead them in the days of trial and temptation.'

In Paris in September she launched her other famous phrase: 'The Spanish would rather die on their feet than live on their knees,' which was coined in Mexico's Revolution for Land and Freedom by the great guerrilla chief, Emiliano Zapata. The French crowd were so moved they shouted down the interpreter so she could continue her speech uninterrupted. She ended prophetically: 'If today it is our turn to resist Fascist aggression, the struggle will not end in Spain. Today it's us. But if the Spanish people are allowed to be crushed, you will be next. All of Europe will have to face aggression and war.'

The fall of Bilbao in June 1937 was a terrible blow to her but she drew the political lesson: 'They refused to understand something fundamental – the Basques had no regular army.' When her native Asturias fell next, she cried: 'We have shouted until we are hoarse at the doors of the so-called democratic countries, telling them what our struggle meant for them, and they did not listen.'

In May 1938 she was chosen to give the keynote speech to the Spanish Communist Party congress, which sought to save Republican democracy by foregoing revolution, accepting Negrín's war aims defending freedom of religion, property and universal suffrage. Vincent Sheean was there, and saw a deep-bosomed Spanish woman of about forty, with a hearty laugh and a firm hand, a certain noble profile but her face sad in repose. She spoke for over three hours although it seemed short. Her voice not musical but what made it unlike any other he'd heard was its passionate sincerity, alike in her slightest remarks or great sweeping statements. It was impossible to disbelieve anything while she was saying it: she was carefully reasoned and analytical, and the party's text in that voice had the taste and substance of truth.

Confronting them with bitter results of nearly two years of war, mistakes and failures, she didn't minimise the danger. She went through President Negrín's thirteen-point programme step by step, demanding total support for his principles of constitutional law and parliamentary democracy – either that or a Fascist victory. They were shocked and silenced at first, being asked to sacrifice everything, even Communism itself, but at the end they cheered with enthusiasm.

Later she was devastated by the implications of the Republic's sending home of the International Brigades. They were the living symbols that the Spanish Republic did not stand alone. At their farewell parade in Barcelona in the last days of October 1938, she gave the speech which Brigaders remember as her greatest: 'You are history, you are legend. We will not forget you. Come back to us.' As she spoke the onlookers threw flowers at the passing Brigaders. What could have been a march of defeat became a celebration.

She escaped from Spain to Russia and a thirty-eight-year exile. An ex-brigader who met her there before the Second World War began, in her small hotel room guarded by the Red Army, felt she was in tears as he left. She had spent long years directing underground work in Spain and now she accepted the dissenting documents from underground Madrid executive members. But she devoted her time with their delegate to hearing everything of the Madrid she loved: its people, their daily lives, the changes to the city she knew. She shared her stories of the Madrid she first saw, coming from the north in the 1930s. Even when the exiled party leadership split, with two executive committees, they shared one president, herself.

20

DUBLIN HONOURS THE BRIGADES

Eric Fleming down in Liberty Hall wanted to see me. He'd been a great supporter on our outing to Barcelona in 1988 and now three years later, when Dublin was having its year as 'Cultural Capital of Europe', he was implementing the resolution voted by Dublin Trades Council when they came back fresh from Barcelona: to erect our own memorial to the sixty Irish who died for the Spanish Republic.

Eric had arranged a whole week of events to be opened by President Mary Robinson. The highlight at the end would be the unveiling by the Lord Mayor of the Spanish Civil War memorial, a bronze plaque in the forecourt of Liberty Hall with all 60 of the Brigaders' names. He filled me in: he would provide an office there in Liberty Hall, and I was to find veterans, arrange whatever needed to go with the unveiling, generate support and raise the funds to pay for all this. Eric himself would be busy running the events of the rest of the week. After organising Buswell's and Barcelona with Bob, I seemed an obvious choice to him.

I rang Bob, who was a real tonic. We began to consider whom we could get to come, which veterans would travel. I put down the phone and started the endless chore of drawing up target lists for mailing our appeal for funds and began the biggest job of all: starting to write the first draft for that appeal. All our cash would depend on it. And that cash was vital. The Trades Council wasn't broke. They just had no money – the old union story and it's always true. I opened a reply to our first mailing from John Taylor, a veteran of the Civil War and the Second World War whom we'd met in Barcelona's Plaza Real.

I'd mentioned the Battle of Jarama, where nineteen of the sixty Irish were killed.

'Jarama,' wrote John, 'how well I remember it, how poor we were there': their lack of all essentials, the out-of-date weapons they had to defend Madrid as Franco tried to cut the Valencia road in what became one of the key battles of that decade. While John couldn't afford to give us money, he'd actually provided something much more important: the vital quotes.

Now we'd got an appeal that worked, all I needed was to find the right people and adapt the basic letter for each one. The replies started coming in. As a gamble, I'd asked people to sponsor a name for £50 or jointly for £25. It turned out that £25 was a winner, and every political party in the Dáil wrote in support of the memorial. Donations came from all levels of society: from a cabinet member, Attorney-General John Murray who was an old friend from the UCD Law Society, through trade union branches to pensioners. The NUJ upstairs at Liberty Hall wanted to sponsor Frank Ryan's name: 'After all, he was one of our members.'

François Mazou was just recovering from breaking a leg in his native Pyrenees but would travel if his veterans' association nominated him. I rang their chief, Ossart, in Paris, who said he'd love to send someone but with key events coming up for the anniversary of the 1944 liberation of Paris, nobody was free.

But we had someone. Who? Mazou! Excellent choice, a very suitable representative. So François set out, as did three from the USA and John Taylor (an anglicised form of his name which he'd adopted on settling in the UK) representing his native Czechoslovakia. Jim Ferguson got a group of his UCATT union members to sponsor him. He'd spent hours listening to John's experiences on the stone benches of Barcelona's Plaza Real: on the first day at Jarama, as a raw recruit, he'd been seventh in the team manning a heavy machine gun, carrying ammunition. By the end of the second day he was third man; the others hadn't survived.

Bill Alexander and a group of Bob's UK veterans association were coming, including Michael Economides from Cyprus. I realised we'd have to do more than provide an afternoon's unveiling, so Eric agreed we could organise a dinner in the Clarence Hotel the night before, and I tried to get freebies to fill the rest of the days our guests would stay.

Bob arrived at last into the tiny office, now crammed with files and materials. He brought one of the large flags of the Spanish Republic made by his wife Lola, which the two of us hung on the office wall. He and I were in great glee: his successful campaign for Barcelona was leading to a memorial in his native Dublin. He'd the mouth organ in his top pocket and his father's gift for music.

Manus O'Riordan dropped down with nuggets of history, contacts and encouragement. It helped my spirits to see allies from the warren of glass floors above. And the main text I was relying on was his father Mick's book *Connolly Column* on the Irish fighting Franco, the record we all consulted at these times.

The three Americans were fascinated by Big Jim Larkin's chair in the Trades Council office. They each had to sit in it once. Bill Van Felix was tall, big-boned, with a New York twang, a man who remembered the Woolworth's Dimestore strikes of the thirties and now was president of the largest Democratic branch in New York. Sam Walters was the opposite: quiet spoken, easily over-shadowed at first, busy in the US movement for Central America, while Julius Margolin was small, dark, wrapped like the TV detective Colombo in a raincoat, a survivor of the McCarthy-era blacklisting in the film industry. Julius still regretted that while active in supporting the Spanish Republic, he had not gone to Spain.

François Mazou turned out to be a shrewd charmer. He'd been political commissar in Spain, was wounded at Jarama, then became a colonel in charge of a military hospital. When he came back from fighting Fascists in Spain 'I found they were here in France' so he joined the Resistance. He began making clandestine return visits to Spain. We'd find afterwards that he'd recruited Bob and me into a new campaign of his own.

Michael Economides had felt lonely as one of the few Greek Cypriots in his time in the battalion and chose to stick with the Irish.

He told us about the period when he was recovering from wounds in Figueras and about a French officer who'd been in charge, a great commissar. The night that the news came that Chamberlain and French premier Daladier had flown to meet Hitler for what became the Munich Agreement, everyone spontaneously assembled with this commissar in the main hall to debate its effect on them and on Spain. But Economides couldn't remember that Frenchman's name. Someone translated the conversation for François, who suddenly sat up exclaiming, 'But I was the commissar in that hospital – that was me!' And so, to Michael's delight and surprise, it was. They'd met in Dublin now after all the years.

Belfast Trades Council invited some of our veterans up north to march in their May Day procession. Limerick Trades Council arranged a special meeting to listen to them and we did a tour in our car from Hertz via Galway. To Connemara we went, the Burren and the Cliffs of Moher down to Jim Kemmy's Limerick where François and the Americans spoke. François took the tough final question: 'Given the outcome of Franco's victory, do you think all your efforts were worthwhile?' The same question that always gets asked and François was the right man to answer it. Two third-level colleges in Dublin held sessions for the veterans, providing the sort of young and intelligent audiences where Bob and François were at home.

The Clarence Hotel banquet was packed. Mick O'Riordan presided and Bob sat looking around cheerfully at all those gathered here in his native Dublin. He felt proud that he and the Irish veterans were now the ones entertaining guests. The unveiling ceremony was one of those unforgettable experiences; you could feel the emotional build-up. Eilís Ryan was there; Sheevaun Lynam, who'd been in her finishing year at school in Madrid when the war broke out, and whose book on the Basques got her banned for life by Franco; Antonio Serra, director of the Instituto Cervantes – a breakthrough, as the socialist government was continuing the policy of having nothing to do with the Republicans in the Civil War.

The German Miners' Union band played. Robert Ballagh filled in with timely words, pretty good since a few hours before he hadn't known he'd be speaking. Paddy Coughlan presided for the Trades Council, Lord Mayor Michael Donnelly prepared to unveil and Maurice Levitas read the roll of honour. His fellow veterans looked like a portrait by a twentieth-century Rembrandt, with their faces set against the banner of the Irish in the Brigades, the Connolly Column Banner, inaugurated long ago by that Republican priest Fr Michael O'Flanagan with the words 'Their deed was as noble as that of the men of 1916.'

That brief moment of the actual unveiling was intense, silent, timeless, the line of old comrades united by all they had fought for and by all who had died. The differences that had developed between these strong-willed men of principle over the sixty years disappeared.

When almost all the visitors had left town, François, Bob and I were invited to the annual Trades Council dinner where we began to come down from our cloud to the real world. Eric Fleming explained that we'd more than covered basic costs and he'd enough left to help each veteran with a contribution to travel expenses.

I never did find out how much money I had raised; all replies went up to the Trades Council secretary on the thirteenth floor. But John Taylor's words had carried far. He could never forgive the English establishment for their sacrificing of Spain and then Czechoslovakia.

For Bob it was recognition by his own native city of all they fought for so many years ago. The photo of him meeting President Robinson caught what was the second most moving moment of his visit for him. As he told the SIPTU journal, 'Meeting the president was an honour I never thought I'd live to see – especially as I'd never heard of a president entering Liberty Hall. I thought of the times I spent in raggedy clothes fishing for crabs over the Liffey wall, and later being batoned down in the many demonstrations against unemployment and Fascism around the corner in O'Connell Street.' Looking at the recording later I noted the expression on Mary Robinson's face, as if she was the one meeting the dignitary.

When the dust settled I foolishly thought it was all over, but of course the next stage was about to get going: François, like Bob, made clandestine trips after the war into Franco's Spain and with the return of democracy he'd become more adventurous. In the small town of Morata de Tajuña, south of Madrid, where in 1937 he was based during the battle of Jarama, François had located the rubbish pit on the edge of the cemetery where the remains from the Republican war dead had been gathered and dumped under broken pots, dead flowers and assorted junk.

Through his own efforts, bringing classes of school kids to visit, getting his story into Spanish and French papers, calling on officials and writing from his tiny apartment in Pau across the border, François had achieved a lot. The regional assembly of Madrid Province voted a special budget to restore the pit – '*El Corral*' – as a proper war grave. But they were blocked by the old-style Franco supporters on Morata town council, so the Madrid socialists decided to spend the money in nearby Arganda, which just happened to be represented by their party and was delighted to have a monument.

François felt betrayed, but as I pondered the problem I noticed another angle: the Spanish authorities might be entitled to do what they wished with their own war graves and their money but these were Irish dead too, and British and French – there could have been up to fifty nationalities in the Brigades. The terrible slaughter at Jarama meant that the dead of many lands were now lying in the rubbish of El Corral. Whatever might happen at Arganda, these were our dead in Morata.

21

THE JARAMA VETERANS' MEMORIAL ASSOCIATION

In London Bob and Walter Greenhalgh formed the Jarama Veterans Memorial Association to campaign for the restoration of the graves. Once again Bob's friends found their UK war veterans' association was not with them, supporting instead the alternative monument proposal at Arganda. They later learned it was to have Republican dead, including Brigaders, on one side and Franco's dead, including the Nazis, on the other.

Walter said such a 'military-thinking memorial' was in conflict with the idealism which brought their comrades to Spain – not to fight as mercenaries but as an expression of their deeply held anti-Fascism. Franco understood this, and showed it by his standard practice of shooting captured International Brigaders. The news about the Arganda monument shocked many veterans but it spurred on Walter and Bob.

Walter had been in the early battles of the Brigades in Andalucía, where his rifle had a brass date on its stock – 1877 – and would fire a single round at a time. During the battle of Jarama his mate Tony Larlham was killed on his first day under fire but there were lighter moments too: their cook had been told to prepare a frontline dinner for VIPs including the American writer Ernest Hemingway, so he prepared a 'rabbit dish', which they learnt was prepared with one of the few cats left in the town of Morata.

When Walter found he'd have to serve under Wally Tapsell, a commissar for whom he'd lost all respect after Wally's public outbursts in the aftermath of the battle of Brunete, he went to see

Frank Ryan, for whom he worked as adjutant. 'A former IRA leader, a big man, fabulously brave in action yet extraordinarily gentle, he was a man with sympathy for everyone's troubles.' Frank got Walter out on a mission to Barcelona.

When Walter was back in his unit and about to go into action in Aragón, Frank turned up with orders transferring him to the base at Albacete, where linguists like Walter were urgently needed, and also got him promoted to lieutenant. 'You'll need that officer's rank; They're all bloody officers down there,' Frank told him. 'I'll take your rifle. You make your way to Albacete.'

Walter was sensitive to others and full of common sense. He told me how the famous row with the Irish in the British battalion, which led to them transferring to the Americans, was finally sparked off. The 1st Company, then largely Irish with many ex-IRA men, had distinguished itself in heavy fighting. The British Communist papers arrived out at the front perhaps a month later, with headlines about the company's success ascribed to 'Our British Boys'. As Walter recalled it, this was the umpteenth time and was just one straw too many.

He reckoned there were more Irish volunteers who'd died in Spain than were recorded: young Irish from Manchester, Birmingham and the like who turned up on the eve of battle. They went into action with the battalion, and were lost among the huge casualties. Later when things became organised again, not all were remembered and listed among the dead. (Research published in 2005 by Ciaran Crossey indicated the total of these Irish volunteers was over 300).

In Ireland there was great support from all sections of society for the campaign of Bob and Walter. If there was one event in twentieth-century history that seemed to unite all Irish traditions, it was the death of the nineteen Irish at Jarama. They included Billy Tumilson from the Shankill, whose last postcard home ended with 'Impossible to do other than carry on with the slogan of Cathal Brugha: "No Surrender"; 'McGrotty' an ex-Christian Brother from Derry; Church of Ireland minister R. M. Hilliard from Killarney; Charlie Donnelly from Tyrone; leading IRA men like Kit Conway. With the gradual slow moves towards peace in Northern Ireland, the relevance of their dying together defending another Republic's freedom was clear in 1993.

My own campaign was based on getting as many heavyweight supporters as possible to write, trying to keep up the pressure through friends and sympathisers snowing Madrid with the most impressive stationery we could, Spain being a land that sets great store by formalities and appearances.

We had letters from a widening geographic circle – Labour history societies, universities abroad, party leaders, government ministers like Ruairi Quinn and Michael D. Higgins, MEPs, Lord Mayors of Dublin, trade union leaders and clergy. Dr Caird, the Church of Ireland Archbishop of Dublin, was supportive, remembering the Rev Hilliard. So was Fr Austin Flannery, whose hallway had that wonderful quotation that Bob loved by the Brazilian Archbishop Helder Camara: 'When I feed the hungry, they call me a saint; when I ask why they are hungry, they call me a Communist.' He wrote to the parish priest at Morata, reminding him that many practising Catholics wanted to see their dead relatives there given Christian burial. François called on the priest and found him favourable to the project.

The breadth of support in Ireland was historic: Jimmy Deenihan, Fine Gael TD for north Kerry, took it up with his party, which had been co-founded in the 1930s by General O'Duffy. The reply from his party leader John Bruton was a classic: the party did support this campaign to restore graves of these Irish volunteers – then a final line, 'It was true of course that Irishmen fought on both sides in Spain.'

I remembered Eilís Ryan's account of how she went to meet General O'Duffy when he was back from Spain and her brother was under death sentence in Burgos. She asked him to send an appeal for clemency to Franco. He met her in Wynn's Hotel. They had coffee 'and he let me pay for it,' added Eilís. Then they went over to the GPO to send the telegram. She wrote out their agreed wording and passed him the form to sign. O'Duffy shook his head. 'No, you sign my name.' She did, the telegram went off and O'Duffy had covered himself against any leak that might have embarrassed him in the future.

The discourtesy of the Madrid officials who never acknowledged our letters was a real downer, all the more so since I knew only too well how punctilious Spanish officials normally are in these matters. This was a tactic: ignore us and eventually we'd just fade away. But with a team like Bob and Walter, and François urging us on, they couldn't have been more wrong.

Bob often came over to Dublin. One night he decided he'd try Christy Moore's concert in the Gaiety but it was sold out when he arrived minutes before curtain time. He nipped round to the stage door and banged. Someone came: 'Tell Christy it's Bob Doyle from the International Brigades, will you?' The door slammed. A minute later it shot open again, a hand grabbed Bob and dragged him inside. 'OK, this way…now, just sit there and don't move or the audience will see you!'

Sitting on the edge of the stage, hidden by the curtain, Bob had the best view of the night. Near the end Christy suddenly announced, 'This next song is for my friend Bob Doyle, sitting just offstage.' Christy's own ballad, 'The Fifteenth International Brigade', followed, with Bob cheering louder than anyone.

One day Bob mentioned Edward Heath's stance during the 1991 Gulf War about how much this Tory ex-Premier had developed in his politics, adding that he once saw Heath interviewed about his early life, and when asked if he'd ever demonstrated back in the thirties, he'd said, 'Only for Spain.' Bob remembered that Heath had made a personal visit as a young Tory to the British in the trenches. He decided to write to him about Morata. He asked Heath to support the cause of the British war dead in Morata, quoting Heath's recent comment on the Gulf War.

For months nothing happened, while Bob lobbied his local Labour MP who got the Minister of State at the Foreign Office to send British embassy staff to the graveyard itself. This began to have an effect on Madrid. Finally Heath's reply arrived attached to a letter from Felipe González, the Spanish Prime Minister, which said:

I read your letter of 25 March carefully in which you enquire about the state of the graves in Morata de Tajuña of the British members of the International Brigades who'd died during our Civil War.

I sincerely regret that such a state of abandonment has occurred. I have asked the President of the Madrid Provincial Assembly to let me know about all this, and he has told me that there are ongoing talks with an association of Republican Army veterans with a view to erecting a monument to the Brigaders. Also it's intended to set up a commission which will take charge of getting this project underway and to decide on its location.

I hope this affair will soon be settled and that the fighters of the International Brigade in Morata will be remembered with the dignity which they deserve.

The spotlight was well and truly on those socialists in the Madrid assembly and the old guard on Morata town council.

Bob himself was full of surprises! He'd been nominated by a young friend for the BBC2 series of home-produced programmes, *Video Diaries*. The friend was Cluna Donnelly, niece of Charlie Donnelly, the Irish poet killed at Jarama. She and Bob ended up travelling through Spain with a BBC camera, filming their encounters with locals in Morata, exposing the evasiveness of Madrid bureaucrats, and showing reactions good and bad to Bob's campaign in Spain and in Britain. It was a revealing programme and kept the spotlight on Morata, whose clock tower still says 'To the Victory of 1939'. At the graves, in what Bob thought looked a rich cemetery with expensive tombs, the 5,000 Republicans had only the dinner-plate sized stone placed by François. Bob wondered would they ever see their own unveiling ceremony here?

The most moving moment came as Cluna tried to speak the lines she'd written for the camera, and Bob left her alone at the old rubbish pit, the mass grave where her uncle's remains lay. She left a personal note, made out with his photo like the mortuary card the family never got printed half a century ago, for her uncle who, she said:

> Lies somewhere in this cemetery, without a grave, his bones strewn with the remains of the other anti-Fascists. I place this note here, as a memorial to him and his comrades who died in the olive groves and battlefields of Spain

Her hope was to show that he had not died in vain and that many would try to ensure that the past would neither be forgotten or relived; and to see a proper memorial here, acting as a warning to her generation of the real and terrible face of Fascism, honouring Charlie and all the others in Spain, who gave their lives. 'Their fight then is our fight now. *No pasarán!*'

They had a friendly meeting with the parish priest. Bob said, 'Even though I'm an atheist, I wanted to get his commitment.' The priest saw no problems from the town; he understood it'd been discussed at the ministry. Bob joked that he'd quote his assurance that none of those buried here were going to object.

In Madrid the regional minister's assistant assured them the Brigaders were the last heroes who always had a special place in 'the hearts of all of us who struggled'. Yes, they were working on a monument. The official seemed positive about the project. Cluna felt if she'd not met Bob, she'd never have known of Spain's experience of prisons and concentration camps, unlike the Holocaust.

They went to stay in San Pedro. Only recently had it been admitted that there were once concentration camps in Spain. Bob admired the new fittings: 'It wouldn't half make a good dance hall!' Everything in the monastery had been changed except the statue of El Cid crushing Moors. As at Jarama, nothing showed what had once happened to prisoners from so many nationalities here.

Back home, Bob's brother Peter died of cancer. Two of his brothers and a sister had now died in the last few years and Bob thought, 'As we seem to be dying in order of age I suppose it'll be my turn next.' The last time he'd seen Peter was when he crashed on the bike going to visit him in hospital, and Peter was astonished to see Bob arrive on a stretcher. 'So the last time I saw Peter, he had a smile on his face!' Reflecting on life, Bob murmured, 'The best religion to me, my wife, to my brother, would be the preservation of everything that is good in this world, and particularly for the unborn generations to come.'

He read Heath's reply on the Morata graves: 'It shows Heath's got a conscience and is quite humanitarian.' Meanwhile after an appeal for Morata at a meeting of the Labour History Society in Dublin, I was approached by Pat Feeley of the Irish Labour Party. He knew Dick Spring, the party leader and then the Irish Minister for Foreign Affairs, well enough to draft a letter for Spring to send to the three Madrid assembly officials involved. There was no reply to his three letters and Dick Spring needed another draft. This time, as he told Pat Feeley, 'The Spanish foreign minister and I have to meet regularly at European meetings and I will have a reply.'

I knew from this that we'd finally outflanked the local political interests that had blocked us for so long. This had now become an issue at international level. Spain had recently joined the European Community and there were now too many vital Spanish interests to be defended. There was no way their foreign minister could avoid talking to Dick Spring, and on the other hand, Felipe González had already committed himself to move on this for Edward Heath.

News of progress came from an unexpected direction: a typed sheet in Spanish on plain notepaper from the Republican veterans' association in Madrid (to whom we'd never written) announced the imminent unveiling of an inscribed plaque over El Corral in Morata cemetery on Saturday 8 October 1994. We had to rush off a note of thanks to everyone who'd written. Then there was the scramble to get everyone off to Madrid.

Despite their condemnation of Walter and Bob's Jarama Memorial Committee as 'redundant and divisive' now that there was going to be a ceremony, the UK veterans' association organised a large delegation and a speaker. By this time Bob had been excluded from association membership and Walter appeared to have been blacklisted. He sent out a final message of thanks and wound up the Jarama Memorial Association.

François decided that wasn't enough. He'd now got his heart set on having a centre for the dead and a battlefield historical site established, as had been done in France at Verdun, the First World War battlefield. Like Bob and Walter he was upset that some people who had been opponents of his efforts were now heading up the forthcoming event.

The last Irish survivor from Jarama, Peter O'Connor from Waterford, was to speak for the Irish. Mick O'Riordan came. At the last moment François agreed to travel with just a handful of close friends.

Early on the day a few pals and I arrived in the square at Morata just before the first scheduled event, a reception by the mayor. The square itself was empty; it still bore the Fascist titles from Franco's regime and the town hall was locked. The mayor had waited until that morning to cancel his welcome with maximum impact. But radio and TV crews were rolling in, press photographers unpacked cameras, coaches of our people began arriving, as did staff from the Irish and Cuban embassies.

We strolled out to the edge of the town and got our first sight of the cemetery with a huge covered marble plaque ready to be unveiled, right along the top wall looking down on the graves of generations of Morata's worthy families.

Manus recognised an elderly man at the back being approached respectfully by people in the crowd. It was the legendary Republican General Lister, aged and feeble, on his own today. Gently, Manus approached and asked if he could bring him through the crowds. Lister assented and, for the last time, with Manus guiding, Lister 'went to the Front'. He died two months later.

Peter's speech recalled that his native Waterford had sent ten volunteers to Spain, five had fought in this spot and one, Mossie Quinlan, was buried here. He added the only lines spoken in all the day's events recognising the key role of François – all in English.

Next the Minister for Social Affairs, Cristina Alberdi, spoke. She explained the emotional effect that watching Peter had on her, as she began to appreciate what this part of her own history really meant. She spoke with that sincerity I had noticed before whenever people of her generation found this hidden history had pierced the amnesia in which they'd been reared.

Peter, standing close by, didn't speak Spanish and had no idea of the effect he'd had on her. Significantly she mentioned the Madrid veterans' request for citizenship for the Brigadistas, which she thought couldn't be done – but she would look now at their proposal. Lequina, President of Madrid Provincial Assembly, unveiled the memorial which read (in Spanish):

> To the memory of the heroic Spanish and International
> Brigade anti-Fascist fighters who offered their lives to
> the cause of liberty of Spain, of Europe and the world
> in the Battle of Jarama, February 1937

Bob and François were deeply moved. Both of them were here only as onlookers in the crowd – in Bob's words:

> On Saturday 8 October together with some 700-800
> other men and women from many countries, I stood in
> the cemetery of Morata de Tajuña to watch and listen
> as a platform of representatives of the Comunidad de
> Madrid supported by other 'important personages'
> dedicated a memorial at the former rubbish tip
> where lie scattered the remains of the 5,000 Spanish
> Republican militia men and International Brigaders
> who were killed here in 1937.
>
> The fact that I and others of the Jarama Memorial
> Association who have campaigned for many years to
> bring about this result were but a part of the crowd of
> onlookers, whilst on the 'official platform' there were
> those who bitterly opposed us, brought only a wry

smile. Maybe it has been and always will be so. When the cause which the rebel has for so long held to his heart becomes 'policy' there is no shortage of important personages ready to jump on the bandwagon. This is the time for the rebel to move on to a new cause.

There were many reunions of old comrades among the cemetery's tombs and some surprises. Vincent Tonelli was amazed to see a hand stretched out to him by his old commander from Madrid, Comandante Muniz, whom he hadn't seen for fifty-six years.

After the gleaming plaque with its gold lettering had been unveiled, we had a huge meal in El Cid, the local restaurant. It was a noisy banquet, packed with famous guests, visitors, local friends of François and their families, and the grave-diggers who'd first helped him to locate the grave site.

When the set speeches were over, a speaker from the floor, a Spanish veteran now living in France, called for a few words from 'the man who made all this possible – François Mazou'. François finally, slowly, rose with the clatter of glasses and voices growing less until he stood in the silence looking around, and began a few short words of acknowledgement, cigarette drooping from one hand, his voice emotional at times. François was being honoured as ever, if not by the top table, by his rank and file – like a true commissar still.

La Pasionaria's daughter Amaya read her mother's famous farewell speech to the Brigadistas from their last parade in 1938, over the resumed clatter of glasses and conversation. Mick O'Riordan's son Manus delivered Alberti's elegy 'If My Voice Should Die on Earth' with translations in Irish and English.

Bob dined at a distance from the UK association. During the visit he never spoke in public but when we got the next day's papers there was his photo on the back cover of *The Sunday Times*, a lone veteran lost in the crowd, his head in his hand, by a tombstone at the emotional climax in the graveyard. The story in a picture.

22

THE BRIGADERS ARE MADE CITIZENS OF SPAIN

In 1938 the president of the Republic, Juan Negrín, formally promised the Brigaders Spanish citizenship, and La Pasionaria had told them in her historic farewell speech to the Brigades:

> We will not forget you; and when the olive tree of peace puts forth its leaves, entwined with the laurels of the Spanish Republic's victory, come back. Come back to us and here, those of you who have no homeland will find a homeland, those who are forced to live without friends will find friends, and all of you will find the affection and gratitude of the entire Spanish people who today and tomorrow shout with enthusiasm. Long live the heroes of the International Brigades!

In 1996 to everyone's joy and surprise it happened. The Spanish cabinet approved legislation offering citizenship to every surviving Brigader. The efforts of associations in Madrid, veterans and friends whose request was noted at Morata by the Minister for Social Affairs, Cristina Alberti, had now borne fruit. The vote in the Spanish parliament, the Cortes, was deemed unanimous. Anyone who observed the tensions in Spain through the 1970s and into the 1980s could appreciate the deep change that brought about this vote.

When the Brigaders arrived in Madrid for the ceremonies to mark the bestowal of citizenship, premier Aznar's newly-elected Partido Popular (conservative) government honoured the commitment of their Socialist predecessors – it truly was from 'the entire Spanish people'. The Irish veterans went on to the Basque celebrations in their honour in Bilbao.

François Mazou travelled against doctor's advice and fell seriously ill in Barcelona. His hospital room became the scene of political discussions, history lessons and reunions with visiting student groups, veterans and old friends.

Bob missed the Spanish ceremonies. At seventy-nine he started painting his first-floor windows, climbing a ladder with paintbrush in one hand and paint in the other, leaving no hand to hold on. He fell twenty feet on to concrete, broke his pelvis and one arm and had a hole in a shoulder blade. He suffered massive internal bleeding and needed seventeen pints of blood.

The family were brought in; the end seemed near. His son Julian was alone with Bob for a moment and Bob whispered, 'I'm a prisoner.' Julian wondered if his father was wandering mentally as a result of all the drugs, and said gently, 'What do you mean, Dad? You're not a prisoner.' With a tiny gesture Bob indicated the drips and monitors whose wires and tubes surrounded him, saying 'I'm a prisoner of science.'

'I was very lucky, I didn't know I was so near death,' Bob said later. Lola was astonished and relieved to have him home while Bob was simply grateful to be able to celebrate Christmas, after having been unconscious for most of his stay in hospital.

The official granting of Spanish citizenship is now framed and displayed prominently in his room in London.

Bob Returns to Tarrazona

In October 2000 Bob went back with friends, Jane from Barcelona and Seve from Madrid. Before the Civil War, Tarrazona was as it had been for centuries: land was owned by the wealthy few. Most of the ordinary people either had small plots or were day labourers employed seasonally. Land reform was attempted during the Republic but when Franco won, the land went back to the wealthy landowners again.

The first two battalions of Brigaders trained there went to defend Madrid in November 1936. The Fifteenth Brigade was formed for English speakers; later there was the famous split in the British battalion. Within weeks both units were plunged into the Battle of Jarama.

Tarrazona was in use from June 1937. The recruits were normally enthusiastic and 'desertion to the front', as in Bob's case became a habit. When Bob arrived in December 1937, soldiers were billeted in four houses and officers in a fifth, all expropriated from rich locals. Their mess was the Socialist Party hall. The church had become a 'Casa del Pueblo' for meetings, film shows and social events. There was a pine grove nearby that gave cover from any enemy planes overhead.

Brigaders used an old stone threshing floor for exercises – old men over seventy today remember with admiration how the recruits did their exercises in sleeveless vests in mid-winter. Their friendliness gained a warm response from locals, especially the children. The small wartime airfield still exists, with its underground storage shelters, where about ten Russian Katyushka bombers were based. But there are no physical memorials to the Brigades.

Bob went straight to the Plaza Mayor to see what the atmosphere was like after an absence of sixty-three years. The first time he was here, he felt what the Anglo-Irish poet Cecil Day Lewis described in 'The Volunteer':

> Tell them in England, if they ask
> What brought us to these wars
> To this plateau beneath the night's
> Grave manifold of stars –
> It was not fraud or foolishness,
> Glory, revenge or pay:
> We came because our open eyes
> Could see no other way.

Most Brigaders had supper in local homes. An old man, Cresencio, remembers: 'A Czech lad came to our house to share my mother's cooking, a well-behaved man. When he left for the front he gave us a leather raincoat.' Another Brigader, Harry Fisher, recalls that the Spanish would not allow them go hungry. When they returned from daily drill a group of children would be waiting. A boy of ten came to his side, telling Harry his parents wanted to invite him to share supper, which continued every evening from then. Fisher liked his evenings eating with simple honest families after a day with the other recruits.

The most dramatic memory of these one-time children was of the Brigader who climbed the church tower with his army boots on. At the top he tied on a red flag and sang the 'International'. Locals believe that the future ruler of Yugoslavia, Marshal Tito, spoke from the balcony of their town hall. Some can remember brigaders marching to the trucks outside town, heading for Madrid and the war.

In the provincial capital, Albacete, the Brigade's headquarters during the war, Bob and his friends visited the local cemetery to see any monuments to the post-war repression under Franco. There is a memorial inscribed to 'Those who died for Peace'. On either side are lines of bullet marks on the cemetery wall from the execution squads that shot Republicans here.

Bob's group called on the Provincial Archives, donating photos and records from Britain, then went into the air-raid shelter which is still in the town centre. The entry was uncovered. They went down steps into a humid atmosphere, finding the warning which said 'Come in slowly and take your place quietly.'

Coming out they were met by an old Republican soldier, Alberto Martínez. He wouldn't go down; the place had too many memories for him. He recalled how, when war broke out, the Fascist Falange and the Civil Guard joined the generals' revolt, and kept everyone indoors under curfew, until aircraft and sailors arrived from the Cartagena naval base and liberated the town. Bob was in his element as Alberto talked about the war and Madrid's trenches.

23

MEMOIRS IN MADRID: REUNION IN NEW YORK

On Tuesday, 10 December 2002, *Memorias de Un Rebelde Sin Pausa*, the Spanish translation of Bob's autobiography, was published by the Spanish Friends of the Brigades. He came with family and friends from Ireland. A packed hall waited on an upper floor of the elegant nineteenth-century Círculo de Bellas Artes, once a wartime Checa base for hunting Franco's Fifth Column and used by the Falange after the Civil War until the end of the 1970s but now restored as a focal point of cultural life in Madrid. The young novelist Manuel Rivas launched Bob's book. Ana Pérez of the Friends of the Brigades presided, and Bob spoke of his aim that day: 'To pass it on.' There was, he said, a real need to encourage and inspire people today, to show the next generation what was worth defending in life and to restore their full history to the people of Spain.

Tribute was paid to Walter, to François, and to Maria McLaughlin who had worked patiently over his text in London, and lastly to his friend and supporter here, schoolteacher Seve Montero, an expert in the history and landscape of Madrid's wartime battlefields, who had done the translation. The Irish embassy's Pádraig Mac Coscair bought everyone drinks downstairs, and the book itself got a full-page review and interview with Bob in the daily paper, *El País*. Bob's family and friends took copies back to Dublin and London.

In May 2003, the Spanish embassy's cultural centre in Dublin, the Instituto Cervantes, held a reception to celebrate Bob's autobiography, their second reception for a Brigader. We heard Pearse Hutchinson's resonant poems of the Spain he had found in 1952: 'A girl with the oldest face I ever saw – She asked me if I wanted her – "Un duro", a five-peseta coin. I asked her age. "Eleven."'

Bob thanked everyone, and pointed out that his aim, like the Madrid Friends of the Brigades, was to promote the enthusiasm of Spaniards today for the Republic's fight for survival, and to reveal the human cost of Franco's triumph, concealed for forty years. He had gone to Spain to avenge Kit Conway, and to take his place. He saluted the huge popular anti-war protests held recently in the main Spanish cities. Now he was bringing his life story, and his three granddaughters, Tabitha, Margarita and Jessie, to his native city. He said that what happened in Spain wasn't any different to what was happening in the 1980s in Nicaragua. 'The young people should not forget, the young must not forget.'

His granddaughters then drove him down to the house in Sandymount where he'd once worked. Standing on the steps in front of the hall door, with the girls and the flag of the Spanish Republic wrapped around him, Bob had his souvenir photo of the day taken.

In Madrid Seve organised commemorations on the low hills of the Jarama battlefield on the weekends closest to Kit Conway's death, with Bob as guest speaker. In the wind and cold of February 2004, an enthusiastic group of fifty Madrileños turned out among the olive trees and wild grass, twenty-five kilometres from Madrid, on the spot where so many poorly armed Irish and British volunteers died in one of the war's bloodiest and most heroic scenes. Leaning on his stick Bob spoke with tears of that fight and of those who died.

Everyone added fragments of old weapons and shells to the memorial cairn which had grown there over the previous three years, around a hand-painted notice with the names of Kit Conway and three others, recalling the battalion's 200 dead. The lines by the wartime poet Miguel Hernández were read:

> If there are men, whose souls know no frontiers,
> a scattered forehead of universal hair
> covered with horizons, ships and summits,
> with sand, with snow – you are one of those.

There is now, as François Mazou wished, a project for a museum in the restaurant El Cid where we dined in 1994 and a national park to conserve the entire Jarama battle site.

Bob's First Visit to America

Bob said: 'As soon as I read about the reunion of the American veterans in their magazine *The Volunteer* I decided to go. I saved up. My son Robert got the tickets for me and my grandaughters Margarita and Tabitha. He wrote to Richard Branson, the guy who owns the airline, asking for upgrades and I don't know if he got a reply but we got first-class tickets. I told Robert afterwards and he didn't believe it. Branson was an admirer of the Brigades. He wanted to name one of his trains after our Fifteenth International Brigade but our association didn't support it.'

'We'd no problem flying,' said Tabitha. 'We had free champagne in first class and we drank them out of it! We tried everything on the menu during the trip over. There was a hitch about Bob when we got to check-in. He needed a visa and we were told to go to the US embassy and come back next day, when Virgin bumped the three of us from first to the super class.

'We were put into this lounge at the airport where everything was free: the bar, food, massage, hairdo, and phones – we girls were calling all our friends. "Guess where we are!" Everywhere we went in super class we were getting these looks – we two girls and then Bob – guys going, "Well, *he's* done all right!"

'On arriving in New York it was like the reunions in Spain. People weren't there at first – it was all a bit messy – but a reunion helper got us to where Moe Fishman, the veteran organiser, had arranged for us to stay out in Brooklyn.'

Bob remembers: 'I met the Irish Republican girl, Bernadette Devlin, who was over to address a meeting for a birthday of an Irish Republican in New York. She said she was pleased to meet me. The two Doyle girls wanted to get dresses and everything. They knew the biggest second-hand clothes shop in the world. The hotel cost a hundred pounds a night, a beer £3.50 or £4.

'I had an interview with the New York paper, the *Irish Echo*. We met their people on May Day when I was having a good Irish breakfast. Jack Bjoze who had come on his own to the ceremony at Morata, had his photo taken with me. Jack's hair wasn't as long this time.'

Tabitha remembers the theatre-sized reception: packed hall, speeches and songs and stage performances. Jane came from Barcelona. That's how the two girls got to know everyone they met later at events back in London and in Spain, such as the commemoration for the crossing of the Ebro, where they threw flowers in the river. She found the Lincolns event was 'really well organised with people from every nationality, even Japan, and lots of Jewish guys. Their stories were really worth hearing. So were the Americans' accounts of their experiences in the McCarthy era when they got back, being followed by the same FBI agents whom they got to know personally. They'd see them shadowing and go into a bar and stay as long as they could, to see if they could outdrink them. I thought the Lincolns were real flirts. One of them signed a copy of my book, adding, "Wish I was sixty years younger."'

Brooklyn was too far out so they moved into a cheap noisy hotel in Greenwich Village, with an Irish bar opposite, for the second half of the trip. The girls did the flea markets and Bob could get his siesta. Friendly locals wanted to give Bob some 'very special grass' but the girls wouldn't let them. 'Couldn't you just see him, hanging over the balcony, having his smoke!'

They did the tourist spots like the Empire State Building, the Statue of Liberty, where all three bought the daft yellow sunglasses and hats. Tabitha and Margarita took Bob for his first sushi. They found life in New York with their grandad was so different and great fun. Tabitha had never laughed so much in her life.

Margarita realised the extent of her grandfather's heroism only on this trip: 'In Spain today my grandfather is treated like a rock star – people can't get enough of him.' And the question she asks is: 'How many kids nowadays, who can't get off the sofa, would fight for a cause?'

24

FOR KIT AND SPAIN'S REPUBLICANS

Kit Conway 'Por la Libertad de Irlanda y de España'
Bob had missed the 2004 unveiling of a memorial to the eleven
volunteers who left Waterford for the Brigades. One was Johnny
Lemon, who shared his prison bunk in San Pedro. Sean Kelly,
the memorial committee treasurer and friend of Brigader Peter
O'Connor, found they had cash left over and paid for a memorial in
Kit's native village of Burncourt in County Tipperary.

On a sunny Saturday afternoon in June 2005 about 100 people
gathered at the corner in Burncourt village, where the road forks
for Mitchelstown Caves. Beneath the Galtee mountains we heard
Councillor Mattie McGrath welcome relatives of all who'd fought
with Kit in the local flying column. Some wore their family medals
from the old IRA. Relatives of Brigaders had come from Waterford,
Scotland and Dublin; friends from Howth, Bray and Laois were
standing in the sunshine.

Seán Ó Cearnaigh, whose father was Kit's best friend, recalled
their exploits in the IRA war against the Black and Tans and the
Auxiliaries. One of Kit's first attacks was on the RIC station in
nearby Ballyporeen, whence US President Reagan's people had
emigrated.

Bob spoke of the man who was his hero and inspiration, who
trained him when he joined the IRA as a teenager in 1931, who had
taken him in when his father threw him out and how he followed
Kit into the Republican Congress, for the fight against poverty as
well as Irish unity. In Spain he used Kit's training to instruct other

volunteers. Bob's friend Seve, one of four Spaniards there that day, had organised the commemorations of Jarama on Kit's anniversary.

Mick O'Riordan recalled that it was here that Kit first defended a Republic chosen democratically by the electorate in the 1918 election. He was a patriot and internationalist. Unlike most volunteers who left quietly in those pro-Franco times, Kit told his fellow workers from the top of a barrel: 'Sooner than Franco should win there, I would leave my body in Spain to manure the fields.'

He did that, commanding three companies at Jarama, where eighteen other Irishmen died. The honorary Spanish citizenship awarded to Bob and Mick, the only surviving veterans, in 1996 acknowledged that they had stood by the Spanish Republic in its hour of need.

Seve said he came from where Kit lay: why there, and not in his own land? Because of a personal decision: to fight Fascism, for the Spanish people and for social justice for those oppressed by landed gentry. Tipperary was far from Spain, but thanks to him and more than 200 Irish who volunteered, Ireland and Spain today were closer, Kit buried there was now the bond between Tipperary and Madrid.

Bending down, he poured around the base of the memorial the pale sandy soil which he told us he'd taken the previous Thursday from the hill where Kit died. It fell against the dark Irish earth. There was a hush among the children, their parents and the clustered groups in the streaming sunshine. The gesture caught everyone else by surprise, leaving a lump in our throats.

Manus sang the local ballad 'The Galtee Boy', with added verses composed for the occasion, Bobby Gardiner, a musician from Clare, played 'Slievenamon', a lament that Waterford brigader Frank Edwards had sung while burying fallen comrades in Spain. Then everyone was invited to the community hall and a warm local reception, with home-made scones and jam, each with a copy of Annette O'Riordan's beautiful brochure for the day. It was a day that was 'pure magic' as one visitor from Laois said.

The fresh stone pillar at the corner under the shade of an ash tree now bears a panel dedicated to Kit and all the Burncourt IRA volunteers, with its last phrase in Irish and Spanish: 'For the freedom of Ireland and Spain'. In the pub tales of Kit's youth emerged: how he'd worked for a local's father until one day he didn't come in for his meal, and they found written in the sand of the farmyard: 'Christy Conway. Now a man. Gone far away.' He never came back to his childhood spot, but isn't forgotten there, nor where his body lies, far away.

Spanish Republicans Restore the Lost Memories

Bob had a framed poster on his lap as he sat for the Burncourt ceremony for a concert in homage to Republicans in a town near Jarama in June 2004. Special buses went from Madrid. Admission was free to this first celebration of Spanish Republicans which ran from 7 in the evening until all hours. 25,000 came from Asturias, Cataluña, Galicia, Andalucía and Canarias – and Madrid.

The front four rows were filled by 700 veterans. There were elderly speakers remembering, reciting a poem about a dead beloved with firm voice and shaky hand. As the night fell, the songs and speeches were accompanied by series of photos of those who had fallen, projected on to each side of the stage. Those listening were filled with memories of the incredible efforts, the sacrifices made for their war. Folk singers and movie stars were interspersed with veterans, survivors and their children: great names of modern Spanish entertainment and music, Ana Belén, Paco Ibañez, film star José Sacristán, singer Victor Manuel, writer Manuel Rivas. Poems by Cernuda and Alberti poured from the bright stage into the packed crowds and the warm night air was full of of sadness and joy, of pride and tears. Thousands were doing what Bob Doyle had sought for so long – proclaiming their Spanish traditions.

The Spanish state had never organised an official event for its fallen in the fight against Fascism. Now it was the Spanish people who were holding a mass Republican event, reading, recalling, singing songs of yesterday, today and tomorrow, their aim 'to show dignity for those who never lost it'.

Finally, as the night was about to end, the last two guests came onstage. Two elderly men were brought to the spotlights, two brigaders: Theo Franks and Bob with his usual black cane and beret. Bob had a few lines written but the atmosphere, the event itself at last, had moved him too much. Seve stood beside him and read the short speech Bob had begun the day before in London: many years ago, he came inspired by their heroic struggle to fight shoulder to shoulder with these people in their fight which resounded throughout Europe and the world. Now he was grateful they'd allowed him this opportunity to be with them again, here honouring those who fell. Today they were a free and united people but sadly once more forces of militarism and totalitarianism were menacing the peace of all. And once again the Spanish people's recent elections made a gesture echoing round the world. The fight goes on!

The explosion of applause from the 25,000 present ended a unique night, simply yet dramatically. Asked what his thoughts were sixty years later about all that happened during and after the Spanish Civil War, Bob said:

> Our average age was twenty-three; we believed we were the conscience of mankind. Spain is democratic today. We didn't win. Franco won a military dictatorship over the Spanish people. But when Franco died, as my old friend in Spain said, many candles were lit all over Spain. We are remembered for contributing to the long fight for democracy.

25

TEA WITH THE NIECES AND NEPHEW IN DUBLIN

After the visit to Burncourt, Bob was asked to his niece Bernie's home on Dublin's North Circular Road. Over cups of tea and a big fry with his nephew, Father Peter the Jesuit and his other niece Carmel, they produced a photo of grandfather Aldridge with Bob's mother Margaret. It shows a young woman with attractive features, wearing a floral hat, beside an older, dark-haired man with his hair brushed back. Bob has no memory of his mother. Was she blonde or dark? 'No, I don't remember.'

She used to suffer from post-natal depression after each child. The last time she was fourteen years in Dublin's Grangegorman mental hospital. It was a family trait on the female side. Bob's cousin Lily lives in OAP flats in Crumlin, still active and smartly turned out in her old age, but her daughter suffered from postnatal depression and apparently committed suicide.

Grandfather Aldridge was of Huguenot origin. The family details may be recorded in the church facing the Guinness Brewery. He was an electrician, married an O'Hara, and retired to a home for the elderly run by nuns in Kilmainham. The Aldridges had lived in Mount Brown, near Kilmainham, but Cissie, one of the girls, got pregnant by a married man, so they moved for the shame of it. When Bob's parents married, it wasn't an easy match. She was from a respectable family; he was a labourer from Rush. He'd walked all the way into Dublin at the age of ten to get a job as a telegraph boy at the GPO.

Bob was baptised Andrew by his mother but his father wanted

him called Robert so his name was registered as Robert Andrew. Just three months after the next child, Eileen, was born, Margaret was signed into Grangegorman by her husband. Bernie's mother, Josie, was the eldest. All her life she remembered that last time her mother was taken away: they came at night in white coats for her. She was dragged down the street with her long hair flying, screaming, 'Don't take me! Don't take me!' Josie was haunted by that scene.

Christy and Peter were sent to the Brothers in Baltimore, County Cork, treated very badly and so hungry they used take the turnips out of the fields. Finally they decided to escape and set out to sea in a small boat. They were missing all night, the story making the news. but they were located offshore after daybreak next day. Peter was put into a bath and flogged with a leather strap and Christy jumped on the Brother's back to stop the beating. He was older and doing valuable work making fishing nets so he wasn't beaten. The two boys talked all their lives of writing a book about the bad times in care, but they never got around to it. Josie could never forget the day the nuns came for young Bob and Eileen. They went off in the cab and Grandfather Aldridge got in a taxi and followed them to Wicklow to see where they were brought. But the nuns insisted on no contact.

Josie used to be sent down to the aunt's home in Dorset Street every week with the shillings for the nuns' care fee. The aunt was 'a real holy one' and paid it over to the nuns in Eccles Street. Left alone when her father went off to work each morning, Josie was locked into their rented rooms. Her aunt had told her father Josie shouldn't be mixing with the children down in the street. A young lad had a key and would let her out to play. She'd get him to lock her in again before her Dad came home.

Years later as adults Josie and Christy tried to have their mother released, even going to their TD, but as their father had signed her in, only he could get her out and he refused. So they got a letter sent notifying him that she was about to become a private charge at his expense and she was out in a few weeks. She loved to sit with them around the fire. She'd play the melodeon and they'd all sing until 'Old Doyle', as she called their father, came home. Her husband had a good deep singing voice himself and later when Josie heard Paul Robeson singing she exclaimed, 'That's like my father!'

Grandfather Aldridge called to see Margaret and gave Christy and Josie a gold sovereign but they didn't know what it was and flushed it down the toilet just to watch it disappear. Margaret died in her house in North Great George's Street aged forty-six and her husband remarried. He used come down to see his grandchildren and give them a shilling, a big sum for a child, telling them to stay away from where he lived with his second wife. He didn't want her to know he'd been seeing them or how much he used give them. He was a stoker on British Merchant Navy ships during the war. He used to bring back a parcel of tea, which was strictly rationed, and give the grandchildren their shilling with some tea for their mothers. His ship was bombed, the bombs fell fore and aft, port and starboard, but every one missed. 'It must have been someone praying for them.' Bob says he was on at least one Russian convoy.

Bob's uncle Sonny O'Hara was the one who got young Bob into politics. He'd been excommunicated for taking the IRA side in Ireland's Civil War. When he died in his basement room in Dominic Street, relatives found he'd built an altar there 'as good as any in a church' as he was still barred from the church itself.

Bob's father came over to stay with Bob and Lola in London. Bob said, 'He came to our place. We ignored everything from the past. He slept there for a good few weeks. He thought we'd done really well for ourselves and he said he'd go back and tell them we were the best of the lot. He even asked about joining the Party. We made it up and were friends; we let bygones be bygones. You know Lola, what she was like.' He went back to Dublin full of his visit. Christy got fed up hearing how well young Bob had made out in London. He was in the Irish army. Nephew Peter remembers his father in uniform with leggings. He was selected for the guard of honour at the official opening of the rebuilt GPO in 1929. According to the family, Bob and Christy's grandfather Doyle had been a stoker on the British naval gunboat *Helga* when it sailed up the Liffey and shelled Dublin in 1916, including the rebel headquarters in the GPO.

PART III

JULIAN AND ROBERT ON THEIR FATHER

26

BOB'S SON JULIAN ON HIS FATHER

It was getting dark. I sat in the back of the car, scared stiff. My father drove and my elder brother sat next to him. It was 1957 and I was just fifteen. My father turned into Portobello Road. A group of big nineteen-year-olds were gathered on the corner. We drove slowly. I watched them, wondering what would I do if anything happened.

The news had been reporting gangs of whites beating up blacks in Notting Hill. Race riots they called them. That night my father had decided to tour round Notting Hill to try to break up any attacks. Our instructions were that if we saw anything we should rush over and save the guy. So there I was, a scared fifteen-year-old watching these big nineteens, praying they wouldn't start anything. Luckily, as I remember, we never found any trouble. But we probably frightened a few black blokes by trailing them in the car, to give them protection.

It was only one of the many odd events I was involved in by my father. The first memory of being scared was when I was about six and he brought home some posters from a demonstration with the devil on them. He stuck them up in the sittingroom, saying jokingly that they should call up the devil. To this day I don't know what the demonstration was about, probably a visit from US secretary John Foster Dulles, but I stayed awake all night under the covers waiting for the devil to come.

Obviously I didn't understood much about politics at that age but I seemed to have a different view about things from other kids. This was partly because we had a bilingual household. We travelled abroad, which was unknown in working-class areas in those days. I had a funny name, Julian, which I hated because it sounded like a girl's name, and nobody else was called Julian.

I later realised when a friend had a kid and named him Julian that maybe it wasn't so bad after all and then John Lennon named his son Julian but I put an accent on the 'a' as a tribute to my Spanish grandfather, a miner who'd died of silicosis.

In primary school, the teacher was going round asking the kids what their father did for a living? A carpenter, a plumber... When it came to my turn I announced quite proudly that my Dad was a Communist.

And of course before television there were the family visits to the cinema. In those days of the double bill and the Movietone News, I remember my father having a shouting match with Winston Churchill. Churchill was making some budget statement on the news and my father replied to every other comment out loud, sometimes raising applause but most often a hushing.

He spoke at Hyde Park. I can still recall sitting on the grass watching the large crowd he drew. He must have been a good speaker because I sometimes go down to Hyde Park and get on a platform, just to test my wits out. And let me tell you, it's real hard to keep your audience.

He had a good singing voice too; now it's a hoarse whisper. But a very fond memory is my brother and I getting into our parents' big bed on a Saturday morning and singing revolutionary songs with my father. I was filming in Russia recently and we were in a car travelling from Leningrad to the Finnish frontier to film in a castle. I surprised my Russian crew by dragging from memory the 'Partisan Song' in English. The old chauffeur, a war veteran, was so moved he gave me a coin with Marshal Zhukov on it, which the others told me was quite valuable.

My father was a self-taught writer; he has a skill which I will always envy. My writing is dour and functional; he has a wit and natural skill that in another time could have been put to TV or film. I remember a letter he wrote about a new motorcycle that kept failing him. The piece was called 'That Was the Bike That Was'. It was hilarious and had a wicked sarcasm. How do you aquire that? You probably can't. It's not a mechanical thing. I only wish I had inherited some of it but I suppose you just have to find the things that your nature makes easy.

As a person who likes his privacy there is an aspect which I find quite strange in him. In my garden I grow high bushes and trees to give it privacy. Looking at my father's garden and noticing the flats built at the back, I suggested he grew some tall bushes so that they couldn't see into his garden. 'Why?' he answered. 'I want them to see my garden; it looks nice. I'm proud of it.' It's such a different view from mine. It reminded me of a Russian friend I met filming. I bought her a winter hat in London. When I asked if the hat had kept her warm, she said, 'Yes.' A woman at a bus stop had asked about her it. 'Did you tell her where you got it?' I asked. 'No,' she said, 'I didn't like to boast that I'd been abroad.' It's an attitude I'd totally forgotten that was prevalent after the war here. Now we never stop boasting about what we've got or where we've been.

One thing he suffered from when we were young was a duodenal ulcer, said to be a common complaint among sailors, but why, I never found out. He had several bad attacks and I remember his hospital stays, his medicines, one of which exploded, and the boiled food we were forced to eat for his sake. He spent one Christmas in hospital and I remember Roger Bannister coming through the wards. As a long-distance runner this was a treat for me. The attacks finally stopped when they invented an operation that cut the nerve from the brain to the stomach. The idea was not to allow any worries to stimulate stomach acid production. However unlikely, it seemed to work for him. Although his digestive tract is still pretty sensitive, he enjoys every now and then a good drink and the sociability of bars. But the stomach usually plays up on him. My brother and I decided to try him on cannabis instead of drink and cigarettes. It seemed to work. At the age of seventy-two he took it up with a relish and began to grow stuff in his greenhouse.

The hypocrisy about cannabis annoyed him, and as is his way, he soon took it up as a cause, writing letters and even getting on to talk-ins on the radio about it. He grew a pretty good hybrid that reached up to the greenhouse roof and had quite a punch. The 'Neasden dope' we called it. Part of his subversive activity was to take a plant and attach it to his moped, drive past the local police station and drop it off. I'm not sure what he was trying to do, other than get the cops high. He finally had to stop growing the stuff because he was so open about it that the local kids used to jump into the garden at night and pinch his plants. Now he just smokes my kids' stuff.

Any cause he thought valid would soon involve him. Euthanasia became such a one. And when my mother was dying he told me she wanted to go. I stupidly took her to hospital in an attempt to save her. She was very disappointed in me. Her last words were: 'Why did you bring me here to die?' She wanted to die at home.

His lifelong struggle for freedom from colonialism, for peace, against racism and for the democratic rights of all people, has been inspirational. But it has not been without its problems. The path is complicated but huge advances have been made. Even the Conservative Party waves the flag of democracy now. But the fight for a better society, against capitalism and the amoral demands of the market, is not easy. Mistakes are made. As 'father of the chapel', a quaint term for a union leader in the print trade, my father fought to protect jobs against redundancies threatened by new machinery. The success of their struggle led to ten workers for every job. It was a mistake. Protecting non-existent jobs, having workers sit around all day, does not make good people let alone good socialists. People need to be challenged, to be involved and to be useful.

But the fight for the shorter working week was right. The demonstration outside Odham's Press in the 1960s led to my father's arrest on a charge which could have landed him in prison for ten years. He was accused of jumping up and down on a policeman shouting 'We want the forty-hour week!' The case went to the Old Bailey. In those days the Metropolitan Police hadn't gone through any reforms. People who shared my outlook would have thought they were riddled with racism and political bias. We knew there had to be reforms. Good cops left; bad cops were rewarded. But I blame the judges and magistrates who encouraged them. A policeman once told me on the Lumumba demonstration: 'I could nab you and invent any charge and you'd be sent down.' This is what we thought had happened in my father's case and that the police had gone in viciously and then said they'd been attacked. Usually it would be your word against theirs and you would lose.

Luckily they arrested a newspaper photographer before they realised he was nothing to do with the demo. The photographer went around Fleet Street and collected all the news photographs of the demo. My father was clearly visible because he was carrying a banner with 'We want the forty-hour week.' The case lasted days but slowly it turned into farce.

'Where was Mr Doyle when you arrested him?' The police would say one thing, the photos would show another. One line of questioning I remember really well. The lawyer kept asking this cop: 'You say you arrested Mr Doyle on your own?'

'Yes.'

'You're sure?'

'Absolutely positive.'

The lawyer kept on; the cop insisted. 'Yes.' Then out came ten odd photos of him and four others nabbing my dad and throwing him into the van.

They won the forty-hour week but since Thatcher's time they have lost the battle for reasonable working hours. I recently worked on a documentary with Terry Jones of Monty Python fame. Terry argued that we have not actually progressed in medicine, in law. For example we filmed a reconstruction of a libel case from a medieval court brought by an ordinary villager. Today, it was pointed out, only the rich can afford to take a libel case.

Another section of the film was a comparison of the life of a Cowley car worker today with a villager who lived in medieval times on a strip of land where the car factory is today. From existing documents Terry was able to calculate how many days the villager had to work to make his basic subsistence: his rent and his food. It worked out about a hundred days a year. The Cowley car worker on the other hand, had to work some 250 days a year just for his basics. More than double the medieval peasant.

But there has been so much progress. A baton has been passed from the Tolpuddle martyrs fighting for the rights of working people to those who went to fight Fascism in Spain. And on to the tens of thousands of forgotten Germans who fought against Hitler and were the first to be murdered in the concentration camps.

These men and women made a conscious choice. My father is one of them; he might have died in Spain with the hundreds who gave their lives. He survived but continued the battle for a new society. They may do things wrong, they may be impatient, but they must succeed, not only for the good of mankind but it is now clear – for the good of the planet.

27

BOB'S SON ROBERT ON HIS FATHER

My father was away at sea when I was born and my mother named me after him, in his memory, as she didn't expect him to return from the war. She hadn't known Bob long enough to know what a survivor he is. The first time my father and I met is recorded photographically. There he is, handsome with a wide smile and in his petty officer's uniform. I'm maybe three months old, looking at him with a surprised curiosity. That was the pattern of our relationship for the first five years of my life. My mother Lola, younger brother Julian and I were evacuated to Ironbridge in Shropshire during the Second World War and saw my father only occasionally. Not until we returned to London at the end of the war did I really get to know Bob. Even then, time with him always seemed special as his various political activities kept him away from home a great deal.

Nowadays we might take a different attitude to the situation of a young mother left alone much of the time to bring up two small boys – especially one so alone in a foreign country without a network of family and friends to support her. From a young age Julian and I knew about Fascism and concentration camps, the struggle for independence in the colonies, and the fight for 'peace'.

I never questioned that my father's activities were important and his absence from home necessary. He explained that he had to struggle for us, and all of the other children, to make the world a better place. In fact we participated as a family in demonstrations, even making our own banners and marching proudly with our parents against German rearmament, for the restoration of Paul

Robeson's right to travel, and to get British troops out of Malaya or Kenya.

Life was made a lot easier for Lola when her sister joined her. Our aunt, Tia Josefa, came from Spain to live with us in London as soon as travel was practical following the war. Thereafter the two sisters were rarely seen apart, talking to each other in Spanish. Their very close and supportive relationship continued until Lola's death in 1997. With her down-to-earth sense of humour and common sense, Josefa was a valuable addition to our family. Lola's English never got much beyond the needs of shopping – although she always seemed to understand complex forms to do with things like tax and rates better than any of us. Once Josefa arrived, Lola's English stopped advancing, and Josefa's always remained basic. Consequently Julian and I always spoke to them in Spanish. In my case I didn't really start speaking English until I went to school, and by that time Lola had already taught me to read a little in Spanish. Although Bob spoke Spanish very well, with Julian and me he would soon slip into English, so it's thanks to Lola and Josefa that Julian and I acquired so easily an entry into another language and culture, and such a tremendously rich one at that.

One of Bob's main political activities was public speaking. Street-corner meetings do not seem to happen much these days, although John Major in one general election revived the soapbox tradition as a sort of gimmick. Bob and his party comrades put quite a bit of their efforts into these meetings. Bob had his own wooden platform that folded down into a sort of suitcase. On Sundays I would often go to Hyde Park Corner with him. I think that the idea was that I should play in the park and sometimes I did. But usually it was more interesting to hang around the platform listening to the meetings. Bob was a very funny speaker. He encouraged hecklers and the witty banter that he could keep up would often attract huge crowds.

Sometimes he spoke on the Communist Party platform, but more often for the Connolly Association with a huge Irish flag attached to the platform flying beside him. He made friends with many speakers from the colonies and would speak as a guest on their platforms.

The only one I can remember now was, I think, called the Nigerian Workers' Association. Bob felt strongly that the struggle for African and Irish self-rule was very much part of the same fight.

When speaking on these 'other' platforms, sooner or later someone in the audience would accuse him of being a Communist. This was one of his favourite heckles. He would turn the question round and ask, 'Well what is a Communist?' Usually the heckler would come up with a fairly inarticulate but very derogatory definition of a Communist. Bob would wait patiently for him to finish, and then say, 'No, I'm not one of those.' Then he would launch into what for him a Communist was.

Bob has a great sense of humour and will often do something just for the fun of it. I remember when Jimmy Carter launched his 'Entebbe-style' raid on Iran in an attempt to release the US hostages. As neither Stallone nor Schwarzenegger was on the mission it ended in fiasco, due I think to a helicopter breaking down. Because Iran bordered the Soviet Union, many people at the time worried that this was a provocative act that could have caused the Soviets to intervene and consequently lead to a great power confrontation. Bob mounted a lone demonstration outside the US Embassy in Grosvenor Square holding aloft a poster that said, 'World War III Postponed – Due to Technical Hitch.'

Neither Lola nor Bob had much idea about bringing up children. Both of them had been brought up under the supervision of nuns in Catholic orphanages. I sometimes wonder if this was coincidence or a reason for their marriage. Lola desperately wanted a little girl to dress up but we were both boys and troublesome ones at that.

Bob had no special language or register for children. Presumably this was because he had been forced to grow up so fast. He always talked to Julian and me as if we were adults. When he read stories to us at bedtime they were not children's books but whatever he happened to be reading for himself. Once he read *Alice in Wonderland* to us, but I think that this concession was only because it was a book that he enjoyed.

More likely we listened to the writings of authors like Maxim

Gorky. Often he would read things or use words that I could not understand but it didn't seem to matter. In fact I think it was good for us, stretching our imaginations. I know that I have always tried to be the same with my own and any other children that I have come into contact with.

We were left to our own devices much of the time. Bob had his work as a packer at the Book Centre as well as his political work, while Lola and Josefa worked in clothing sweatshops. We got ourselves up for school and our parents came home long after us. In the school holidays we roamed the streets and played in gangs on the many bombsites around us. There was an absence of supervision but also a freedom that no parents – including myself – would allow their children today. We were, like most of our school friends, 'latch-key children', quite wild and streetwise.

We easily outmanoeuvred our parents in their attempts at discipline. Once Lola in desperation at something we had done tried slapping us across our legs. This feeble attempt at corporal punishment was totally undermined by my father repeatedly saying, 'Don't hit them.' Bob was never one of the 'I was thrashed and it made me the man I am' school of child rearing. He remembered his own pain and humiliation at the hands of the Irish nuns too vividly.

In spite of his own treatment and harsh upbringing, Bob was a very gentle man. I can remember him trapping birds in the garden where we lived in Maida Vale. He would hold the tiny creatures carefully in his huge Irish navvy's hands for us to stroke and then let them fly away. Having spent so much time in the Irish countryside Bob had a great deal of country lore and knew how to catch animals. Some of my best memories are of trips to the country and learning from him.

These trips were usually combined with other activities. There were temporary barracks in Oxfordshire for the hundreds of Irish workers imported for the construction of the Harwell nuclear centre. Bob and comrades would sell the *Irish Democrat* to the workers as they left Mass. He and his friends would try to get public meetings going. Looking back on it, this seems to me a foolhardy if not provocative thing to do. Indeed once they had to flee for fear of a beating after a priest had denounced them from the pulpit.

Bob also used his knowledge of the countryside to put food on the table. I know that we were poor but we were not starving. I don't think that he really needed to go poaching; it was more for the crack at the expense of rich landowners and the establishment. He would go off with a friend from the Party like Alfie Bass who lived in a railway carriage in Reading or his brother Peter on the back of his motor bike, and return with trout or pheasants. The nearest thing we ever had to grace was when Bob would start the meal with a 'thank you to Lord So-and-So', or whoever's estate he had poached from.

Once Bob and Uncle Peter returned to the motorbike to find a policeman waiting for them. He told them that he had evidence that they were poaching; he had found feathers in the pannier bags. 'Feathers!' exploded Peter. 'There were four birds in there.' They were sent home with a warning. Bob was a clever poacher and although there were many stories of escapades and tight scrapes, he was never caught.

Singing was important in our family. My mother always sang Spanish songs as she did the housework. Bob could sing very well as a high tenor and held this part in the Communist Party choir conducted by Alan Bush. Lola also had a very good voice, much lower than Bob's, and they were often asked to sing at parties and socials. They sounded great together.

On Sunday mornings Julian and I would get into my parents' double bed, and we would all sing. They taught us Spanish popular and Civil War songs, Irish Republican songs, Russian partisan songs, Negro spirituals, suffragette songs, union songs from the USA, and folk songs from all over the world. Often the songs told of events or characters in what Bob called the struggle for 'progress' or 'the liberation of mankind'. These terms may seem quaint or even naive today but we sincerely believed in them; Bob still does, and the world would be a better place if there were more like him.

Sometimes the songs had a personal connection to my father. A song that we could never finish without tears in all our eyes was one he had learned from a fellow-prisoner in Spain. He was a young Spanish Republican, and although they were kept segregated from the International Brigaders, he and Bob had communicated through a pipe or hole in the floor. They never met or saw each other and their short friendship ended when the young man was shot.

Bob greatly admired Paul Robeson and he was very much our hero. He had met Robeson when he visited International Brigaders during the Spanish Civil War. He met him again on one of his visits to London just after the Second World War. The meeting was arranged at the last minute and Bob told me about it the next day. I was already asleep in bed and Bob told me that he had thought about waking me up so that I could also meet Paul Robeson but unfortunately decided that it was too late. I still feel the disappointment today.

We followed Paul Robeson's struggle with McCarthyism closely and of course learned all his songs. I remember sitting with Bob in St Pancras Town Hall during the time that Paul Robeson was not allowed to travel. He spoke to the packed meeting over an amplified transatlantic telephone call, technology defeating those who tried to restrict communication – a bit like the Internet today.

When Robeson was finally given his passport back and came to Britain, we went to the celebration rally at Trafalgar Square. I will never forget the reaction of all of us in the crowd when Paul Robeson said his first word of greeting. His incredibly deep and rich voice shook the square like the bass pipes of an organ shaking a church. We all burst out laughing and then cheering. This man of huge physical and moral stature was among us again. How sad it was that the rest of his life was short and dogged by ill-health. Was he poisoned? We may never know, but, unlikely as it seems, I will always be suspicious until the relevant and still secret files held by the US government are made public.

Bob instinctively hated racism. In the house we had books about the Holocaust with photographs that gave me nightmares. From a young age Julian and I were told of the East-End marches, and how many London Jews had gone to fight in Spain. We were taught that the Spanish Civil War, opposing Mosley and Hitler, racism and colonialism were all part of the same fight. As the post-war West Indian immigration got under way the focus of the racists changed. Bob would remind us of his time looking for digs when he first came to London, and the adverts that said, 'No Irish or dogs'. He made us aware that he and Lola were also immigrants.

Fascism had a bit of a revival with all this in the 1950s and Mosley appeared on the scene again, amazingly, just after the war. He had a big rally, at the Albert Hall I think, – I was just ten or twelve at the time – and Bob ran up onstage and grabbed the mike from Mosley and started haranguing them. Haranguing a hall that was full of Fascist supporters!

When the 1958 race riots broke out we lived close by Notting Hill in Paddington. The riots went on for several evenings with many white people on the streets jeering and threatening West Indians on their way home from work. Sometimes the threats turned to violence and beatings. Bob and I went out every evening, sometimes with friends, in his Ford Popular to pick up West Indians and drive them home, so that they did not have to walk through the dreadful streets.

When he saw a commotion, Bob, never afraid of physical confrontation in the right cause, would plunge in with me following nervously behind. He would pluck out the West Indian and get him into the protection of the car. Once he got himself bundled by the police into a Black Maria and was released only after I pleaded that he had been trying to help the victim.

It was sad to see the reactions of many West Indians. They were just ordinary people like ourselves but they sat in the back of the car bewildered and uncomprehending. They were severely shaken up. I don't think that it was just the shock of the violence but the crashing down of their whole world. These hard-working bus drivers and nurses had been fed and believed in concepts about the Mother Country and white paternalism but now they were meeting ugly racism face to face. Irish people like my father had no illusions about British Imperialism, an empire, as he taught us, maintained from Ireland to India by the policies of divide and rule.

The race riots were eventually stopped by a heavy police presence in the area. For the following Saturday, Bob organised an anti-racist march. Only about six people turned up, and three of these were my father, mother and I. We each carried a large placard – Bob's said 'No Little Rock Here' – and the police made us walk some twenty metres apart. I don't know the reason for this, but it meant each of us walked virtually alone. Feeling vulnerable and conscious of the hostility of the crowd, I had cause to reflect on the effectiveness of demonstrations and my father's activities as a way of changing society. I was beginning to see some of my beliefs as illusions.

For a long time it had been easy for me to dismiss much of the comment in the media as 'capitalist propaganda'. After all I could see for myself that the press was hardly objective. However, these were the rock-and-roll years and I too had bought 'Rock Around the Clock' and signed on for the youth revolution. Questioning received wisdom was very much a part of this. Things became quite strained between Bob and me. I could not understand why he and other respected Communist Party mentors reacted so defensively to my innocent questions.

The first question that I tried to get answered was why we were defending the obviously wrong theories of Lysenko as against those of Darwin? As I pushed my question up the party hierarchy, instead of an answer I found myself accused as a 'class traitor'. I was confused; after all, Communist theory was supposed to be scientific, not based on faith.

Events in Hungary, Nikita Khruschev's revelations of the abuses under Stalin, reading wider, discussions with old school friends who were now Young Socialists; all these contributed to the slow stripping away of childhood beliefs. I tried for a while to believe that it was just in Russia that things had gone wrong, but this idea went the way of the rest when the Communist leaders of the Electrical Trades Union – my union at the time – were found guilty of ballot-rigging. It was hard for me to acknowledge their cynicism.

I had a couple of heated rows with Bob over politics but these stopped after my mother told me how much they hurt him. We remained friends but we were no longer 'comrades in arms'. What was the point in arguing. He would never change – I thought.

In the late sixties I went to college as a mature student and adopted the drugs and music attitudes of the time. I lived with my family in the King's Road at the time of the swinging London scene. Bob would arrive on his motorbike at our Chelsea flat and join my college friends and myself smoking dope and listening to music. Bob was never a puritan and was always prepared to try anything. He would sit there saying, 'Should I be feeling something?' and 'This doesn't have any effect on me.' It went on for quite a while until one day he suddenly announced, 'This music is great, isn't it?'

After that there was no stopping him. He became a marijuana proselytiser and increasingly interested in the Green Movement and alternative life styles. He began growing organic vegetables on his allotment and recycling everything. He wrote letters to the local paper suggesting among other things that marijuana be made available to old-age pensioners on the National Health. Always an avid radio listener he would use phone-in programmes to spread the message. Bob of Neasden became a regular on some radio shows.

Already into gardening, he was very interested when I showed him my marijuana plants. Soon he was growing prize specimens in his green house. Enormous plants with stems like tree-trunks. He would gather huge harvests but was wise enough never to sell any and only give it away. Within the family and close friends this was fine but the trouble was he would give it to anyone that asked. He also could not resist bringing people to his greenhouse for them to admire his dense crop. Before long his activities were common knowledge in the neighbourhood. I warned him that this could only lead to one thing but it made no difference. I think that he wanted to get 'busted'. Always a rebel and a fighter, he wanted to confront the establishment as an old-age pensioner defending his right to use the least harmful of all drugs, the consolation of his old age!

What happened in the end was not what I had predicted. One year his greenhouse was broken into and his crop stolen. Lola hadn't minded his smoking it but at this she put her foot down and that was the end of his illegal gardening activities. (But not before the 'Stoned Christmas' when Lola and Josefa, who were curious about the others smoking this stuff, let Bob put some in the Christmas cake. Not just a few leaves, more like a small bag full. They thought since it was cooked in a proper cake, and they weren't actually smoking it, it'd be fine just to taste a bit. But they weren't fine when they ate it and poor Lola had to go and lie down before everyone started dinner.)

In spite of our political ups and downs, Bob often brought the texts of his speeches and articles for me to check. Working on these over a pint in the local, I began to realise that he had always had some doubts and differences with the Party. It was just that when under attack, he fell back on the Party line. I learned of a number of rows between him and the Party leadership and that he had always been selective about the issues that he would fight over. This he had not revealed to me or anyone else – except perhaps my mother – because of his notions of Party discipline and loyalty. He accepted the concept of 'democratic centralism' that effectively gagged criticism from within the party. But Bob's sense of humour and down-to-earth perspective always rubbed pompous Party and union officials the wrong way.

Once we needed a soldier in a film for Julian when he was a student, so Bob got made up as a wounded soldier with make-up blood, latex skin falling off, dust and cuts, even a fake bullet hole. When he'd finished he had to go to a union executive meeting down in Kings Cross. He changed his clothes but wouldn't take off the make-up. When he walked in, the whole lot were aghast – he'd do anything for a laugh, and yes, he loved the attention but they would have to throw him out at times. He was an idealist who just wouldn't shut up.

I helped him in his campaign to change ideas in the party and the print union of which he was an official. Neither of us could see the point in defending a situation in which hundreds of workers stood around doing mind-numbingly trivial tasks which could easily be handled by machines. Bob promoted a rational approach based on early retirement and retraining. He knew that defending restrictive practices had nothing to do with working-class progress. In fact he saw these practices as reactionary and corrupting.

As his son, I was entitled to join the union, and Bob got me a ticket. So for a while I worked in the print room and on the presses in Fleet Street. At first, because of Bob, I was popular with my workmates. They liked him because he was a thorn in the side of the union executive, and with his witty speeches he was a good turn at union meetings and conferences. But why, his workmates asked, was he wasting his time with resolutions on apartheid and nurses' pay? These workers actually did not want to see other workers improve their conditions, as it would devalue their own privileged position.

Their attitudes ranged from right-wing conservatism to outright Fascism. Of the hundreds of workers hanging around Fleet Street, earning more than an average week's pay for one night's work a week – if indeed it could be called 'work' – not one was a woman, never mind black. Not having my father's patience and tolerance, after a few flaming rows in the canteen, I gave up my union card and went back to work on building sites. How ironic that Bob should find himself in this union and obliged by the party to defend this absurd situation and these corrupt and selfish workers. His campaign for a rational approach had no success and when the crunch came, he was loyally on the picket lines at Wapping. While I had no liking for Rupert Murdoch, I thought that these were the very workers who had elected the Thatcher government and they deserved all that they got.

As I grew older I came to see my father in a different light. In spite of his Communist ideals, I understand now that he could never have carried out or condoned the inhuman policies of the Communist dictators. Early in his climb to power Stalin had to murder the very Communists who would have opposed him and who might have created a real alternative to the rampant corporate capitalism that dominates us all today. Bob would have been among the first to be shot. It was his hatred of human suffering that led him to be a Communist in the first place, and these feelings have always been above doctrine in his actual practice.

Late in his life, Bob was to make a *Video Diary* for the BBC. It was called appropriately enough, 'Rebel without a Pause'. In it there is a scene in which he talks to a Spanish Fascist who fought for Franco in the Civil War. The Fascist makes it clear that he approved of shooting of 'people like you'. A friend of mine once asked me, 'How can your father stay so calm and even talk to the man?' This is to have no real understanding of Bob. He is a real humanitarian who loves people. He would say of an individual, 'He's someone you can talk to,' and that for him was what counted. They may not think like him but that was because they were confused or misled, or perhaps they were even right. It was the fanatics, the ideologues, the arrogant, the self-righteous, and those who could not see beyond self-interest, with whom you could not have a civilised conversation who had to be opposed and, as a last resort, fought. A humanitarian yes, but Bob has never been a pacifist.

In spite of Bob and Lola's inexperience of family life, they didn't do a bad job. They may not have been perfect parents but they were a wonderful father and mother. Bob's total lack of arrogance and almost childlike openness meant that we all learned how to be parents and children together. Ultimately Bob and Lola's lives were not guided by doctrine or political correctness but by love, and so everything turned out OK in the end. I think that it was easy for Bob to relate to 1960s youth culture because he instinctively agreed that you can only change society by changing people, and you can only change people with love. It's all you need.

A FINAL WORD FROM THE MAN HIMSELF

I never feel old, I might feel less energetic physically now but I don't feel old in mind and that must keep you young. Maybe I'm an idealist. I don't see anything wrong in that. To me being an idealist means you're concerned about everything that is going on in the world. I know it sounds like a lot of bravado but before it gets to my time to depart, I want to make use of my time in doing something useful. My favourite quotation (from Nikolai Ostrovski, 1904–1936) is still:

> Man's dearest possession is life, and since it is given to him to live but once, he should so live as to have no torturing regrets so that when dying he can say, all my strength was given for the finest cause in the world, the liberation of mankind.

Hasta Siempre
Bob

NOTES

Kit Conway (p. 31)

Kit was an orphan, brought up with his brother in a Tipperary workhouse and hired out to a farmer near Burncourt in about 1910: youths worked two years for nothing, after that they might get a few shillings if kept on. He was popular and well read, especially in Irish history. When the First World War came he surprised everyone by joining the British Army in 1915, but quickly had second thoughts and got out of it by pretending to have gone mad, fooling officers and medical staff.

Back on the farm he joined the local IRA flying column in the War of Independence and fought well. When the Truce was signed he again surprised all by joining Collin's new Free State army while most of his colleagues were anti-Treaty. He was soon disillusioned but his previous escapade leaving the British army was too well known to be repeated, so he finally deserted and headed for Dublin where he rejoined the IRA until the Civil War ended in April 1923.

He then went to the USA, where he served in the National Guard, returning with the defeat of the Cumann na nGaedheal government by de Valera. Jobs were tough, pay bad. He was often unemployed yet full of humour and generous although firm, even grim, in politics. A socialist, he left the IRA with those who set up the Republican Congress and was instructor to their armed units. He was among the first to go to Spain when the Spanish Civil War broke out and proved a first-class soldier under fire.

The Economic War and the Depression (p. 41)

The Great Depression of the early 1930s was worldwide, but in Ireland its effects were worsened by the 'Economic War' with Britain, where Ireland sent 96 per cent of its exports. The value of these fell from £36 million in 1931 to £18 million within a few years, as British tariffs penalised them and prices for cattle and sheep collapsed.

This trade dispute was sparked by de Valera's policy of refusing to pay to London the annuities collected from Irish farmers as repayments for their land purchases under pre-Independence schemes. Many farmers couldn't pay during these hard times. Ironically de Valera hadn't chosen this policy on annuities. It had been foisted on him by Peadar O'Donnell, a left-wing Republican who was later among the founders of the Republican Congress.

De Valera's dispute with London was bankrupting the class of grazing farmers who were bedrock supporters of Cumann na nGaedheal, the party which Fianna

Fáil had replaced in government. The Depression also closed the safety valve of emigration, leaving young unemployed men hanging around, waiting for something to turn up. The Blueshirt movement emerged under the leadership of General Eoghan O'Duffy, the commissioner of police whom de Valera had sacked.

Bob's contemporary Eugene Downing, then in the fledgling Commmunist Party, felt that most of the working class were 'looking at Dev's policies through green glasses, supporting him on national rather than economic grounds. He was doing all the popular things with the support of small farmers too.'

The Outbreak of the Civil War and the Catholic Church (p. 44)
When the Spanish Republic was declared in 1931, the first liberal government had largely avoided the crisis of land reform, focusing instead on a new constitution with articles on religion which lost them the support of the peasants in Galicia, Castile and Navarre. Meanwhile Spain's colonial wars in Morocco had brought elements of brutality and aggression to overshadow politics, favouring the group of senior officers with African experience who planned the army revolt which sparked the Civil War.

Franco and his colleagues began by shooting fellow officera who refused to actively support them, then wiping out members of unions and parties supporting the government, often including Masons and even Protestants. The main conspirator, General Mola, sought to create 'exemplary terror' through ruthless bloodshed, in order to cow potential opposition.

Apart from Galicia, Navarre and Castile, which, together with the Moors, were to furnish Franco with his front-line Spanish forces throughout the war, the rising failed in mainland Spain. The reaction it provoked elsewhere was the very revolution which the generals' rising had been intended to prevent. While the Basque provinces were among the few areas unaffected by the bloodbath, in Republican zones, the Civil Guard and the priest were usually the first targets – many landlords and right-wing Party organisers, aware of the plot, had disappeared or were involved in the attempted military risings which had been crushed by ad hoc combinations of armed workers with loyal Assault Guards, and some army officers.

Before the Republican government restored control of arrests and executions, over 6800 religious were slaughtered, many in dramatic circumstances. In the uncertainty of Civil War, the French poet Claudel believed it was 16,000, although Franco's brother-in-law would claim 400,000 were killed. Speakers on public platforms in Ireland emphasised only the horrors on the Republican side, even creating vivid fantasies of 'nuns crucified' which added to public fervour for Franco.

Bob's sister-in-law Josefa had childhood memories of the outbreak of war in traditionally left-wing Asturias: a nearby village had two priests. One had spent his time hobnobbing with the wealthy and the landlords, the other did normal parish work for everyone, the first was killed and the second was left alone to carry on as usual. Irish priest Fr Mulrean remembered a Spanish colleague out reading his breviary on a country road one evening, when a labourer came up behind him with a scythe and lopped off his head. Stopped at checkpoints in besieged Madrid, Fr Mulrean had to show his passport. In those days it gave your trade or profession. The armed anarchist militia would read 'Priest,' and then reassure him 'Don't worry, father, you're Irish – this is just a Civil War.' Interviewed in 1983, Luis Buñuel recalled those Madrid days: 'I can still hear the old cry "Come down and see – there's a dead priest in the street."'

Though popular anger continued at the Church links with landlords, and its support for right-wing politicians, the aim of Republican authorities was to end mass killings, while General Franco on his side continued it as a policy driven from the top – even in the face of appeals by bishops and his own generals.

Among the first and the fiercest supporters of the military rising were the Carlists based in Navarre, royalists and smallholders with strong religious traditions. They fought in their own units, their banners reading '*Viva Cristo Rey*' and wearing religious emblems on the heart as '*détente balas*' (to ward off bullets). Had the Republic's constitution been less extreme in its religious clauses, their narrow majority vote against joining the Basques in supporting the Republic's reforms and autonomy might have been reversed, and their effect if they had fought against the military devastating.

From an early date, Franco's military conquest for landlords and a very primitive form of capitalism needed some fig leaf. He found it in traditional Catholicism, hence his welcome for O'Duffy's Irish volunteers who lent international credibility to his new role, claiming to protect the faithful.

The issue of religious persecution was used by right-wing media and supporters worldwide to deny recognition or support for the besieged Republic, by suggesting there were no social or class issues of poverty, of landless peasants and democratic rights involved. But 20,000 landowners held over half the land, while two million labourers worked barely half the year.

The Republican Congress and the War in Spain (p. 45)
At the Rathmines meeting Bob attended, the Congress had divided and failed to win trade union or wider public support. A hard core remained on, under strong attack from individuals using religious slogans and with Christian badges worn on blue shirts.

At first the Congress didn't campaign strongly for the Spanish Republic. This brought Charlie Donnelly back from London and at a heated meeting he demanded its support, despite Frank Ryan's insistence that it just didn't have the resources to fight the Franco tide. Frank agreed to send a telegram of support to the Republican government, which provoked Cardinal McRory to call for the Congress to be suppressed.

Frank responded publicly that the cable was one of support of sympathy and support for the Spanish, Catalan and Basque peoples in their fight against Fascism, and that 'as an Irish Catholic, I will take my religion from Rome but as an Irish Republican I will take my politics from neither Moscow nor Maynooth.'

No Irish Republican had forgotten the bishops' pastoral during the country's own Civil War fourteen years previously which condemned the Republican side: 'no one is justified in rebelling against the legitimate government...all those who in contravention of this teaching participate in such crimes are guilty of the gravest sins...we desire to impress on the people the duty of supporting the national government, whatever it is...'

The Cardinal's rebuke inspired the Congress to send out volunteers. Ryan and Gilmore organised the first eighty, including Bob's flatmate Kit Conway. They joined the 35,000 volunteers from fifty-three countries supporting the popular resistance to Franco in the International Brigades.

The Non-Intervention Policy (p. 46)

Although proposed by France, this policy was created in August 1936 by Britain. Early that month Britain told France that if France were attacked as a result of supplying the Spanish government, the British guarantee to support France would not operate. As British premier Chamberlain said in June 1937, 'Our policy has been consistently directed to one aim – to maintain the peace of Europe by confining the war to Spain.'

It was feared if the Republic won, the left would damage Anglo-French trade interests in Spain, while the Spanish generals seemed to stand for law and order and, it was believed, if Franco did win, he could be detached from his German and Italian allies by financial assistance. The pressure of these elements and the wish to confine the war to Spain, brought about the Non-Intervention Committee, where Germany and Italy were represented but not Spain. It prevented the Republic buying arms from other democracies, but had no significant effect on Italian or German supplies to Franco, which is what Britain intended.

In December 1936 Britain had to support a resolution in the League that Spain's situation was a breach of Article 10, and a similar one in 1937 adding that there were foreign army corps in Spain. The true nature of British 'non-intervention' was shown in January 1938 when Spain proposed acting on these resolutions. Lord Halifax voted 'No!'

The Labour Party went along with this defence of Tory business interests in favour of Fascism. The effect of this one-sided policy on the battlefield was critical, as one Franco officer said, 'What won the war for the nationalist army was its superior artillery and bombing capacity (both provided by Germany and Italy). You could almost say the Condor Legion won the war.'

Texas Oil provided Franco with unlimited oil supplies and British mining firms condoned Franco's exporting half of Spain's ore to Hitler at low prices. Spanish wolfram was a key ingredient of German tank armour during World War II.

At the start of the Spanish War, fear of a repeat of the 1914–18 slaughter was strong everywhere, especially in Germany, where Hitler had continually to reassure both the army and the public that he would not lead them into another war. The 1935-36 betrayal of Ethiopia had made dictators aware that the democracies weren't worried about small interventions. Spain proved they would tolerate German and Italian interventions however blatant, as long as the threat was directed elsewhere.

This led to continued hypocrisy by British politicians. Two decades earlier, the same British cliques had declared a blockade on the new Bolshevik government while supplying the White Russian forces which they were fighting, also in the name of 'not taking sides'. The historian Paul Preston quotes a Foreign Office official on Spanish non-intervention as 'an extremely useful piece of humbug'.

Thanks to Italian and German aircraft, the world's first airlift brought over 14,000 troops of the crack Army of Africa for the rebels in some eight weeks. Without the twenty Junkers 52 and nine Savoias, it would have taken nine months. France closed its Spanish border to arms supplies, without waiting to see what German and Italian intentions were, on 8 August.

The historian Helen Graham reckons Non-Intervention inflicted a disaster on the Republic at the start of the war: it forced their buyers on to an international black market for arms, of unreliable types and of uncertain calibres, at inflated prices and often unrelated to specifications. Much Soviet help wasn't made in the USSR but bought by them on the same highly priced black market. The first Soviet purchases arrived on 4 October. The entire Soviet manpower in the war was just 3,000.

Germany sent a complete battle group under General Sperrle known as the Condor Legion with their latest fighters, bombers, tanks and artillery. But Goering told Franco that fears of international repercussion meant a full regular division as such wouldn't be sent. Mussolini added two groups of three thousand Blackshirts each, with their own artillery and transport, which arrived in December and January, when their commander requested another 9,000. By mid-February 1937, there would be nearly 50,000 Italian regular troops and militia with Franco.

Franz Borkenau, who twice visited wartime Spain, considered the defeat of the Left was not by Franco but by German and Italian planes, tanks and artillery. Unlike earlier revolts, every revolution now was likely to meet the attack of the most modern, most efficient, most ruthless machinery yet in existence. 'It means the age of revolutions free to evolve according to their own laws is over.' The final issue of the fight would depend on foreign forces. If Franco won it would be a military dictatorship.

Did Chamberlain have any justification for his policies? In the eyes of the British establishment, he certainly had. They had just seen off the threat from organised labour in the 1926 general strike, and weren't too worried if Germany was 'saved from going red,' by someone who might not be the kind they'd invite to dinner but still did any unpleasant tasks that might need doing. Hitler's *Mein Kampf* had been published in English and made clear his intention of coming to terms with Britain, leaving her the role of overseas Aryan empire, while he took on mainland Europe.

From the point of view of 10 Downing Street, there were three great threats to the Empire emerging in the 1930s: Japan in the Far East, a re-arming Germany and finally Italy in the Mediterranean. They reckoned at best they could fight only two at any one time, making great efforts to avoid a conflict, placating Hitler, while encouraging Mussolini to maintain Italy's First World War alliance with them and France.

Italy was astride the vital routes to Suez and Britain's empire, and its oil, and also had conflicts of interest with Austria over provinces gained at the end of the last war, and then over its being reunited with Germany. But in the end, Mussolini like Hitler respected only strength. The total lack of determination from London fatally undermined French will to resist, and Spain, which might have proved the limits of Fascism, became one more victory for it.

Ireland was the exception: Chamberlain, on the very eve of war, negotiated a return of the vital Irish ports with de Valera, to ensure a friendly Irish Free State to Britain's rear, and in the hope of being allowed use them in time of war. Though Churchill remained bitter when they were denied, and thus lost the extra aircraft and naval mileage in the U-boat war, Britain's gain was enormous.

Not only did almost the entire resources of Ireland, north and south, now become available for Britain's wartime economy, but thousands in the south volunteered for her armed forces, including some seven thousand members from the ranks of the Irish Army, or like Bob for Britain's merchant navy. All this without Britain providing a single soldier or sailor to guard the Irish Free State, whose ships were now included among the British merchant fleet.

The Irish neutrality despised by Churchill also prevented Germany from attacking these economic resources and at moments like the Battle of Britain, when fighter numbers were stretched on both sides to breaking point, this lack of dispersal was of real significance. In his volume on the period, Robert Fisk wrote that many wartime British ministers realised that the Free State's benevolent neutrality was of more use than her participation in the war would have been.

Valencia and the Tory Sympathisers (p. 46)
When Madrid appeared to be about to fall to Franco, the government fled to Valencia. The city attracted foreigners who hung around claiming to be connected to the International Brigades if questioned. Unlike Madrid, food there was good and plentiful, with market prices that startled visitors from elsewhere. Englishman Chris Lance was smuggling out right-wing refugees from the port, one of whom was asked confidentially by a senior policeman to take out a letter addressed to Franco's chief-of-staff.

The British ambassador Sir Henry Chilton was very pro-Franco. 'I hope,' he told the American diplomat Bowers, 'that they send in enough Germans to finish the war.' Now based across the French border, he left John Leche, the chargé in Valencia, to be named Minister with the Republic. According to Lance, British officials at Valencia had smuggled out Spaniards in British naval uniforms.

Winston Churchill much later deplored Franco's coming victory, pointing out the illusions and misconceptions which had made well-to-do-society so prejudiced in Franco's favour, and saw with foreboding what this might mean for England. A Franco diplomat confirmed that the Duke of Alba, their agent in London, was given information on shipments of arms to Republican ports by an Admiralty officer.

Dubliner Joe Monks, fighting with the Republican forces down in Linares about this time, describes how the local British consul hung pictures of Hitler and Mussolini on the wall above his desk.

Paul Robeson (p. 57)

Paul Robeson, the first American black to become a true world celebrity, a fearless upholder of the dignity of all men and women, made a tour of the areas with International volunteers when he visited the Spanish Republic to support its fight for survival. Everywhere he went, often catching everyone by surprise, Robeson was immediately recognised by the troops. They had read about him, seen his films, heard his songs. Astonished to see him here in Spain, they crowded around his car whenever it stopped. Each time he sang without accompaniment, as the soldiers called out favourite songs.

At the International Brigade training quarters in Tarrazona, he was warmly welcomed by soldiers from a dozen countries; some five hundred men packed the church to hear him sing. When he arrived in Spain, he had stated: 'As a black I belonged to an oppressed race, discriminated against, one that could not live if Fascism triumphed in the world.'

Robeson brought back songs from the Civil War, which he sang at concerts. He reckoned his trip to Spain 'a major turning point in my life. I have never met such courage in a people. We must know that Spain is our front line…If we allow Republican Spain to suffer needlessly, we will ourselves suffer as deeply.' These were exactly Bob's sentiments.

In the post-war McCarthy era in the USA, he was summoned before the notorious House Committee on Un-American Activities, but far from being intimidated like many others, still less turning informer against old friends and colleagues, he roundly abused the committee for its unprincipled abuse of power, proudly declaring his solidarity with all who fought for democracy in Spain, and on the picket lines at home. Like the other veterans who heard Paul Robeson sing for them in Spain, Bob never forgot that experience.

Explosive Bullets (p. 59)

Jason Gurney, an earlier member of the battalion, described the enemy's high-expansion bullets, which exploded on impact with as much noise as a rifle being fired, and inflicted appalling wounds. The bullet was the same size as an ordinary one and was a super dumdum. It had a nickel alloy shell and at the point a slug of metal with a high coefficient of expansion, the rest filled with lead. The heat set up by the friction of impact caused the inner slug to expand more rapidly than the jacket so that the whole bullet exploded.

Belchite and Franco's Breakthrough (p. 60)

Bob's comrade, Carl Geiser, wrote of this battle: 'Artillery barrages on a one-hundred-kilometre front began Franco's drive to the sea to cut Republican Spain in two. Hundreds of aircraft bombed the front as 150,000 Fascist troops attacked 35,000 Republican defenders. They broke through in hours as defenders who stood and fought were killed or captured. The enemy tanks were running on fuel supplied by Texaco.'

The British were the last Republican unit through Belchite, which fell on 10 March. The anti-tank battery had to abandon its three 37mm Russian anti-tank guns there, and the crews joined infantry defending across the Lecera road. The British battalion never had an anti-tank unit again. The German tank corps under von Thoma was accompanied by thirty anti-tank companies with six 37mm guns each.

After the war Franco had the ruins of Belchite preserved, as a memorial to 'the horrors inflicted by the Red hordes'.

Bob's Group of Recruits (p. 60–1)

Bob's group of volunteers joined the recruits company at Tarrazona on 16 December. The battalion had over 480 members including the recruits, commanded by an ex-professional soldier in the US Army, Allan Johnson. Training took two months and the recruits were led by Lt Paddy O'Sullivan, an ex-IRA man like Bob. Laurie Lee was among the comrades who stood on the parade grounds in Tarrazona and Figueras. He was found to be unfit for military service and left Spain with an honourable discharge on 19 February 1938.

In Eugene Downing's view, Laurie Lee's memoir *A Moment of War* (1991) was: 'Absolute fantasy, a fine piece of writing and there's no way of checking up because he doesn't mention anyone's surname, they've all got nicknames, he doesn't tell you what unit he was in or who was his captain – he waited until everyone was dead practically. He's quite genuine but at the same time he created something in his own life that never happened. Now that it's in print, it's a history book!' So it might have been, except for Barry McLoughlin's discoveries, quoted above, from the Moscow archive.

Dubac survived and returned to New York, Michael Goodison from Salford was killed near the Ebro in April 1938, Jack Tomkins was wounded three times and finally repatriated with the remainder of the British Battalion in late 1938. The 'true red, white and blue' Fred Smith from Manchester was listed 'missing, believed killed' during the bloody retreats of April-May 1938. Seven were jailed for deserting and reached Britain with help from the British Consul or were readmitted to the Battalion just before it was repatriated.

Their worst record of indiscipline was that of an Irishman, Patrick Tighe. He was arrested at Figueras for insubordination, starting fights and drinking. He was put in detention at Albacete and sent to the labour battalion at Tarrazona. He deserted at the front in August 1938 and was still in detention when the brigades were dissolved. Repatriated with the British battalion, he was the holder of an award for bravery at Belchite.

The POUM (pp. 60–1)

The POUM (*Partido Obrero de Unificación Marxista:* United Workers' Marxist Party) were an independent Marxist force, rivalling the Soviet-backed Spanish Communist Party, in which George Orwell served. It was later crushed by the Republican government in fighting around Barcelona in May 1937, together with anarchist units.

The Role of the International Brigades (pp. 60–1)

The International Brigades, as some of the few disciplined units available to Republican commanders early in the war, were used as shock troops, to plug holes caused by enemy breakthroughs, which led to extremely high casualty rates. At Jarama the Battalion's 500 men had been reduced to 160 in three crucial days fighting, at Brunete only forty-two were left standing out of 300 at the start of that battle, and later their final action on the Ebro would see 377 men reduced to 173.

Even in 1937, when the armies of the Republic were several hundred thousand strong, they constituted a quarter of the army's shock troops. A Franco newspaper boasted at this time that Bob's Brigade had been destroyed, but it was restored to a battle-ready unit within the next two weeks.

The Press Association correspondent reported that Franco's centre column which took Alcañiz had two complete divisions of Italian 'volunteers' with 12,000 men each and a Foreign Legion division with soldiers from two élite Italian units, plus the First Navarre Brigade. The northern column was composed of Spanish and Moroccan regiments, the southern column was entirely Spanish. They totalled about 180,000 men in all.

US Ambassador Bowers told Washington that 'man to man, the Republic's army can hold its own, but when Franco's rebels are backed with the latest weapons on a huge scale, no army can stand against such odds. This was all due to the non-intervention scheme of the British which has tied the hands of France and the other democracies while not even pretending to enforce the agreement on the Fascist Powers.' (See also note, *The Non-Intervention Policy,* p. 213.)

Wally Tapsell (p. 64)

Wally was thirty-three, older than most, when he came out to Spain. He had been leader of the Young Communist League in Britain and later circulation manager of the Communist Party's *Daily Worker.* Claud Cockburn describes working there with Wally, on print-day a man half-crazy with worry and frustration, shouting about trains leaving and peering over his shoulder towards the leader-writer's room with a mix of rage and awe.

Payday was like a lottery with more players than prizes; there was rarely enough in the cash box on Friday to pay everyone full wages. So Wally, tough and humorous from the Elephant and Castle area of south London, shared it out on a kind of means test: anyone whose wife was expecting or had some urgent house repairs or financial crisis, got priority. He was a member of the SOGAT print union, which Bob would join after the Second World War.

After the fighting between the POUM and anarchist units against Republican government forces around Barcelona in May 1937, Wally was sent from Albacete to link up with the British group of the POUM in Barcelona as eight, including Eric Blair (George Orwell), indicated they wanted to join the international brigades. He met Jock McNair to discuss their joining the British battalion, but McNair failed to turn up for later meetings.

With the breakdown in communication and the losses during the battle of Brunete west of Madrid in July 1937, Wally found his role changed: commanding a group in the attacks on Mosquito Ridge. He took over as battalion commissar, and when the British had been reduced after six days intense fighting to less than a hundred men in two groups he took command of one and organised a fighting withdrawal that brought other Spanish units to link up.

Just forty-two men of the brigade's 300 were left standing at the end. When ordered to return to the front, Wally loudly protested that the forty-two were too exhausted and it was left to others to order them back. Arrested for questioning the ability of other units, he was one of four sent back to England but allowed to return. In October 1937 he became Battalion commissar again.

Following the visit of Clement Attlee, the leader of the Labour Party, to the battalion, Wally organised a sports fiesta, including a bomb-throwing competition. When he was in charge of food in the front line, meals were delivered by a grub party sent by each company to collect their food, reheat it at a given spot on the way back and finally deliver it to the hungry front line. They often came back well fed, but without enough food for every one else. Poor Tappy tore his hair out over this old soldier's trick.

In the extreme cold of the winter fighting at Teruel, he was commended by the Fifth army corps. While the remnants of the units were in the trenches, a simple board was fixed at night on the hill overlooking the valley, commemorating their dead British comrades whose bodies couldn't be recovered. The Brigaders moved stealthily by starlight. The Fascists were too close for singing and Wally began softly to recite the 'International' but broke down in a smothered sob.

Merry del Val (p. 70)

Alfonso Merry del Val was the son of a Spanish ambassador in London, where he and his brother were entertained by the Countess of Fingall: 'so good looking and charming, the family was of Irish descent'. He was denounced in Spain's parliament for his role in the murder of a young socialist woman, Juanita Rico, in June 1934,, using his own car in the pre-war death squad of the Fascist *Falange de Sangre*. The murder and that of another socialist were covered up by the right-wing Minister of the Interior at the time.

Reporters and the War in Spain (p. 70)

When Mussolini's crack units were leading attacks on Guadalajara, north of Madrid, the foreign correspondents reporting this from Madrid found their reports censored by their editors back home – the fiction of non-intervention had to be maintained. US reporter Herbert Mathews was told, 'Don't always speak of Italians; you and the Bolshevik papers are the only ones who use that propaganda tag.' Only when Mathews threatened to resign did *The New York Times* agree to let him name the Italian forces. It was found later that most other British, American and French papers changed the 'Italian tanks (or infantry)' to 'nationalist forces' to eliminate the awkward evidence of direct Fascist intervention in the attack. When the Italians were then defeated at Guadalajara, the hundreds of Italian prisoners and thousands of military documents made for a Republican media coup.

The *Daily Mail, Sketch* and *Observer* printed no news that did not discredit 'the Reds', the *News Chronicle* was just as one-sided for the Republicans, *The Times* decided not to print articles by its military correspondent, who pointed out the extreme danger to Britain of a pro-Fascist Spain, reporting this as the first campaign in the coming war. The *Telegraph* was relatively impartial. Filmed commentaries like *England Expects* that showed the bombing of British ships were banned for revealing the danger of war.

The 'Army of Africa' and Franco's Moors (p. 72)

When the war began, Franco had the 'Army of Africa', the only experienced Spanish troops: 5,000 Spaniards in the Foreign Legion, 9,000 Moorish Regulares and 8,000 Auxiliares. Once the rising on the mainland had failed to take over most of the country, his forces became the shock troops for reconquering Republican Spain.

Recruitment stressed the common fight against 'godless unbelievers'. The main impetus was poverty and unemployment. They earned 50 per cent more than normal recruits during the war. Morocco's harvest that year was bad, and work and food were scarce. Many were simply forced into trucks by local chiefs and sent to the ports. By the spring of 1937 over 35,000 Moors had crossed to Spain,the number reaching 75,000 by war's end. The total recruitment was equivalent to one tenth of the local population. Casualties averaged 1,000 a month, with about 11,000 dead by the war's end.

The sole experience of war of Franco's rebel officers was their colonial war in Morocco. In 1936 the 'disaffected tribes' to be crushed were left-wing elements and parties, trade unions and peasants.

These colonial forces used mobile columns which easily outflanked and outgunned the raw militia facing them in the south and west of Spain. Then they practised their usual 'cleansing' to ensure order. Troops were normally granted the first hour in a captured town to scour for loot (Singer sewing machines were prized) and women. Lorry loads of Regulares and Legionnaires would collect and execute suspects then move on, leaving a devastated population behind. Franco's propaganda staff saw countless dead Republican sympathisers at the outskirts of villages and towns, cemetery walls pock-marked by the executioners' bullets. One of Franco's press officers told a US newsman that 'cleansing' exterminated one third of the males, thus purging the proletariat and eliminating the problem of unemployment.

Franco wrote to General Mola of the need to destroy all resistance in 'the occupied zone', a slip which contradicted his official line, that they were liberating Spain from Marxists. When his army took Badajoz on 14 August, where they suffered their first heavy losses, there was an immediate uncontrolled massacre of the wounded, and over the following days of suspected Republican sympathisers of either sex in the town's bullring.

Colonel Yagüe at first denied that so many had been killed, but later declared, 'Of course we shot them. Was I supposed to take 4,000 prisoners with me as the column advanced?' Such brutality was a normal part of their colonial warfare.

From the siege of Badajoz in August 1936, Army of Africa casualties rose sharply and recruitment of Moors intensified. US journalist John Whitaker said it was never denied that the Moors had been promised white women when they got into Madrid. One officer, El Mizzian, met him at a crossroads near Navalcarnero, on the outskirts of the city, as two young girls were brought in. After questioning, he brought them into a small building where forty Moorish soldiers were resting. As they reached the door a deep howling came from the troops, and El Mizzian told the horrified Whitaker, 'Oh, they won't live more than another four hours.'

Failure to storm the militia lines in the streets of Madrid changed their tactics: they suffered huge casualties in conditions similar to the First World War's trenches, as Russian tanks and aircraft matched their Italian and German ones. Their lack of any idea of modern warfare hampered Franco's advance, while greater efforts were needed to find replacement troops in Morocco. This failure at Madrid caused a collapse of morale. Yagüe and Varela told the German observer von Stunk they they were finished. Von Stunk then persuaded Hitler to send emergency reinforcements. The combined German and Italian aid came just in time to save them.

The next attempt to cut off Madrid led to the battle of Jarama where the Republican forces, including the International Brigades, fought the colonial army to a standstill. The Moors' use of knives caused terror: Republican forces dreaded being caught by them. An eyewitness in the International Brigades saw them coldly work slowly with their long triangular knives, stabbing the wounded in chest and stomach, unmoved by the cries of fallen Frenchmen. Returning, they'd exhibit testicles of castrated enemy dead.

Jason Gurney with the British battalion remembered the Moors as the scruffiest soldiers he'd ever seen, covered with a poncho blanket and rope-soled shoes, ideal for skipping on the slippery hillsides. It was terrifying to watch their ability to exploit the slightest fold in the ground for cover and make themselves invisible. They popped up briefly all over the place, too quickly for anyone to get a shot at them, ferocious bundles suddenly appearing out of the ground near you, backed by German artillery and machine guns. But they failed to break through. From then on, like the Brigades, they were used as shock troops and to plug holes in emergencies.

The Spanish Bishops and the War (p. 77)

The first battle between church leaders and the Republic predated the Civil War, when the primate Cardinal Segura was expelled from Spain, after the first churches were burnt in Madrid in 1931. This caused a rift between most Catholics and Republicans which widened with events. The second was over Article 26 of the Republican constitution, as liberal ministers concentrated on religion instead of land reform and the desperate plight of rural labourers, which they considered secondary issues. This constitution was not accepted by the entire country. Spain moved into a phase of each government revoking the policies of the previous one until the outbreak of the Civil War. Then the idea of a crusade was launched by Plá y Deniel, the bishop of Salamanca, although the honour of first proclaiming religious motivations for Franco's cause went to the Moslem chief of Spanish Morocco, Muley Hassan, declaring holy war as his men sailed for Spain.

The switch of emphasis to Christian motives greatly increased support abroad, although the Basques, roughly a third of practising Catholics in Spain, were with the Republic. The Basque leader, Aguirre, never hid his people's faith as Republicans: 'We are faced with Fascism and imperialism on account of our Christian spirit… we assure you that we do not fear social progress.' He wanted 'a poor church preaching real Christianity which identifies with Spain's humble people' and admired the Irish people's Catholicism.

After the outcry caused by the bombing of Guernica, at Franco's request Cardinal Gomá drafted the 'Letter to the Bishops of the World' which denied that the war was a crusade but called it an 'armed plebiscite' to save the 'principles of religon', as Communism had enabled a revolutionary militia to seize power. It denied that any class or social issues were at stake and ignored repression by Franco's side. Its effect on international opinion was said to have been worth more than the capture of Bilbao.

Forty-three bishops signed it; six did not: the bishop of Menorca was elderly, blind and under Republican control; Cardinal Segura, expelled in 1931, was in Rome and was never asked to sign it; and the Bishop of Alicante, a Basque, was living in England. Bishop Múgica of Vitoria refused (he never forgot that Franco had shot his priests). The other Spanish cardinal, Cardinal Vidal i Barraquer, was to pay for his refusal to support Franco by being exiled for life. Finally Bishop Guitart of Urgel, who was close to Vidal, refused for some time to sign the letter.

Vidal i Barraquer defended the use of Catalan by his clergy, and said that the church should never allow itself to be used by one side, however praiseworthy, that people should choose their politics themselves. He foresaw a religion of public ceremonies, processions, funerals for 'our glorious dead', mixing propaganda with the Mass: an external worship as a political reaction, with short spiritual effects, which risked arousing the hatred of the conquered.

A Catholic deputy who helped plan the rising felt that the Church's failure to denounce the crimes of the Right and its leaders' acceptance of Franco's repression and generous state benefits had betrayed him: 'We had to discover God for ourselves.'

Cardinal Gomá saw his post-war pastoral appealing for social justice and forgiveness for the defeated, banned by Franco. Shortly before he died, Gomá admitted privately that in the question of the bishops response to the war, Vidal was 'the only one with vision'.

When Gerald Brenan visited Spain ten years later, he found a church divided between many displays of public devotion and splendour, with just a few bishops and nuns of charitable orders who followed 'the path of St Francis'.

Thirty-five years after the war began, the 1971 Spanish bishops' conference voted 137–78 for a statement 'humbly recognising and asking pardon, for failing to be truly ministers of reconciliation amongst our people, divided by war between brothers.'

The Sudeten Germans and the Munich Agreement (p. 83)

Hitler had occupied Austria in March 1938 and claimed the Sudetenland, the Czech borders, with their German populations, strategic natural defences and fortifications in May, but a strong Czech stand, supported by France, Britain and Russia, forced him to back down. However, British appeasers did not want Russia as an ally; they preferred to turn Hitler loose. They sent an uninvited mission under Lord Runciman to recommend handing over what Hitler assured the world was 'the last territorial claim I have to make in Europe'. A loan of a billion pounds was to be raised in London to help Anglo-German co-operation. The Czechs were to relinquish their border defences and renounce the treaty with Russia; what remained of the Czech state would be guaranteed by Britain and France.

The Czechs had one day to accept; if a refusal caused a German attack, Britain and France would stand aside. Then Hitler raised the stakes: British plans would take too long, German troops must move in at once. Chamberlain, Mussolini, French premier Daladier and Hitler met to settle this at Munich on 30 September 1938. They agreed to allow Hitler to take the Sudeten. The following March he went on to take the rest of Czechoslovakia. Chamberlain returned claiming that he gained 'Peace for our time. Go home and get a nice quiet sleep' and that he had an interval to re-arm, although allowing no acceleration that might provoke Hitler. Churchill pointed out that this had robbed the allies of twenty-one regular divisions and the Skoda works, whose arms output was almost equal to all of Britain's, and whose weapons had proved among the best in Spain.

The Czechs were not allowed to attend the Munich conference that decided their fate, just as Spain had been excluded from the Non-Intervention Committee. They believed like the Spanish that it was better to die on your feet than live on your knees and had mobilised their army. Though geographically isolated and at Germany's mercy, the Czechs were resolute in facing certain war. Prague was filled with people demanding resistance to Hitler, but when France and Britain informed President Benes that they would no longer support the Czechs. When the news got out, women wept, men stood with set silent faces, cars with GB plates were jeered with the word 'Chamberlain' by a stunned grief-stricken population mourning their nation. Their war had been lost without them being allowed to fight.

Munich proved to Germany that nothing Germany did in Spain would now risk British or French action, and the effect on the Spanish War was decisive. Hitler and Franco made a massive 'ore for weapons' deal: Spanish mineral rights were exchanged for German arms and a major new offensive began almost immediately after the Republic had exhausted its supplies in the battle of the Ebro. In a few weeks Franco and his foreign allies captured Barcelona.

After Hitler took Prague, Britain guaranteed Poland, a country with no natural defences and an outdated army, isolated from any French or British help to the west and without any defence agreement with Russia to the east. Britain and France now risked war against Germany, in the weakest possible conditions. Munich meant that Bob's anti-Fascist Sudeten comrades and thousands like them had been handed over to Hitler without their consent. Chamberlain's 'peace' cost lives, but elsewhere.

John O'Beirne (p. 87)

John O'Beirne, known as 'the guy who jumped through the drum' among Sinn Féin supporters, disrupted a British Army recruitment parade through his home town of Balbriggan during the First World War. An IRA volunteer during the War of Independence, he climbed the town's mill chimney one night and hung the illegal Irish flag from the top. The British Army couldn't believe anyone could have climbed it. They had to shoot it down.

After the Truce he emigrated to the USA where he helped train Palestinians in guerrilla warfare (they were then rebelling against the British administering Palestine) before joining the American volunteers coming to Spain. He never took out an American passport, so he wasn't eligible for repatriation to the US and went back to Ireland, bringing his strong sense of equality, and a love of Jazz and Negro spirituals, especially the songs of Paul Robeson.

He rarely spoke of the war even to his family but had recurring nightmares of the time before being captured when he was hiding in a cupboard and searching Moors killed a comrade hiding in the same room. His favourite Spanish phrase became a family saying: '*Muchas mañanas, sí sí camaradas.*'

Guernica (p. 89)

The ancient Basque capital of Guernica was the third urban area of the Republic to be terror-bombed, but the scale was much greater than at Durango on 31 March 1937, and Ochandiano days later. On Monday 26 April, a local market day, German and Italian planes began bombing from 4.40pm until 7.45pm. The town had no anti-aircraft defences, and was wiped out in these three hours by the Condor Legion and Italian Aviazione Legionaria under Richthofen, a cousin of the Red Baron of 1914-18 fame.

People who tried to flee were machine-gunned by low flying aircraft. High explosive, then incendiary bombs were used in patterns to maximise destruction. This was the world's first open town to be destroyed from the air. A survivor, Maria Goitia, said, 'At 4pm when the crowd was busiest, a plane came and dropped a few bombs, causing the first victims. People fled from the market to hide in houses. New planes then appeared and bombed the houses and churches. People were dying under the ruins of demolished houses, which were burning from the incendiary bombs.

'People had to run from the houses. Then they were machine-gunned…many were burned alive under the ruins…they were running across the fields trying to escape the bullets that continued to pursue them…at 8pm it grew dark and the planes left; Guernica by then was a terrible bonfire.' There were over 1,600 killed, nearly 900 injured.

'And to think that we shall be blamed for this,' said Sr Epalza to Dr Junot, Swiss Red Cross representative, as they walked through the burning ruins hours later. 'No, said Junot, 'that's impossible.

'You don't know the enemy we face,' replied Epalza.

Within 24 hours Franco's HQ was denying the role of their forces, Radio Salamanca claiming there were no German or Italian aircraft in Franco Spain. Franco's side then blamed 'the Reds'.

This controversy made Guernica a symbol of the horrors of modern war, inspiring Picasso's great painting. It was a propaganda disaster for Franco: there had been three British reporters and a Belgian nearby, who with Fr Onaindía, dean of Valladolid cathedral, gave internationally reported accounts. On 18 July 1938, Franco celebrated the second anniversary of his rebellion with a speech where he declared that the destroyers of Guernica had lost the right to call themselves Spaniards. Bob and his comrades supported Franco entirely on this point.

Confession for Execution (p. 90)

At the time of the famous bishops' pastoral of July 1937, Cardinal Gomá claimed that 'on dying, condemned by law, the immense majority of our Communists reconciled themselves with the God of their fathers: in Majorca only 2 per cent died impenitent, in the south no more than 20 per cent, and in the north it probably didn't reach 10 per cent. This is proof of the confidence trick which our people have been victims of.'

Bishop Miralles felt satisfied at being able to say 'just 10 per cent of these beloved sons of ours refused the sacraments before being shot by our good officers.'

A Spanish theologian published advice on the question – not the killing, but on annointing the condemned: the sacrament was reserved for the sick who were at the point of death, the condemned weren't sick, but they certainly were at the point of death. To avoid doubt, 'one should be generous and give it conditionally, the best moment would thus be after the squad had fired, and before the officer gives the coup de grâce.'

Irish Church Aid (p. 93)

Of the £43,300 sterling collected for 'Spain at this moment fighting the battle of Christendom against the subversive powers of Communism' by the Irish Catholic church 'for the relief of her suffering Catholics' only £32,000 reached Franco's army, who spent it on weapons, not medical supplies. Spanish sources appear to have no information on the missing £11,300. O'Duffy's Brigade lent credibility to Franco's claim to be defending religion, and not merely landlords and Fascists. The atmosphere which encouraged them can be gauged from James Dillon, a future Fine Gael leader, speaking to the Dáil: 'We want the pinks and the semi-reds and the muddleheads in this country to understand that there is no use wobbling at this stage…Your sympathies must be on one side or the other…the issue in Spain, the fundamental issue, is God or no God.'

O'Duffy's recruitment office at 12 Pearse Street was in the same area where Bob believed the Animal Gang had a HQ. They had suffered seven dead, about one per cent, and a similar number agreed to stay on as volunteers in the Foreign Legion when O'Duffy withdrew his men. Frank Ryan and one of their chaplains, Fr Mulrean, independently gave similar opinions of the rank and file of this unit – 90 per cent were decent Irishmen.

As the Dust Settled in Spain (p. 94))

The refugees in France from the collapse of the Spanish Republic were meanwhile interned behind barbed wire in mass prison camps, guarded by colonial troops, but their horrors were not allowed to appear in the Tory papers, to avoid damage to Britain's relations with France. When Mussolini was told of Italian Republicans captured, he replied: 'Let them all be shot. Dead men tell no tales.'

Britain made sure the Royal Navy didn't help Republicans to flee, as the navy had done earlier for right-wingers on its own account: their diplomats in Valencia channelled refugees down to Alicante with vague promises. The last desperate thousands were trapped there on the docks, still awaiting ships that would never arrive, when Franco took over the city.

'As the dust settled,' Robert Graves and Alan Hodge wrote in *The Long Weekend*, their social history of the period 1918–1939, 'British military opinion, and Conservatives generally, saw Franco's conquest as "a triumph for professional armies over an undisciplined Red rabble, not as the victory of a rather clumsily handled mechanized army, supported by inferior infantry, over superior infantry with no air or artillery support worth mentioning.'"

Only Mexico and the USSR had provided significant aid to the besieged Republic. An American assistant Secretary of State, Sumner Welles, wrote: 'Of all our blind isolationist policies, the most disastrous was our attitude on the Spanish Civil War', which he felt was 'the worst error in Roosevelt's foreign policy'.

Claud Cockburn, the *Irish Times* columnist who fought there in the first days, said his generation saw Spain as the decisive point of the twentieth century, when your actions have to follow your words, a moment of truth: it proved that when some talked of dying for a cause, they meant it. It was where democracy was going to have to stand up to the enemy or else take a terrible beating, after which there would be a bigger and worse war.

The Phoney War (p. 95)

The name given to the period from the declaration of war by Britain and France on Germany in September 1939, until the German Blitzkrieg which overran the west in May 1940. During the first four weeks, Germany was left free to conquer Poland while France, which had promised Poland to launch attacks in 3–4 days with 'the strongest army in the world' and was facing only twenty-three German divisions, did nothing. The first British casualty on the front was a corporal shot on patrol – on 9 December.

Just before the May Blitzkrieg began in the west, Chamberlain announced his view of Hitler's strategy: 'One thing is certain: he missed the bus.' French General Bilotte felt: 'Nothing will happen before 1941', and his colleague General Gamelin stated: 'We are not Poles. It could not happen here.' At the post-war trials in Nuremburg, German generals said, as they only had a military screen, not a real defence, they'd expected but could not prevent an allied attack across the Rhine, threatening the decisive area for the German war effort in the Rhur. They considered that the failure of France and Britain to attack them in the west during their Polish campaign had lost the allies their golden opportunity.

The Battle of the Channel (p. 100)

War correspondent Vincent Sheean watched events from land: the air attacks seemed very successful; the navy had to cease using Dover port after 3 August 1940. Off Deal the masts of sunken ships dotted the waters. The huge port of London became of secondary importance. The Stuka was the main instrument in attacks and was deadly accurate. The Battle of the Channel, a preparation for the Battle of Britain, was a German victory. Like Bob, he had first seen the Stuka used over Republican trenches and retreating troops in Spain, and in 1940 it could deceive the British anti-aircraft gun predictors almost with impunity.

Communazi (p. 101)

Bob's sense of his comrades' suspicions was not just because he'd fought against Fascism in Spain, but that since the Munich Agreement, which betrayed Czechoslovakia to Hitler, Moscow was abandoning its policy of promoting alliances with France and Britain. 'One might think that the districts of Czechoslovakia were yielded to Germany as the prize for her undertaking a war against the Soviet Union,' Stalin said a few months after Munich.

Seeking to protect the Soviet Union itself, although trying to negotiate with Anglo-French delegations, Stalin also accepted a German delegation. The Germans were eager for agreement in order to free themselves for an attack on Poland. Meanwhile the allies continued to prevaricate, and in August 1939 they were surprised by the Nazi-Soviet Pact of Non-Aggression. This was Hitler's master-stroke: the right-wingers in Britain and France who never wanted to fight him now saw their left-wing opponents demoralised, with local Communists obliged to support this sudden alliance. Once war began, British Communists were considered unreliable until Hitler attacked Russia in June 1941.

While Frank Ryan in his cell in Burgos condemned the pact, Eugene Downing felt Stalin had long been trying to get a pact with the West and couldn't do it, although he was later shocked by Molotov's congratulations to the German army when they overthrew French democracy. But he remembered how 'it all came right when Russia was attacked', the Party's terrific enthusiasm in favour of the war. They were delighted and felt at ease at last. They had made themselves right with the working class in Britain.

The Free French under de Gaulle recruited many Spanish Republicans, unlike wartime Britain and America (who labelled them 'premature anti-Fascists'). Among the first tanks in Leclerc's division liberating Paris in 1944 were those with the names 'Madrid', 'Guernica' and 'Teruel'.

'Estraperlo' (p. 120)

The *estraperlo* was a pre-war scandal. Promoters of a new roulette wheel, which could be controlled to avoid wins by punters, were allowed set them up in prominent casinos by the right-wing Partido Radical but revealed this after their crooked wheels had later been banned and they were refused compensation. The first syllables of their names, **Stra**uss and **Per**lowitz, went into this word symbolising the widespread corruption in the final years of Spain's monarchy and the Radicals' government of 1934-36.

Hardship in Post-War Spain (p. 120)

Gerald Brenan revisited Spain in 1949. He reckoned the only thriving industry was the *estraperlo*, while the controls served to keep up the black-market prices.

It was assumed the ministers who imposed controls were paid by racketeers. Franco's motto then was 'Bread and Justice' and people said, 'We've seen his justice and don't like it – but where's his bread?'

Wages were too low for officials to be honest. Black-market bread cost 12 pesetas a kilo, a day's wage. Even barley coffee was on the list; people roasted it at 2 or 3 am so the smell wouldn't be detected, then hawked it around on bikes or handcarts.

In Lucena in Andalucía, Brenan found the streets filled with gaunt dejected men, standing silent against the walls and staring in front of them. There were crowds bargaining for shreds of fish or vegetables sold off cheap when they were no longer fresh, swarms of children pestering women dressed in rags and caked in dirt with emaciated babies.

The streets of Córdoba had children of ten with wizened faces, women of thirty already old wearing frowns of anxiety from constant hunger and uncertainty. He had never seen such misery before, even among beggars in Morocco. The symbols of the regime were the Civil Guards and the *Estraperlista*.

Franco's ignorance of economics and disastrous plans for self-sufficiency caused the continued hardship. Spain's economy, ravaged by war, was supposed to substitute imports, increase exports, rely on their own raw materials and do it all without free trade or loans.

Visitors in the late 1940s saw harvesting done by hand on the central meseta. Families had to prop up the elderly who collapsed in the heat against cornstacks, and the rest continued with their sickles, bent under the sun, as in medieval times.

The Second Inquisition (p. 125)

General Mola began the war with a deliberate policy of public bloodshed to intimidate opposition but became shocked at the continuing killings, while Franco, who took over leadership of the rising, made sure they remained as a deliberate weeding out of left-wing, separatist or democratic elements.

Once prisoners were taken by Franco forces, their names were publicly displayed in his recruiting offices, allowing them to be denounced or accused of 'armed rebellion', membership of a trade union or a banned political party. Spain was viewed as two separate populations, the good and the bad – the enemy included those who were neutral; their crime was 'non-rebellion'. To avoid the firing squad, captured officers and commissars had to have gotten rid of badges of rank, which were as good as a death sentence.

At concentration camps systematic 'cleansing' began with those who had already been accused before being captured. The remainder were placed in labour battalions, but if news arrived from their home areas of anything damaging they had done or said since 1934, their files were re-opened. Zealous fact-finders in the Fascist party were used to build the cases for summary court martials. Over 700,000 prisoners went through the 'cleansing'. Half of Spain was involved in this Nazi-style process, on one side or the other, with waves of accusations, often false.

Apart from the frequent unofficial killings by Fascist death squads, there were over 192,000 death sentences passed between 1939 and 1944. In July of 1939,

Madrid had between 200 and 250 executions daily, Barcelona 150, Seville 80, all of people being tried speedily in summary tribunals. On his 1940 visit, Himmler was shocked at the scale of post-war repression. The official bulletin recording executions didn't resume publication until 1947.

The Spanish Inquisition had ended barely a century earlier after 350 years. Like Franco it overrode resistance of local authorities and the rights of regional assemblies. Franco ruthlessly suppressed the Republic's autonomous regions and languages. He saw the army as the modern enforcer of national unity.

Both agencies ordered lay people to inform on others, seeking anonymous denunciations and allowing nobody to be neutral. Franco even set up prison camps in post-war Spain solely for clergy who offended his regime. The policy of leaving bodies of those shot at the side of roads, and the orders for 'exemplary punishments' recalled a member of the Inquisition who declared that autos-da-fé were 'for the public good and to strike terror into people'.

Franco's regime considered you guilty until you could prove otherwise, while the Inquisition began your trial only because it had already concluded you were a heretic. Both arranged that afterwards you were 'reconciled' to God by clergy acting in coordination with your executioners. Just as the Inquisition had done, Franco threatened those who persisted in opposing him that 'there [would] be no pardon' and demanded 'blind faith' in his cause'.

He told US correspondent Jay Allen, 'There can be no compromise, no truce...I shall save Spain from Marxism at whatever cost.'

'That means you will have to shoot half of Spain?'

At which a smiling Franco said, 'I repeat, at whatever cost.' After the fall of Barcelona he declared there could be no amnesty for defeated Republicans – only punishment and repentance would open the way to their redemption. He disliked Italian ideas on gaining a quick victory. 'I must not conquer but liberate, and liberating also means redeeming. The only possible solution (to the war) is the absolute victory of pure and eternal principles over bastard anti-Spanish ideology.'

His 'Law of Responsibilities' was promulgated just as the war as about to end. It classed wide areas of normal public life as criminal, and those who took part in them became guilty retrospectively. Special tribunals were set up, with positions as judges reserved for victims of acts of violence by Republicans or their next of kin – in other words, those least likely to be objective and most desiring vengeance.

It was estimated that two million passed through his prisons and concentration camps by 1942. When the war ended Faustina García was denounced by her employer, who wanted revenge on someone for her own husband's execution by Republicans. In her prison there was one toilet for 600 women. They slept on the ground, and endured five days in August without water. She was sentenced to twelve years by court martial although she was never involved in politics or trade unions.

She witnessed a woman with lungs crushed, one with her toenails pulled out, another with electric shocks to her breasts, an eighteen-year-old who'd been repeatedly raped. There were many similar accounts of prison: hunger, cold and misery for the thousands who voted for the wrong party or whose names were on the wrong membership lists or who were maliciously denounced.

The dictatorship took the children of left-wing families and had them brought up in convents. Emilia Girón's child was taken away for baptism in 1941 and never returned. As a member of a Communist family she was 'unfit to rear him'. Even today researchers can't find out how many children were legally kidnapped. The children of Republicans executed by Franco's firing squads were taken over by the state. Children returning after the war were sent for adoption and separated. One woman was told by nuns her sister 'must have been thrown from the train' and did not find her until sixty years later after an appeal on television. Many names were changed in the registers. Some were given to safe families and never knew they were adopted, in a systematic campaign to eliminate future opposition.

As Franco told Faupel, Hitler's emissary during the war, a negotiated peace with free elections would have meant a government of the left and the end of White Spain. They'd 'rather die than place Spain in the hands of a democratic government.' An idealistic Falangist, Ridruejo, said later that 80 per cent of those being executed in the rearguard were workers. The repression was aimed at decimating the working class, destroying its power. It was a class war.

During the final year of the war, Republican premier Negrín insisted that continuing it would cost fewer lives than surrendering. He was right: as historian Gabriel Jackson later estimated, Franco's side executed perhaps ten times as many as the Republic, 200,000 to 20,000 between 1936 and 1944. In 1938 Franco boasted that he had a list of two million 'Reds' to be punished, once claiming he'd enough victims to last him ten years.

At the war's end senior officers and political forces in Madrid, who believed Negrín was refusing to negotiate peace with Franco, led a successful coup. Like Negrín, they discovered that Franco wouldn't negotiate at all. Not even to allow enemies who were on his black list escape. He wanted revenge not peace, and he wanted it in full.

Between 6000 and 7000 Spanish Republicans escaped and fought for France in 1940. When France fell, thousands more were sent from the French concentration camps to Nazi death camps, especially Mauthausen, where some 10,000 of them died.

US assistant Secretary of State Sumner Welles was one of several observers who saw the negative impact on Latin America of the defeat of democracy in Spain. 'Madrid was their centre of the civilised world morally and culturally, and was led by Franco, who proclaimed his sympathy for the Fascists.'

The Guardia Civil (p. 130)

The Guardia Civil had been founded in 1844 to fight rural bandits, who themselves were a form of social rebellion. Feared rather than respected, they were stationed away from their native province, living in barracks separated from the local population. One writer commented in the 1930s: 'There is no deeper abyss, no more deadly or constant war imaginable, than that waged continually, every day, between the village, especially the Andalucían village, and the Guardia.'

This was an armed paramilitary force, reporting on each adult's social or political involvement, including priests' sermons. They traditionally acted as the enforcers for landlords and local political bosses against the poorer classes.

The poet Lorca's 'Ballad of the Spanish Civil Guard' was a dramatic account of them 'with their souls of patent leather' attacking the poor of Jerez. It included the theme of the wounded horse, which would become a feature of Picasso's Guernica. Many assumed this poem was the Right's motive for killing Lorca during the Civil War. Arturo Barea tells how the local Guardia sergeant confronted him in public for associating with the workers in the small town of Novés in the lead-up to the Civil War. In the war Franco used them in the rearguard, to ensure that conquered territory was well pacified and that it stayed that way.

In this later post-war period, students considered them ruthless: 'If they lower their guns at us demonstrating, it's because they're going to fire and they don't fire to miss. "Los Grises", the regular armed police, are bad but not as confident about shooting at crowds of us unarmed students.' 'Los Grises' were seen as Franco's main weapon in cities, and their special counter-subversion units were dreaded by union and student activists. Amnesty's Torture Report had found all three forces, Grises, Guardia Civil and Brigada Político-Social ,figured prominently in victims' accounts.

Colonel Tejero, the officer who led the 1981 coup in Madrid against Spain's young democracy, however, was commanding Civil Guards, while the parliament he seized was surrounded outside by military police, backed up by Los Grises, who supported the constitution.

The Years of Repression (p. 130)

At the beginning of the 1950s, Spain was one of the most backward countries in Europe: there was one car for every 120 Spaniards, compared to one for every eleven French citizens. The first post-war strike was held on May Day, 1947 in the Basque Country. In 1951 strikes began in Barcelona's public transport with an attempted boycott of the Madrid metro. There were strikes again in Cataluña in 1952 and in the Bilbao shipyards in 1953.

With no remaining hope of change from outside Spain, workers and student movements took the lead. The cost was high: from 1949 to 1953, 300 were sentenced to prison, and at least seven executed for belonging to outlawed unions or parties. Tomás Centeno, secretary of the socialist UGT union, died in a Madrid cell after third-degree interrogation.

A confidential survey of student opinion in 1955 showed 74 per cent thought the regime incompetent, 85 per cent that the ruling classes were immoral, 90 per cent thought the military commanders were ignorant. There was an unending cycle of student protests, riots and university closures from 1956 on, so the Franco regime set up police stations inside the main universities.

The notorious Brigada Político Social was the special police force dealing with illegal union or political activists, responsible for sudden arrests and torture. When Simón Montero was caught on 17 June 1959, through police surveillance of a released Communist Party member, his closest comrades in the inner party core decided to break the rules for these emergencies: immediately to abandon all houses known to the victim. Since the police knew they were torturing in a race against time, to get information before news of his arrest spread, everyone had to assume the victim would be broken, and Simón knew the rule too.

Yet his closest comrades chose to sleep in their own homes that night. As one of them, Jorge Semprún, who had been in Gestapo hands, wrote afterwards, it was the only thing they could do for him. They awoke safe in their beds next morning. Simón had not cracked. When Jorge met him after ten years, Simón's first question was: 'Did you sleep at home that night?'

'Yes.'

'I hoped you would! It gave me strength knowing you'd be at home.'

The number of strikes increased, with one in the Basque country and Cataluña in 1956, a Barcelona tram boycott in 1957 and strikes in Asturias province in 1958 and again in 1962 and in July 1963, and Madrid in June 1966. By 1970 strikes affected almost all major Spanish cities. In the two years 1969 and 1970, eight workers died from shots fired in clashes by police. The Communist leader Nuñez was sentenced to twenty-five years, while another, Soler, died in his cell from 'natural causes' after getting a thirty-year sentence.

In May 1960, 339 Basque clergy wrote a petition to their bishops denouncing the brutality of the police and denial of freedom, charging the Church with 'complicity with the state'.

After the USA had forced the bankrupt Spanish government into new economic measures, growth took off and living standards rose. Spain was developing a modern economy, overtaking Britain in shipbuilding, but without the essential social structures: labour rights, a free press and political parties.

Within a month of Franco's 1964 amnesty for prisoners, police fought a miners strike brutally, castrated one striker, drove another mad and openly admitted shaving their wives' heads. Two young anarchists bombed Madrid, causing injuries. Both were caught, tortured to procure confessions and executed after court martial by garrotte: the victim was seated in front of a post with an iron collar round the neck which was tightened slowly to cause strangulation.

In March 1966 hundreds of Barcelona students held a free assembly in a Capuchin friary setting up an independent student union. On Franco's direct orders, the police assaulted the friary, in breach of the concordat with the Vatican, and arrested them. Two months later, 130 priests gathered in silent protest outside police headquarters but were dispersed with batons. In 1968 Madrid students clashed with police downtown and even the conservative University of Navarre run by Opus Dei was affected with disorder. The same year saw strikes by the Communist-led Workers Commissions which now became the real opposition to the regime. Prisoners' wives shut themselves inside a Jesuit church in Madrid opposite the US embassy, and these *encierros* (sit-ins) became standard protests.

ETA (Euskadi ta Askatasuna) killed its first Guardia Civil in June 1968, and suffered their first death in action. In January 1969, thirty years after the Civil War victory, strikes were still 'sedition' and the whole country was under emergency law. A student was said to have 'jumped' out of his seventh-floor apartment when police were beating him. Finally, 1969 was the year of the Matesa Affair. Billions of pesetas were hidden in Swiss bank accounts or spent on Opus Dei projects, even a donation to Nixon's election as US president, which were supposed to have financed exports of textile looms.

1970 opened with a wave of strikes. In July police opened fire again, killing three building workers striking in Granada. That year saw over 800 strikes, all illegal. During the 1970 Burgos trial of ETA suspects, a defendant revealed how he was tortured following arrest 'for nine days on end, I and two comrades were beaten and tortured by a group of thirty policemen working in shifts, without a break, including the operating table', where the victim is laid on a table with a guard sitting on his legs, the rest of his body hangs down and he is beaten on the stomach and genitals with a steel rod.

The 1973 Amnesty Report on Torture said torture was widespread, regular and unrestricted. Most victims were from one of three groups – workers, students and Basque nationalists. In June 1972 police captured the 'Carabanchel Ten' who were leaders of the Communist union *Comisiones Obreras*, and a Jesuit who got a nineteen-year jail sentence. Camacho, the union general secretary, got twenty years. Bob's veterans' association, the IBA (Internationl Brigade Association), sent Bill Paynter, who attended this trial and reported back to the members, as they had similarly done during other political trials.

Portugal (pp. 132–5)
Portugal had actively supported Franco during the Civil War. Salazar announced he'd help Franco with all available means and he did, sending 20,000 volunteers in the Legion de Viriato, refusing non-intervention observers on his frontier. Republicans who escaped to Portugal were handed over to Franco; German aid was transported through with Salazar personally handling details.

Franco's brother was able to set up his arms-buying headquarters at Lisbon where the Republic's ambassador became in effect a prisoner in his own embassy. Franco described his part of Spain, with Hitler's Germany, Portugal and Italy, as bulwarks of culture and Christianity. The government called for two days of national mourning for Hitler's death and had flags on public buildings at half-mast. In October 1941 a US organiser of escapes from occupied France learnt the British were sending back to Spain those Republicans who managed to get to Lisbon to fight for the Allies.

Amnesty's 1973 Report on Torture confirms that under the dictatorship, torture appeared to be routine, and was done in cells below the courtroom of the Lisbon security headquarters and in the new DGS centre in a wing of Caxias prison. Sleep torture was often used: some prisoners were deprived of sleep for up to 14 days by guards changed every 2–3 hours. A special decree allowed the DGS imprison anyone for up to six years without judicial control for acting 'contrary to the territorial integrity of the nation'.

Spain's Army in Changing Times (p. 135)

Spain's Fascist regime and its pillar, the army, were left isolated and outdated by the peaceful Portuguese revolution, followed shortly by the fall of the Greek Colonels' dictatorship, and many younger officers' families expected to be part of modern fashionable life in Europe and the USA. Outside Spain, European Fascism wasn't in vogue any longer. When visitors questioned Spain's repressive military regime Spaniards claimed that, as Franco's Minister of Tourism said, 'Spain is different.' They'd add, 'Well, look at Portugal,' which was certainly backward and even poorer. Visiting Spaniards felt superior – until its regime unexpectedly fell.

This undermined the extremists trying to organise the survival of Spanish Fascism. They no longer had a significant social base outside the war veterans and employees of the thirty-five state newspapers, forty-five radio stations and widespread local party offices. When these organs lost their state subsidies in April 1977 they withered. A Spanish court martial of the 'movement of officers for democracy' had exposed the degree to which junior officers supported popular solutions within the army. The influence of Portugal's Armed Forces Movement had destroyed the last excuse for denying democratic progress. One could never underestimate the sense of national honour in a country as proud and yet marginalised as Spain then was, especially among traditionally minded young officers. Fascism did revive, for instance among youths in Madrid's private secondary schools, who could be seen leaving class and changing into the dark blue shirts of 'The Movement' at school gates in 1979, but it eventually went out of style for them too.

The 1981 attempted coup against the transition to democracy was supported by a Civil War veteran commanding an armoured division in Valencia. General Milans del Bosch had been a cadet with the famous beseiged garrison in Toledo's Alcázar until it was dramatically relieved by Franco's advance.

In January 2006 there were signs of military tension as Cataluña's proposals for national status and self-determination were being negotiated with the Madrid government. While reviewing a parade in Seville, the Chief of Land Forces, Lieut-General José Mena, warned of military intervention if the constitution's limits on autonomy were crossed. He was sacked and placed under house arrest, but supported days later by an open letter from a captain in the Spanish Foreign Legion in Melilla, the base for Franco's uprising against the Republic in 1936.

INDEX OF TOPICS COVERED IN NOTES

BIBLIOGRAPHY

Principal Published Sources

I am deeply grateful to several authors whose books are more like companions than texts: Hugh Thomas wrote the first reliable general history, a background for everyone since. Eduard de Blaye's volume was essential for the post-war social struggles. Ronald Fraser's *Blood of Spain* has the very feel and warmth of those who lived the war. His is a book unique in its detail, from arms to religious feelings. Paul Preston's works are rich and many, as is his extraordinary ability to write about all kinds of people, from the best in that era to the dullest personalities of Franco's regime. And the man in person is 'a dacent skin'. Carl Geiser's is a moving account of comrades in physical and spiritual struggle, almost poetic in the clear emotions it recalls from the 1930s. The reports from that time included in *The Guardian Book of the Spanish Civil War* have been more than helpful.

Arturo Barea's memoirs, with their tales of earlier hope and frailty, were my company for months after I left Madrid in 1979 during its disturbed passage from dictatorship. Skoutelsky is the great source for French international brigaders, as Michael O'Riordan was for so long for the Irish. Eugene Downing gave his own memories of Dublin and wartime Spain freely, with the vigour of a man half his age. Gerald Brenan was present, a lone witness, when almost nobody outside Spain cared any more. And Severiano, who published Bob's memoirs in Spanish with Ana Pérez and the Amigos de las Brigadas, led the way for us.

There was a heap of my old press clippings, memories of Spain from 1960 on: looking for work, hitching the country roads, watching the transition to democracy from the 'champagne stage' when unions and political parties burst out joyfully into a bright new day, through the later disappointments and, alas, normal disillusionments of mature consumer democracy. As a trucker in the hills north of Barcelona told me, 'We voted for socialism – we got social democracy.'

Books

Alexander, Bill. *British Volunteers for Liberty*. London: Lawrence & Wishart, 1982.

Amnesty International. *Report on Torture*. London: Duckworth, 1973.

Balfour, Sebastian. *Deadly Embrace*. Oxford: Oxford University Press, 2002.

Barea, Arturo. *The Forging of a Rebel*. London: Granta, 2001. (Originally published in Spanish in three volumes: 1941, 1943 and 1946.)

Biblioteca El Mundo. *La Guerra Civil Española: Mes a Mes*. Madrid: 2005–6.

Bilainkin, George. *Poland's Destiny*. Hutchinson, 1939.

Borkenau, Franz. *The Spanish Cockpit*. London: Faber & Faber, 1937,

Brenan, Gerald. *The Face of Spain*. Harmondsworth: Penguin, 1965.

——————. *The Spanish Labyrinth*. Cambridge: Cambridge University Press, 1943.

Brome, Vincent. *The International Brigades*. New York: Mayflower Dell, 1967.

Carroll, Denis. *They Have Fooled You Again*. Dublin: Columba Press, 1993.

Cockburn, Claud. *I Claud…* Harmondsworth: Penguin, 1967.

——————. *The Devil's Decade*. London: Sidgwick & Jackson, 1973.

Coogan, Tim Pat. *De Valera: Long Fellow, Long Shadow*. London: Hutchinson, Arrow, 1993.

Countess of Fingall, Elizabeth. *Seventy Years Young*. Dublin: Lilliput, Press, 1991.

Cronin, Sean. *Frank Ryan: The Search for the Republic*. Dublin: Repsol, 1980.

Cunningham, Valentine. *The Penguin Book of Spanish Civil War Verse*. Harmondsworth: Penguin, 1980.

de Blaye, Edouard. *Franco and the Politics of Spain*. Harmondsworth : Penguin, 1976.

Donnelly, Joseph. *Charlie Donnelly*. Dublin: Dedalus, 1987.

Doyle, Bob. 'The Print Jungle', in *Work*. Harmondsworth: Penguin, 1965.

——————. *Memorias de un Rebelde sin Pausa* (ed. Severiano Montero Barrado). Madrid: AABI, 2002.

Fisk, Robert. *In Time of War: Ireland, Ulster and the Price of Neutrality 1939-45*. London: Paladin Grafton, 1985.

Foot, Michael. *Debts of Honour*. London: Picador, 1980.

Fraser, Ronald. *Blood of Spain*. Harmondsworth: Penguin, 1979.

Geiser, Carl. *Prisoners of the Good Fight*. Chicago: Laurence Hill Books, 1986.

Graham, Helen. *The Spanish Republic at War*. Cambridge, Cambridge University Press, 2002.

Graves, Robert & Alan Hodge. *The Long Weekend: A Social History of Great Britain, 1918–39*. Faber & Faber, 1940.

Gurney, Jason. *Crusade in Spain*. London: Faber & Faber, 1974.

Gutierrez, J. L. 'Dolores: El Largo Adíos', in *Diario 16*, 17 November 1985.

Haigh, Peter and Wildwood Peters, *The Guardian Book of the Spanish Civil War*. London: Guardian Newspapers, 1987.

Hutchinson, Pearse. *Done into English: Collected Translations*. Oldcastle, Co. Meath: Gallery Press, 2003.

——————. *Collected Poems*. Oldcastle, Co. Meath: Gallery Press, 2002.

Jackson, Gabriel. *La Republica Española y la Guerra Civil*. Barcelona: Crítica, 1999.

Letelier, Orlando. *Chile: Economic Freedom and Political Repression*. London: UK Institute of Race Relations, 1976.

Liddell Hart, Basil. *History of the Second World War*. London: Cassell, 1973.

Llarch, Joan. *Batallones de Trabajadores*. Barcelona: Manantial, 1978.

Lucas-Phillips, C. E. *The Spanish Pimpernel*. London: Heinemann, 1960.

McDonald, Nancy. *Homage to the Spanish Exiles*. New York: Insight Books, 1987.

McGarry, Ferghal. *Irish Politics and the Spanish Civil War*. Cork: Cork University Press, 1999.

Madariaga. Ma Rosa de. *Los Moros que Trajo Franco*. Martínez Roca, 2002.

Miller, John (ed.). *Voices Against Tyranny*. New York: Scribner, 1986.

Monks, Joe. *With the Reds in Andalucía*. London: privately published, 1985.

O'Connor, Joseph. *Even the Olives are Bleeding*. Dublin: New Island, 1992.

Ó Duinnín, Eoghan (Eugene Downing). *La Niña Bonita agus an Roisín Dubh*. Baile Átha Cliath, An Clóchomhar, 1986.

O'Riordan, Michael. *Connolly Column*. Dublin: New Books, 1979.

Orwell, George. *Homage to Catalonia*. Harmondsworth, Penguin, 1966.

O'Shaughnessy, Hugh. *Pinochet – the Politics of Torture*. London: Latin American Bureau, 2000.

Poltorak, A. *The Retribution*. Moscow: Novosti, 1976.

Preston, Paul. *Doves of War*. London: Harper Collins, 2002.

——————. *Franco*. London: Harper Collins, 1995.

——————. *The Triumph of Democracy in Spain*. London: Methuen, 1986.

——————. *Las Tres Españas del 36*. Barcelona: Debolsillo, 1998.

——————. (ed.) *La Republica Asediad*. Barcelona: Barcelona: Península, 2001.

Raguer, Hilari. *La Pólvora y el Incienso*. Barcelona: Península, 2001.

Semprún, Jorge. *Autobiografía de Federico Sánchez*. Barcelona: Planeta, 1977.

Sheean, Vincent. *Between the Thunder and the Sun*. London: Macmillan, 1943.

——————. *Not Peace But A Sword*. New York: Doubleday, 1939.

Skoutelsk, Rémi. *L'espoir Guidait Leur Pas*. Paris: Grasset, 1998.

Shirer, William L. *The Rise and Fall of the Third Reich*. New York: Simon and Schuster, 1960.

Stradling, Robert. *The Irish and the Spanish Civil War*. Manchester: Mandolin, 1999.

Tellez, Antonio. *Sabate: Guerrilla Extraordinary* (trans. Stuart Christie). London: Davis-Poynter, 1974.

Thomas, Hugh. *The Spanish Civil War*. London: Random House, 1960.

Torrés, Henry. *Pierre Laval*. London: Victor Gollanz, 1941.

Valenta, J. & E Duran. *1987, Conflict in Nicaragua, A Multidimensional Approach. Boston: Allen and Unwin, 1987.*

Welles, Sumner. *The Time for Decision*. London: Hamish Hamilton, 1944.

d'Ydewalle, Charles. *An Interlude in Spain*. London: Macmillan, 1944.

Zilliacus, K. *Between Two Wars*. Harmondsworth: Penguin, 1939.

240

Newspapers and Periodicals:

El ABC, Madrid.
Diario 16, Madrid.
The *Guardian*, UK.
Interviu, Madrid.
The Irish Times, Dublin.
The *Irish Press*, Dublin.
The *Irish Socialist*, Dublin.
The *Morning Star*, UK.
El Mundo, Madrid.
The *Observer*, UK.
El País, Madrid.
El Periódico, Barcelona.
An Phoblacht/Republican News, Dublin.
The *Sunday Press*, Dublin.
The *Sunday Times*, UK.
The *Sunday Tribune*, Dublin.
Tiempo, Madrid.
The Times, UK.
La Vanguardia, Barcelona.
Voluntarios de la Libertad, AABI, Madrid.
The Volunteer, ALBA, New York.
El Ya, Madrid.